# THE LONG SHADOW OF EXTRACTION

# The Long Shadow of Extraction

## THE ORIGINS OF INDIGENOUS AUTONOMY DEMANDS

CHRISTOPHER L. CARTER

PRINCETON UNIVERSITY PRESS

PRINCETON & OXFORD

Published by Princeton University Press
41 William Street, Princeton, New Jersey 08540
99 Banbury Road, Oxford OX2 6JX

press.princeton.edu

GPSR Authorized Representative: Easy Access System Europe - Mustamäe tee 50, 10621 Tallinn, Estonia, gpsr.requests@easproject.com

All Rights Reserved

ISBN 978-0-691-27115-6
ISBN (pbk.) 978-0-691-27116-3
ISBN (e-book) 978-0-691-27118-7

British Library Cataloging-in-Publication Data is available

Editorial: Bridget Flannery-McCoy, Dave McBride and Alena Chekanov
Production Editorial: Jenny Wolkowicki
Cover design: Heather Hansen
Production: Lauren Reese
Publicity: William Pagdatoon
Copyeditor: Bhisham Bherwani

Cover image: © James Brunker / Magical Andes Photography

This book has been composed in Arno Pro

10  9  8  7  6  5  4  3  2  1

*For my parents, for everything*

# CONTENTS

Online Appendices (see under the Resources tab,
https://press.princeton.edu/ISBN/9780691271163)

ILLUSTRATIONS

# Figures

# Tables

# ACKNOWLEDGMENTS

THIS BOOK would not have been possible without the tremendous support of a number of people. Thad Dunning has been an advisor and mentor, a constant source of support, and a role model for what an engaged and rigorous scholar should be. I would not be where I am today if not for Thad. Alison Post, Kenneth Scheve, Ruth Collier, Andrew Little, and Noam Yuchtman all pushed me theoretically, conceptually, and empirically. The final product owes an enormous debt to their consistent, sharp feedback.

The project's roots grew from my time as an undergraduate at UNC-Chapel Hill, where John Charles Chasteen, Cecilia Martinez Gallardo, and Lars Schoultz inspired a lifelong love for Latin America and provided an example of how teaching and mentorship can change an undergraduate student's trajectory. George Rabinowitz and Stuart Macdonald introduced me to the systematic study of politics and quantitative research. I hope this book would have made George proud.

Melani Cammett, Tim Colton, Alisha Holland, Fran Hagopian, Steve Levitsky, and Pia Raffler provided me with an intellectual home during my time at the Harvard Academy. Their warmth and generosity made that experience two of the very best years of my academic career. Steve chaired my book workshop, where he, Alisha, Evan Lieberman, Jim Mahoney, and Deborah Yashar offered detailed and insightful feedback on an earlier manuscript draft. Their careful engagement made this a much better book. I thank them and hope the final product reflects well their many contributions.

I feel lucky to have completed this project at the University of Virginia, a wonderful academic home where I have been offered consistent professional support and personal kindness. Dan Gingerich has been a mentor, co-author, and friend. I have learned so much from him. Gabi Kruks-Wisner, Anne Meng, Sid Milkis, and David Waldner have made this a better book and—through conversations and their example—have made me a better scholar.

The support of the Karsh Institute of Democracy and my chair, Jen Lawless, provided me with the time needed to finish this book.

Anna Callis and Tanu Kumar have read more versions of this book than anyone else. Their comments have greatly improved the final product, and their friendship has made the process of developing it worthwhile. Others have contributed helpful feedback on the theory and evidence, including Guadalupe Tuñón, Alexandra Blackman, Natália Bueno, Sonja Castañeda Dower, Danny Choi, Anirvan Chowdhury, Kaitlyn Chriswell, Justine Davis, Siobhan Finnerty, Natalia Garbiras-Diaz, Francisco Garfias, Tanushree Goyal, Marcia Grimes, Gabe Koehler-Derrick, Alyssa Huberts, Laura Jakli, Ingrid Luna López, Isabela Mares, Mona Morgan Collins, Lucas Novaes, Neil O'Brien, Mathias Poertner, Emily Sellars, Andres Schipani, Susan Stokes, Jessie Trudeau, Madai Urteaga Quispe, Lisa Wedeen, Elisabeth Wood, and Yang-Yang Zhou. Edgar Franco Vivanco organized a terrific workshop at the University of Michigan, where Karla Mundim, Cesar Martinez-Alvarez, and he offered tremendous feedback on my manuscript. Seminar participants at Princeton, Yale, Texas A&M, Emory, Stanford, Universidad Católica del Uruguay, University of Southern California, Harvard, University of Chicago, Pittsburgh, and University of Pennsylvania provided comments that greatly strengthened the manuscript.

Four anonymous reviewers at Princeton and Cambridge provided brilliant comments that I incorporated into the final version of the book. Bridget Flannery-McCoy and Alena Chekanov have been phenomenal and attentive editors. Kelley Friel made invaluable copy edits. Gabriella Wong provided skillful research assistance for the survey of community leaders in Peru, and Daniel Moreno offered very helpful advice on the survey of Bolivian Indigenous respondents. The research would not have been possible without generous funding from the National Science Foundation, the University of Virginia, the Harvard Academy, the UC Berkeley Center for Latin American Studies, the American Political Science Association, and the UC Institute for Mexico and the United States.

During my fieldwork, many individuals took the time to meet with me and share their stories. I know I will never be able to fully repay their kindness, but I will try. Others provided valuable support to me while researching and writing this book. Julio Cotler was kind and helpful when I arrived at the Instituto de Estudios Peruanos as a confused graduate student. Allyson Benton provided me with an intellectual home at CIDE during my fieldwork in Mexico. Ellen Lust developed an academic community and invited me into the

GLD network, which I cherish. David Collier and Gerry Munck motivated me to think more systematically and seriously about historical legacies. I deeply admire and am grateful for all of them.

Beyond the academy, Angela provided a source of love, understanding, and a reminder of why being *terco* can sometimes be a good thing. As I finish this book, I think especially about my parents, whose hard work and resilience have inspired me, whose sacrifice has sustained me, and whose unconditional love has made me who I am. For these reasons and many more, I dedicate this book to them.

# THE LONG SHADOW OF EXTRACTION

# 1

# The Puzzle of Indigenous Autonomy

Como indios nos explotaron, como indios nos liberaremos. [They exploited us
as Indians, we will liberate ourselves as Indians.]

—BOLIVIAN KATARISTAS (CITED IN ALBÓ 2002B, 80)

THE BOLIVIAN Vice-Ministry of Autonomy, housed in the recently completed Casa Grande del Pueblo skyscraper, overlooks the rugged cityscape of
the capital of La Paz. The 2009 Constitution, which was issued on the same
day the Vice-Ministry was created, provided a path for the country's majority-
Indigenous municipalities to become politically autonomous by replacing
municipal governments with traditional Indigenous ones. On one wall of
the Vice-Ministry's office hangs a map of Bolivia with markers to indicate
the Indigenous municipalities that have achieved autonomy. Just over 200
municipalities—out of over 300—qualify for autonomous status. Yet, as of
2023, there were only three pins in the Vice-Ministry's map. Thirty-six other
municipalities have started the process, but only six remain actively engaged
in it. I asked an official why so few municipalities have pursued autonomy. His
response: "*Cuanto tiempo tienes?* [How much time do you have?]"

Scholars and observers have long regarded autonomy as the central
demand of Indigenous populations (Díaz-Polanco 1998; Van Cott 2001;
Zuñiga Navarro 1998).[1] According to this logic, marginalized native groups
experience unequal access to state institutions and markets, and thus seek a
government-recognized territorial space—within an existing nation-state—
in which they can freely and legitimately exercise authority. The expected

1. Autonomy is also regarded as the core demand of other territorially based and historically
marginalized ethnic groups (Brubaker et al. 2018, 346–347).

benefits of autonomy over other outcomes are several. Unlike assimilation or integration, autonomy does not require Indigenous groups to abandon their cultural identities or their long-standing institutions, thus promising an alternative path to development. Autonomy may also be preferable to independence or secession because it preserves access to costly public goods, such as national defense, which the state continues to provide (Ghai 2000, 8; Hechter 2000, 157). The presumed benefits of autonomy are reflected in the headline of an opinion piece in Canada's largest newspaper, which claimed, "There is only one solution to the complex challenges facing Indigenous peoples in Canada: a rapid move toward Indigenous autonomy" (Coates 2022).

Yet, a growing body of empirical evidence from across the Americas—including the Bolivian case discussed above—suggests that Indigenous groups are highly divided over their preferences for autonomy. In 1995, one-third of Indigenous municipalities in Oaxaca, Mexico opted against replacing municipal governments with traditional, Indigenous assemblies (*usos y costumbres*).[2] In Ecuador, majority-Indigenous municipalities have had the legal right to adopt traditional political institutions for over a decade, but fewer than 3 percent have done so. Only two Peruvian Indigenous collectives, the Wampis and Awajun Nations, have successfully lobbied for political autonomy. Beyond Latin America, the 1934 Indian Reorganization Act, which promised an expansion of Native groups' autonomy, was rejected by a third of tribes in the United States. In Canada, the 1995 Inherent Right Act offered greater autonomy to the country's nearly 700 tribal bands. By 2018, just 32 bands had concluded negotiations with the government, and only about 50 others had started the process.

Indigenous peoples' unexpectedly uneven embrace of autonomy presents a series of puzzles often overlooked in the existing literature. Why do some Indigenous groups demand autonomy while others do not? If not autonomy, what demands do Indigenous groups make, and when? And finally, what are the material and non-material stakes of (not) demanding autonomy?

To understand why Indigenous groups make the demands they do, I explore their preferences over different institutional arrangements, of which autonomy is just one type. *Autonomy* recognizes Indigenous cultural identities *and* the legitimacy of long-standing Indigenous institutions (e.g., communal landholding, traditional political authorities). Other outcomes recognize only

---

2. There is, however, debate over the extent to which Indigenous municipalities had agency over these decisions (Benton 2017; Díaz-Cayeros et al. 2014; Recondo 2007).

one or neither of these. *Assimilation* rejects Indigenous cultural identities and institutions in favor of those embraced by a politically or economically dominant non-Indigenous group. *Integration* recognizes Indigenous cultural identities only within the framework of non-Indigenous, state-sanctioned institutions (e.g., affirmative action programs, electoral quotas). Indigenous groups' preferences over these different outcomes reflect both material considerations (an evaluation of which is expected to most benefit group welfare) and non-material ones (e.g., psychological attachments to specific group identities).

In this book, I argue that historical instances of extraction—particularly those that occurred at the turn of the twentieth century—profoundly shaped contemporary evaluations of the material and non-material benefits of autonomy. During this pivotal (though frequently understudied) period, Indigenous groups developed novel ways to resist political and economic elites' efforts to seize their labor and land. In some cases, resistance occurred through traditional, ethnic leaders, leading to both enduring investments in Indigenous institutions and, ultimately, demands for autonomy. In others, unions and left parties played a more central role in organizing resistance, reducing investments in Indigenous institutions and sparking long-term demands for integration or assimilation.

The primary empirical focus is Latin America, a region in which a growing number of nation-states have enshrined Indigenous rights in constitutions and statutory laws. Yet, as I discussed above, these policy changes have been unevenly embraced at the subnational level; neighboring Indigenous communal or kinship groups (*communities*) frequently take fundamentally different approaches to autonomy. This subnational variation has implications for other key outcomes of Indigenous politics. For instance, divergence in community demands may complicate large-scale Indigenous collective action (e.g., national movements), which generally requires a common interest or grievance (Olson 1971, 7–8; Yashar 2005). Many existing studies of Indigenous politics employ a supply-side approach to explore these decisions of national governments to recognize autonomy.[3] The book's *demand-side* approach endeavors to explain this community-level variation, serving as a needed complement to supply-side accounts. Specifically, it sheds valuable

---

3. Holzinger et al. (2019) provides a notable exception, endeavoring to understand *cross-national* variation in Indigenous demands for autonomy. This book aims to understand *subnational* variation in demand-making.

light on whether autonomy is adopted *on paper* and on whether it is implemented at the local level.

The theory developed in this book also speaks to broader debates in the comparative politics literature. Scholars of civil conflict and nationalism, for example, often seek to explain why groups pursue autonomy. Research in this tradition highlights the primacy of economic motivations but disagrees over whether wealth and privilege (Sambanis and Milanovic 2014; Treisman 1997) or poverty and marginalization (Hechter 2000; Horowitz 1985) best explain demands for territorial authority. This book moves beyond a primary concern with contemporary economic motivations to explain autonomy demands as the product of *historical patterns of mobilization*.[4] Those groups that mobilized along ethnic lines in the past have been more likely to demand autonomy today, while those that mobilized along non-ethnic lines have—for material and non-material reasons—largely avoided making autonomy demands.[5]

## 1.1   What Is Autonomy, and Why Do Groups Want It?

Autonomy has enormous potential to shape key outcomes of interest to social scientists and politicians. The language of autonomy often motivates rebel actors in ethnic conflicts. Debates over autonomy have constituted a key barrier to the ratification of constitutions in Nepal, Sri Lanka, and Chile, among others. Proponents of autonomy highlight its potential to improve natural resource management, environmental stability, democratic responsiveness, and the inclusion of historically marginalized groups. However, the precise meaning of the word is often unclear.

I define autonomy as a territorial right to local self-rule exercised within (and under) the jurisdiction of an existing nation-state. Because it involves a territory, autonomy cannot be claimed by all groups; instead, the group claiming autonomy must be "territorially concentrated," such as the Kurds in Iraq or the Quebecois in Canada, possessing a contiguous, physical space within and over which authority can be exercised (Hechter 2000, 14).

---

4. The relative economic condition of Indigenous groups may interact with historic collective action capacity—an idea I return to in the conclusion.

5. Treisman (1997) notes the importance of cultural and ethnic identities as a "resource" for leaders demanding autonomy (248). The loss of such identities reduces the likelihood that these demands are successful.

Autonomy may be *economic*, involving the recognition of customary landholding institutions (i.e., communal land), or *political*, arising from state recognition of traditional leaders and governance institutions. The latter transfers authority to ethnic leaders, while the former implicitly recognizes the authority of these leaders, whose power to manage and mediate access to collectively held land gives them substantial control over community members. The domains over which authority extends—and the degree of state intervention—vary by context. In theory, however, the policy responsibilities of autonomous, ethnic governments should correspond to those traditionally exercised by local state institutions, and the state should have a relatively limited capacity to preempt autonomous governments. As such, autonomy implies transferring meaningful responsibilities from state officials to leaders of historically marginalized ethnic groups, which may entail creating new procedures for distributive decision-making and policy implementation. This devolution of power could result in either concentrated authority in the figure of a local executive (e.g., a chief) or deliberative and direct democracy through village or tribal assemblies. The latter has been more common in Latin America (Diaz-Cayeros et al. 2016; Magaloni et al. 2019), while the former is more common in Sub-Saharan Africa (Baldwin 2015).

Because autonomy is exercised *within* existing nation-states, the authority it confers is often substantially less than sovereignty, self-determination, or secession. Why, then, do groups demand autonomy over more extreme institutional changes? Hechter (2000, 116) captures this puzzle by asking, "If self-determination is universally valued, why do people ever settle for anything less?" The available empirical evidence, for example, suggests that some ethnic groups reject autonomy *not* because they oppose increased authority, but rather because the notion of autonomy does not adequately articulate the amount of authority they desire. Gurr (1994) argues that the Kurds in Iraq and Tamils in Sri Lanka rejected autonomy settlements that were imposed unilaterally by the government in the wake of civil wars in the 1970s and 1980s, respectively, demanding secession instead (366).[6] Leaders of Bolivian Indigenous municipalities that have started and subsequently abandoned the autonomy process have frequently cited government interference that precludes the meaningful exercise of authority; they lament that "requirements are imposed

6. Horowitz (1981) maintains that the Kurds did not seek secession and independence (169).

on us under the criteria of some bureaucrat, who does not know the reality of Indigenous peoples."[7]

Despite these costs, many ethnic groups embrace autonomy—even as a more limited form of authority—for two reasons. First, it is difficult to achieve, but more expansive forms of authority may be impossible. Rothschild (1981) argues that governments are often unwilling to recognize even minimal levels of autonomy because "they fear that 'the appetite grows while eating'" (152). Therefore, ethnic groups may prefer to lobby for autonomy because it is the most radically transformative demand they can plausibly achieve. Like governments, they may also believe autonomy is a necessary step to obtain more expansive forms of authority. The second reason many ethnic groups seek autonomy is that it preserves access to existing benefits of belonging to a larger governing unit, which provides "collective goods . . . [that] are subject to economies of scale that reduce their cost. . . . Members of peripheral nations may be willing to sacrifice some self-determination to profit from inclusion in a larger, albeit multinational, state" (Hechter 2000, 116–117). Therefore, autonomy might occupy a comfortable middle ground between the privileges of belonging to a nation-state and the benefits of self-governance over local affairs.

In most of the cases discussed in this book, Indigenous groups did not reject autonomy because they wanted sovereignty or independence, but because they viewed autonomy as *too* expansive and saw non-state— perhaps traditional—institutions as a barrier to their inclusion within existing nation-states. Comanche leader Robert Coffey neatly summarized this perspective. In debates over the 1934 Indian Reorganization Act in the United States, he argued against recognizing tribal institutions, asserting, "we protest against the change of the laws . . . and the taking away of individual and property rights guaranteed by treaties and acts of Congress. . . . We feel that segregation which seems the intent of the bill would be a backward step for us" (quoted in Deloria 2002, 291).

This book focuses on Indigenous groups' three main demand-making strategies (depicted in Figure 1.1).[8] The first is assimilation, which entails sacrificing ethnic institutions and subordinating cultures to the economically and politically dominant group; Indigenous *individuals* are given the same

---

7. See Agencia de Noticias Fides (2022, September 23). Author translation.
8. See Rothschild (1981, 150–152).

Recognition of ethnic group rights

Yes　　　　　　　No

Scope of ethnic authority

**Assimilation**

Limited　　　Moderate　　　Expansive

**Integration**　　**Autonomy**　　Secession/ Sovereignty/ Domination

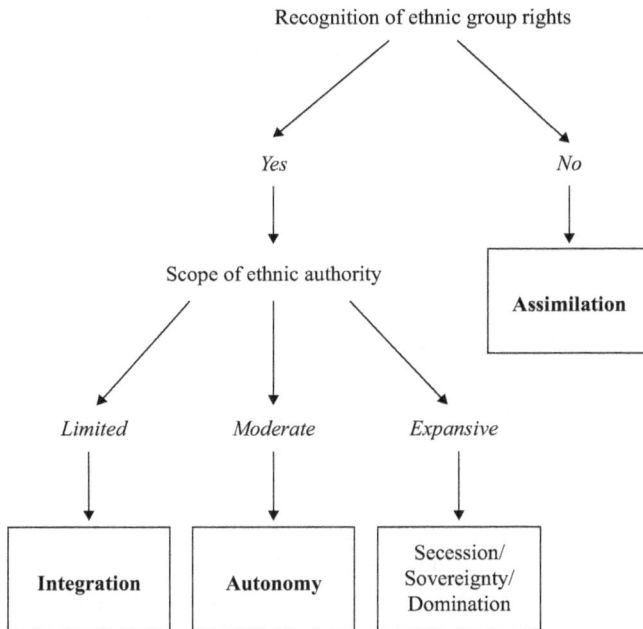

FIGURE 1.1. Typology of demands of ethnic leaders
*Note:* The book's three main outcomes of interest are displayed in bold. Demands reflect preferences for leaders of *territorially concentrated* ethnic groups.

rights as non-Indigenous individuals in an effort to reduce the salience of ethnic difference.[9] Examples include providing education only in a colonial language (e.g., Spanish, Portuguese, English) and imposing private property at the expense of traditional patterns of collective landholding. The second strategy is integration, which allows group "members to rise socially and politically and to extend their economic activities as individuals without impairing the group's ethnic vitality" (Rothschild 1981, 151). Integration policies (e.g., electoral quotas, affirmative action programs, pluricultural constitutions) give ethnic groups authority over cultural matters and guarantee their representation in states and markets. As such, they recognize Indigenous identities but not Indigenous institutions. The third strategy is autonomy, which recognizes

9. As I discuss below, while these are individual rights, they often are obtained through collective, class-based mobilization.

Indigenous identities *and* institutions.[10] The next section develops my argument to explain variation in these three principle outcomes of interest.

## 1.2 Argument

To explain why Indigenous communities demand autonomy in the contemporary period, it is necessary to look to the past. Historical factors such as colonial-era extraction have shaped Indigenous groups' present-day economic welfare (Acemoglu et al. 2001; Dell 2010; Guardado 2018; Lee and Schultz 2012; Mahoney 2010). It stands to reason that variation in other, understudied social and political outcomes, including collective mobilization for autonomy, might also be rooted in these historical experiences.[11]

This book advances two deeply related historical arguments. The first is that colonial and post-independence Indigenous-state relations, which were often characterized by land and labor extraction, inspired Indigenous peoples to invest in collective mobilization to resist exploitation. The second argument is that the form this collective action took shaped later demands for autonomy. State-led extraction often motivated Indigenous communities to invest in *ethnic* identities and institutions, which over time triggered demands for autonomy to protect these same identities and institutions.[12] Extraction by rural elites at the turn of the twentieth century more often led to investments in *class*-based institutions (e.g., unions and left parties) that mobilized resistance to rural elites. These organizations frequently deemphasized or even openly opposed autonomy and instead privileged demands for assimilation or integration.

10. The book does not analyze the more radical strategies of secession and domination (wresting control of the state from the dominant ethnic group) because these have only rarely been embraced in the contemporary period (see Chapter 2). Groups that do not make demands, such as those that have very little contact with the state, and thus enjoy de facto autonomy (Yashar 2005), are likewise beyond the scope of this study. Given the expanded reach of the state in recent decades, the decision to discard this outcome eliminates only a small number of communities from the analysis.

11. This work joins a growing body of scholarship examining these questions (see also Mundim 2022). The important role that memory plays in Indigenous communities further highlights how historical experiences may shape key outcomes for native groups (Abercrombie 1998; Medrano 2011).

12. See, e.g., Honig (2022) on the ways that strong customary institutions can encourage communities to seek state recognition.

While extraction has often inspired short-term resistance, historical factors have shaped whether the effects of this resistance have endured. This book explains the impact of extraction at the beginning of the twentieth century, a period of increased popular sector mobilization through *organizations*. Unions arose to organize Indigenous peoples along class lines, and understudied yet important Indigenous organizations emerged to mobilize communities along ethnic lines. The concessions these groups achieved and the organizational infrastructure they provided created path-dependent forms of mobilization that have often endured into the present. Before the twentieth century, such organizations were absent, and, as such, extraction had more fleeting effects on demand-making.

### 1.2.1   The Divergent Effects of Extraction

Latin American governments have often refused to protect Indigenous institutions due to an overriding interest in extraction—the temporary or permanent capture of Indigenous groups' land, labor, or natural and financial wealth by non-Indigenous actors, usually rural elites (e.g., landowners, mining companies, land developers) or the state (which can be predatory, developmentalist, or liberal). Examples include discriminatory head taxes or tributes levied only on Indigenous communities in the colonial and post-independence periods; various policies in the late nineteenth century that privatized Indigenous communal land for the benefit of non-Indigenous landlords; and contemporary efforts by states to seize valuable Indigenous land and natural resources. The numerous instances of labor coercion were perhaps the most common and harmful.

This book focuses on particularly pivotal instances of extraction that occurred at the turn of the twentieth century. Landowners and the central state competed for access to scarce Indigenous labor. The state, for its part, forced members of Indigenous communities—and frequently Indigenous communities alone—to work without pay to build roads and railways, deliver the mail, and serve in the military, all to project state power. Rural elites sought access to the same labor supply, seeking to trap Indigenous workers in debt peonage arrangements on large estates to take advantage of booming internal and international markets. In the domain of Indigenous labor, the interests of political and economic elites were fundamentally misaligned.

I argue that this extractive competition over Indigenous labor—and, more importantly, Indigenous communities' response to it—shaped long-term community demands for autonomy. The *level* of extraction affected communities' later collective mobilization capacity, while the *type* of extraction determined which rights they demanded. High levels of extraction generally involved exploitation and abuse, sometimes enough to destroy and demobilize communities.[13] More often, however, this extraction triggered resistance from communities and enduring patterns of collective mobilization that persisted through three mechanisms. First, resistance led affected groups to seek organizational allies—such as left parties, labor unions, or Indigenous organizations—that could defend the community against abuses by the state or landowners. These ties to established organizations endured well beyond the period of extraction. Second, the collective memory of exploitation created a shared grievance and potential threat around which social leaders (e.g., Indigenous community leaders, union officials) could mobilize communities in the future. Third, extraction redefined community members' ties to existing Indigenous identities and institutions.

The type of labor extraction that communities experienced is instrumental for understanding the conditions under which this collective mobilization was deployed to demand autonomy. *State-led extraction* played a significant role in eroding community trust in the government, prompting Indigenous communities to turn inward—toward their ethnic identities and institutions—to resist extraction.[14] These investments in ethnic patterns of mobilization and in Indigenous institutions and identities endured through supra-communal ethnic organizations and collective memory, ultimately promoting claims for autonomy—i.e., the recognition and protection of Indigenous identities and institutions.

*Rural elite extraction* generally undermined demands for autonomy. Rural elites (e.g., large landowners) often sought to weaken Indigenous institutions and identities by dividing communal land into private plots, creating privately held debt, and co-opting long-standing Indigenous leaders.[15] The erosion of

---

13. El Salvador's extensive use of repression to enforce coercive labor arrangements discouraged peasant communities from resisting (Wood 2003, 24).

14. State-led extractive efforts historically sought to incorporate Indigenous elites (Dell 2010; Platt 1982). Yet, following independence, as nation-states grew stronger and sought to deploy their authority in traditionally peripheral areas, they began to engage in more direct forms of labor extraction that effectively circumvented Indigenous elites.

15. In contrast to the state, landowners at the turn of the twentieth century were generally less preoccupied with establishing territorial control and more interested in expanding their wealth at the lowest possible cost. As such, these rural elites were more likely to pursue collaboration

Indigenous institutions reduced the need to demand protections for them through autonomy. This form of extraction was also less corrosive to Indigenous communities' trust in the government and thus increased the viability of demands for integration or assimilation. Rural sector unions and left parties, which emerged at the turn of the twentieth century and were especially active in organizing on large estates, reinforced these preferences for integration or assimilation rather than autonomy; they viewed ethnic identities and institutions as a barrier to organizing a peasant-worker alliance.

Whether rural elite extraction generated demands for integration or assimilation depended on whether groups had also been subject to state-led extraction. Communities that experienced state-led extraction made investments in Indigenous identities and institutions and were, therefore, more skeptical of assimilation. In these cases, labor unions and left parties adopted a hybrid strategy that incorporated selective ethnic appeals to recruit and secure the continued buy-in of Indigenous communities. This involved displaying Indigenous symbols in union halls, using Indigenous languages in meetings, and placing ethnic leaders in positions of organizational leadership. Unions and left parties, however, generally refused to challenge the supremacy of state institutions, within which demands for higher wages and better working conditions were articulated. Communities that experienced both state-led and rural elite extraction were, therefore, more likely to demand integration, which recognized Indigenous identities *within existing state institutions* (e.g., affirmative action, electoral quotas).

Demands for assimilation were more common among groups that experienced only rural elite extraction. Groups that did not experience state-led extraction had weaker Indigenous institutions and leaders and were more receptive to organizational allies that emphasized and materially rewarded assimilation. Mobilization along exclusively class-based lines, especially in the twentieth century, yielded benefits from landowners (e.g., higher wages) and governments (e.g., land reform). These successes discouraged groups from investing in Indigenous identities and institutions, which, once lost, could not be easily recovered.

Groups that experienced neither type of extraction have generally preferred autonomy, an assumption I elaborate on in Chapter 3. Yet, because

---

with Indigenous elites to capture Indigenous labor. Owners of large estates frequently offered Indigenous leaders better quality land, exemption from labor obligations, and cash payment in exchange for access to Indigenous workers.

TABLE 1.1. Theoretical predictions

| | | State-led extraction | |
| --- | --- | --- | --- |
| | | *Low* | *High* |
| Rural elite extraction | *Low* | Limited collective mobilization **Demand: No formal demand** | Collective mobilization for ethnic identities and ethnic institutions **Demand: Autonomy** |
| | *High* | Collective mobilization for neither ethnic identities nor ethnic institutions **Demand: Assimilation** | Collective mobilization for ethnic identities but not ethnic institutions **Demand: Integration** |

they have faced no active threat to their territorial integrity or labor, they find it unnecessary to mobilize on behalf of autonomy; only if they experienced extraction (which would shift them to another cell within Figure 1.1) would they need to make demands. Because these cases do not generate active demands, they constitute a limited theoretical focus of this book. They are also empirically rare: the substantial demand for Indigenous labor in the late nineteenth and early twentieth centuries meant that most communities experienced some form of labor extraction unless they were too inaccessible.

To summarize, Indigenous communities that experienced state-led extraction have been more likely to demand autonomy, while those exposed to rural elite extraction have been more likely to demand assimilation. Communities that experienced both forms of extraction have typically demanded integration. Communities exposed to neither type of extraction have been more likely to prefer autonomy but generally have not mobilized to demand it. Table 1.1 outlines my central theoretical predictions.

## 1.3 Alternative Explanations

Two key alternative theoretical frameworks might explain subnational variation in Indigenous demands for autonomy.[16] The first is what I label a

---

16. Cross-national variation in Indigenous mobilization for autonomy has a further set of explanations. As discussed above, large-scale Indigenous movements that have emerged

*distributive* approach, which argues that autonomy demands arise within groups that are "perpetual losers in the competition for state-provided goods" (Hechter 2000, 133). In other words, autonomy solves an inequitable distribution of resources among groups and regions. A long line of scholarship on secession, for example, has argued that

> the modern, mobilizing state's redistributive performance is often either inefficient or perceived as bias, or both, [and] certain categories of citizens and subjects are likely to be alienated from it. If these alienated categories regard and organize themselves as ethnic groups, and if their discontent is sufficiently deep and systemic, they may challenge the very structure or boundaries and domains of their current state. (Rothschild 1981, 233)

Studies of regional (rather than group) wealth also highlight that opposition to the current distribution of resources sparks autonomy demands: for groups from resource-rich regions, the costs of autonomy are lower and the benefits higher (Sambanis and Milanovic 2014; Treisman 1997; Wallerstein 2005, 88).[17] My theory does not dispute that materialist motivations can explain autonomy demands.[18] However, existing distributive accounts cannot explain why groups demand autonomy over other equalizing or redistributive demands. For example, economically disadvantaged ethnic groups will likely be dissatisfied with how the government distributes resources. If autonomy were the only solution to this inequality, disadvantaged groups would be more likely to support autonomy. Yet, in practice, the choice set is more complex. These groups may choose to embrace long-standing ethnic institutions, or they may judge that the best alternative is to invest in integration or assimilation. Extant theories of distributive

---

in recent decades have often been credited with effectively articulating Indigenous demands for autonomy at the national level (Jackson and Warren 2005; Yashar 1998). Scholars have highlighted the role of pluricultural constitutions and peace agreements in providing the opportunity space within which Indigenous communities can mobilize to demand state recognition of rights, including autonomy (Van Cott 2001). Others note the importance of ethnic fractionalization, socioeconomic development, and colonial histories (Holzinger et al. 2019).

17. See also Gourevitch (1979).

18. Scholars have noted, however, that regional resource wealth does not constitute a key rationale for autonomy demands; as Tockman and Cameron (2014) observe, "natural resource control is not a critical issue in many indigenous struggles for autonomy" (63).

politics do not help adjudicate among these options, a key gap my theory seeks to fill.[19]

A second alternative theoretical approach to the study of autonomy emphasizes the importance of sociocultural issues. Scholars in this tradition emphasize that economic and material motivations are "rarely decisive" in explaining demands for territorial authority (Horowitz 1981, 177). Instead, groups advocate autonomy due to a desire for prestige, honor, or control of a "homeland," or due to anxiety about the loss of cultural and symbolic forms of ethnic representation (Hannum 1996, 463, Hartle and Bird 1971; Horowitz 1981). Smith (1985), for example, observes, "it is a sense of discrimination within the larger community that so often forces minority cultural and ethnic groups to seek autonomy" (3).[20] This work generally presumes that groups that are territorially cohesive and share a history of cultural and social marginalization should uniformly demand autonomy.[21] The absence of autonomy demands may thus indicate a lack of group cohesion, identity, or shared history of discrimination.[22] Yet, the examples in this book will show that cohesive, territorially based ethnic groups do not always behave in this way. Their demands—and the degree to which these demands reflect ethnic as opposed to other identity concerns—instead emerge from their response to patterns of extraction.

Thus, existing theories generally fail to make key distinctions relevant to the outcomes studied in this book. Sociocultural and distributive theories are well equipped to address one strategy by which ethnic groups can achieve their material and non-material aims: autonomy. However, these theories do not adequately explain why autonomy is pursued instead of other potential responses to discrimination and inequality, which include integration and

---

19. Specifically, I consider dissatisfaction with the status quo—particularly economic disadvantage—a key scope condition of my argument. Demands arise from a desire to change extant institutions; yet, to understand the form those demands take, it is important to examine historical instances of extraction.

20. This echoes the work of Lawrence (2013), who argues that demands for independence from colonial rule in Sub-Saharan Africa arose only when demands for equality and meaningful inclusion failed.

21. A potential exception to this arises from structural factors such as the distribution of minority and majority populations within a given region (Hartle and Bird 1971; Horowitz 1981; Sorens 2012).

22. This is especially true for scholars who advocate a primordialist conception of ethnicity, which assumes that "groups seek to maintain the integrity and autonomy of the group" (Yashar 2005, 11).

assimilation. They also fail to consider the dynamism of community preferences. Preferences for autonomy are not fixed, as the above theories implicitly
suggest. Instead, they vary over time; initial preferences for autonomy can
evolve into demands for assimilation and integration, and vice versa. Thus,
a new theoretical approach is needed.

## 1.4   Case Selection and Empirical Approach

The book's explanatory focus is on extractive labor institutions that were
common at the turn of the twentieth century. In addition to the unprecedented intensity of coercive labor practices, national and regional popular
sector organizations first appeared during this period. These included labor
unions, left parties, and even early Indigenous movements. For example,
Indigenous Mapuche organizations, such as the Caupolicán Society and the
Araucanian Federation, emerged in Chile in the 1920s. These organizations
wielded considerable influence and lobbied governments to recognize Indigenous cultural rights and native groups' access to communal lands (Crow 2010;
Foerster and Montecino Aguirre 1988). In that same decade, Indigenous leaders in Peru formed the Tahuantinsuyo Pro-Indigenous Rights Committee with
dozens of subcommittees spread throughout the country. In Bolivia, the Oldest Autonomous Mayors formed in the first decades of the twentieth century
and played an important role in increasing the salience of the Aymara Indigenous identity. These Indigenous and non-Indigenous organizations constitute
the primary mechanism through which the posited effects arise and endure.
As a result, it is unlikely that effects from earlier periods of extraction (e.g., the
more extensively studied colonial period) would have persisted to the same
degree.

I examine the effects of this extraction on Indigenous groups' demands in
two emblematic Latin American cases. Peru and Bolivia have large Indigenous populations, and at the turn of the twentieth century, rural elite and
state-led extraction were commonplace. Landowners seized Indigenous land,
capturing Indigenous workers in debt peonage arrangements to toil on large
estates. In each case, governments also used unpaid Indigenous labor to build
roads and railways, and for other infrastructure projects. Yet, exposure to
these different forms of labor extraction varied considerably within the two
countries. In the Bolivian department of Cochabamba, for example, Indigenous groups experienced relatively little state-led extraction but high levels of

rural elite extraction. The reverse was true in the northern region of Bolivia's Potosí department, where hacienda (large estate) expansion was relatively limited, but many Indigenous laborers were conscripted for state infrastructure projects. Similar variation can be observed within the Peruvian department of Cusco. The provinces of La Convención, Paruro, and Paucartambo followed a path similar to Cochabamba's, while the provinces of Quispicanchi, Canas, and Canchis more closely paralleled northern Potosí. Many other regions in these two countries experienced both forms of extraction, including La Paz, Oruro, and Southern Potosí in Bolivia, as well as the capital of Peru's Cusco department.

Within these two cases, I analyze autonomy demands primarily at the level of the Indigenous community.[23] The term "community," which is common in the literature on Indigenous and peasant groups in the Americas,[24] refers to any membership-based unit that is territorially delineated and comprised of individuals who either consider themselves Indigenous or maintain long-standing practices, languages, or institutions that could be considered Indigenous.[25] Members of a community define its borders, often according to long-standing kinship ties, and these boundaries may or may not correspond to administrative units recognized by governments (e.g., municipalities, reserves, reservations, communes). A country often contains hundreds or even thousands of Indigenous communities. Figure 1.2 maps the numerous documented Indigenous communities in Latin America.[26]

My population of interest includes Indigenous communities that existed at the end of the nineteenth century, as identified through census records. This means that communities that are currently labeled as "peasant communities" fall into the category of "Indigenous" for the purposes of this book. I do this for two reasons. First, selecting only those communities that currently identify as Indigenous would eliminate a key collection of communities that are of theoretical interest to this study: those that previously identified as Indigenous but

---

23. Where necessary, due to data limitations, I conduct analyses among larger subnational units.

24. See, e.g., Wolf (1957).

25. Because institutions and cultural practice can change—especially in response to rights that are demanded and received—an Indigenous community in an earlier historical period may no longer be considered an Indigenous community today.

26. This book aims to join a small but growing body of work that focuses on outcomes at the level of the Indigenous community (e.g., Fontana 2022).

FIGURE 1.2. Documented Indigenous communities in Latin America
*Source*: Author's map based on data from Dubertret and Alden Wily (2015).

no longer do. Second, even communities that identify as "peasant" have often preserved Indigenous institutions and customs.

Using the community as my unit of analysis presents a necessary analytic shift. Prior research often highlights the importance of large-scale Indigenous movements for the emergence of autonomy.[27] The Peruvian case, however, demonstrates the need for an addendum to this existing work. Although it was the heart of the Inca empire and is home to a comparatively large Indigenous population, Peru's *national-level* Indigenous movements have only limited

---

27. See, e.g., Andolina (2003); Evans (2011); Jackson and Warren (2005); Yashar (2005).

influence in shaping national-level policy.[28] Yet, Indigenous *communities* in Peru have achieved important and often overlooked concessions. Over 70 percent of the country's Indigenous and peasant communities have communal land titles. A third to half of Indigenous children receive public education in an Indigenous language. And the government has recognized nearly 90 percent of Indigenous communities. That small-scale Indigenous communities—of which there are about 6,000 in Peru—have been the primary level at which Indigenous autonomy has been recognized suggests a need for a renewed focus on these units. I argue that such communities are often equally (if not more) consequential than large-scale movements for achieving Indigenous autonomy.

Identifying *community* demands presents a methodological challenge. While differences may arise across communities, there may also be disagreement within communities around which demands to prioritize. To address this challenge, I rely on behavioral measures that best reflect community demands for autonomy. Costly actions to obtain (or, in some cases, reject) autonomy involve the consent of most community members. For example, a community's decision to apply for a collective land title or political autonomy requires a substantial investment of various members' time and resources. Often, the community must provide documentation to—and engage in prolonged negotiations with—the central government. The community, rather than a single individual, generally pays for hiring lawyers, translators, and enumerators. Examining community-level behavior thus provides valuable insight into community demands for autonomy.

Yet, as I discuss above, examining autonomy provides only a part of the story; evaluating the incidence of non-autonomy demands is also important. To do this, I examine manifestos and organizational membership information for both peasant unions and "hybrid organizations," which advocate assimilationist or integrationist demands, respectively. I also analyze Indigenous community members' preferences and behaviors using original and existing surveys.

The data collection effort for this project presented a substantial challenge, largely due to the aforementioned difficulties of defining measures of autonomy, assimilation, and integration and gathering data that reflects these measures well. I spent a total of eighteen months conducting fieldwork in Peru and Bolivia. This included over seventy interviews with Indigenous community

28. See, e.g., Yashar (1998); Landa Vásquez (2006); Montoya (2006); Albó (1999).

leaders, mayors, and bureaucratic officials in several regions of both countries; a survey of more than 300 Indigenous community leaders in Peru; a survey of more than 1,000 Indigenous Bolivians; and field visits to over thirty Indigenous communities in both countries. These strategies yielded critical insights into community-level demands for autonomy, integration, and assimilation. Extensive archival research provided information on the thousands of Indigenous and peasant organizations and movements in Bolivia and Peru, as did memoirs of Indigenous activists, newspaper reports, and government accounts. Finally, I compiled information from government records on autonomy applications and collective land titles; through a freedom of information request, I obtained community-level data on autonomy from a 2012 Peruvian census of Indigenous communities.

In addition to data challenges concerning the outcome variable, the independent variable—extraction—also presented difficulties. Few comprehensive sources reliably document historical experiences with different forms of extraction. I measure rural elite extraction in Bolivia by examining the change in the population residing in Indigenous communities between 1854 and 1900—data that was collected by McBride (1921) using tribute and taxation data from the nineteenth century and the 1900 Census; most of the community population decline during this period was attributable to large estate expansion. I also examine the prevalence of haciendas across subnational regions of Bolivia in 1950. I measure rural elite extraction in Peru by examining the change in the hacienda population using the 1876 and 1940 censuses.[29] Data on state-led extraction was even more challenging to obtain. The Peruvian government did not systematically collect data on labor conscription or lost it; today, this data exists for only a few provinces. To overcome this issue, I exploit the rules that President Augusto Leguía implemented in the 1920s to determine which communities would provide unpaid labor for road construction. This involved collecting data on road construction and each community's proximity to provinces where labor conscription occurred. For Bolivia, I gathered data on state-led extraction by examining provincial and departmental reports submitted to the national government in the early 1900s. I supplement this data using a strategy similar to that employed in Peru; I code labor conscription based on community location vis-à-vis a large-scale infrastructure project, which serves as a proxy for exposure to labor conscription (communities located closer to these projects should have been more likely to

29. No census was conducted in the intervening period.

be conscripted). These data sources provide a rich, nuanced, and novel picture of labor extraction at the turn of the twentieth century (see Table 1.2).

The most substantial challenge for the project was devising a strategy to reliably identify the effects of historical extraction. Governments and rural elites may have targeted extraction to communities based on baseline characteristics correlated with later mobilization and demand-making. To obviate this problem, I—where possible—leverage natural and survey experiments. This observational and experimental data provides an opportunity to overcome endogeneity issues that would otherwise plague this study of historical legacies. Where I cannot use causal inference techniques to evaluate crucial parts of my theory, I rely on a combination of correlational analyses and process tracing.

Within-country comparisons allow for a test of the general theory I develop in Table 1.1, but my theory can also explain important cross-national differences between Peru and Bolivia. While assimilation has been common in both countries, demands for autonomy have been, perhaps surprisingly, more common in Peru, while demands for integration have been predominant in Bolivia. As I elaborate further in subsequent chapters, these differences can largely be attributed to the timing of extraction ("extractive sequences"). Rural elite extraction happened in similar periods in both countries. However, in Bolivia, labor conscription was adopted in the 1890s, almost thirty years earlier than in Peru. As a result, in Peru, rural elite extraction—where it occurred—almost always happened before state-led extraction, leading to demands for either autonomy or assimilation. Conversely, many communities in Bolivia experienced state-led extraction before rural elite extraction, leading to demands for assimilation or integration.

## 1.5 Contributions

This book offers three key innovations vis-à-vis existing accounts of Indigenous and ethnic politics. First, it challenges an abiding assumption in the literature that autonomy is the central demand of Indigenous communities (Díaz-Polanco 1998). Often, inferences about "Indigenous" preferences are drawn from examinations of large-scale ethnic organizations and movements; yet, this approach ignores Indigenous peoples who may not feel represented by these organizations or by ethnic mobilization more broadly. Examining very local Indigenous communities, I demonstrate that there is, in

TABLE 1.2. Data sources used in the analysis

| | Extraction | Immediate patterns of mobilization | Long-term demands |
|---|---|---|---|
| Peru | State-led extraction<br>- 1920s government reports on road building<br>- Analysis of laws governing eligibility for conscription<br><br>Rural elite extraction<br>- Census data on expansion of large estates between 1876 and 1940 | - Indigenous, peasant, hybrid movements (1920–1930)<br>- Complaints filed with the Office of Indigenous Affairs (1920–1930)<br>- Location of chapters of Tahuantinsuyo Pro-Indigenous Rights Committee (1920–1926) | - Official data on community recognition<br>- 2012 Census of Indigenous communities<br>- 2017 author survey of community presidents<br>- Analysis of content/organizers of movement demands (1956–1964)<br>- 2017 population census |
| Bolivia | State-led extraction<br>- Author compilation of reports issued by local prefects in 1900s/1910s<br>- 1900s registries of conscripts<br>- Location of railways and roads built in early 1900s<br>- 2020 author survey<br><br>Rural elite extraction<br>- Change in Indigenous community population, 1854–1900 (McBride 1921)<br>- 1950 Census<br>- 2020 author survey | - Qualitative analysis of location of networks of "legal chiefs" (*caciques apoderados*)<br>- Analysis of peasant movements (1946–1947) | - Government data on municipalities that have pursued autonomy<br>- Responses to the author's 2020 survey<br>- Petitions for land restitution in 1950s<br>- Support for Katarista Party (1980s) |

fact, considerable heterogeneity in the rights Indigenous groups want. This demand-side approach not only challenges a key assumption in the literature but also suggests that the prevailing focus on supply-side factors (e.g., neoliberalism, democracy's third wave, large-scale Indigenous movements) may be insufficient for explaining when Indigenous autonomy occurs.

Second and relatedly, my theory demonstrates the critical ways in which autonomy, assimilation, and integration are co-produced outcomes by state and society. Much prior work analyzes state policy toward Indigenous communities as a fully top-down endeavor.[30] Yet, these arguments assume a high level of state capacity, which is inconsistent with the observation that countries in the region have rarely been able to project power so fully into peripheral areas (Cárdenas 2010; O'Donnell 1993; Soifer 2015). As Yashar (2005) observes, even though states privilege specific identities, "they have been too weak to impose them" (7). Without a strong state, grassroots buy-in becomes essential for understanding where government policy is faithfully implemented. The demand-side approach of this book can explain why some Indigenous communities responded to state incentives to assimilate or integrate while others have sustained demands for autonomy.

Finally, the book provides a potentially important addendum to broader theories of ethnic politics, which often focus on *electoral* determinants of ethnic mobilization. Much of the existing scholarship argues that political entrepreneurs shape the incentives of groups to mobilize along ethnic lines (Bates 1983; Chandra 2004; Dunning and Harrison 2010; Horowitz 1985). This is particularly true during elections, when politicians seek to mobilize the identities that will deliver the most votes (Posner 2005). Elections can also activate more contentious and violent expressions of ethnic identity (Bates 1983, 61). Yet, given that most ethnic mobilization and demand-making for autonomy occur outside of electoral contexts, it is important to shift to the non-electoral sphere and explore the role of local, regional, and national organizations that constitute civil society.[31] I argue that these organizations often play a more central role in shaping ethnic identities and demands than elected officials do. Furthermore, a focus only on the contemporary salience of ethnicity ignores important past events that determine political officials' choice sets.

---

30. Yashar (2005) makes a similar observation to the one I make here, arguing that twentieth-century policies that emphasized peasant identities "fostered the fiction that the state had turned Indians into peasants and stripped indigenous ethnicity of its salience" (61).

31. See, e.g., Mundim (2022).

Whether ethnicity is a viable identity to mobilize—i.e., whether enough voters identify with a given ethnic group—is a product of the historical formation and erosion of group identities (Yashar 2005, 12–13). Careful consideration of key historical moments in which ethnic, class, and other identities become salient can provide an important—and necessary—complement to existing electoral theories.

## 1.6 Outline of the Book

The remainder of the book is organized as follows. Chapter 2 establishes empirical variation in the primary outcome—demands for Indigenous autonomy, integration, and assimilation across Latin America. To measure Indigenous peoples' preferences, I compile historical and contemporary data and draw on information from original as well as existing surveys. I examine the cases of Mexico, Chile, Peru, and Bolivia. I demonstrate that while Indigenous peoples often want autonomy, they vary greatly in their desire to prioritize it over other costly demands, including assimilation and integration. Those who are wholly opposed to autonomy often cite the fear that their children will experience exclusion and discrimination.

Chapter 3 develops an argument to explain the variation in autonomy demands outlined in Chapter 2. It begins by situating the forms of extraction I analyze within a broader typology of colonial and post-independence extractive institutions in Latin America. I then present my argument: state-led extraction—often through labor conscription—triggered increased community investments in Indigenous institutions and ethnic patterns of mobilization. These near-term effects persisted, increasing the likelihood that communities would demand *autonomy*. Rural elite extraction more often undermined Indigenous institutions, leading native communities to seek alliances with class-based organizations, such as unions and left parties. These organizations represented communities' interests as peasant workers, increasing the likelihood of *assimilation*. Where both forms of extraction occurred together, Indigenous identities persisted but Indigenous institutions were subverted to class-based organizations—leading to demands for *integration*.

Chapter 4 outlines the post-independence history of state-led and rural elite extraction in Bolivia and Peru. It provides the first comprehensive effort to fully map variation in extractive experiences in both countries and documents when and where rural elite and state-led extraction were likely to occur. It also explains *why* different forms of extraction happened where they did—ideas that are developed further in the empirical chapters that follow.

Chapter 5 demonstrates how experiencing only rural elite extraction promoted demands for *assimilation*. Using historical data and a careful analysis of the areas affected by hacienda growth, I show that peasant unions were most likely to emerge in Indigenous communities that had lost land to large estates. These unions then served to link Indigenous communities to left parties, including the Revolutionary Nationalist Movement in Bolivia and the military government in Peru, which advocated assimilation. I demonstrate that, today, communities affected by hacienda expansion assign less value to long-standing Indigenous institutions and are less likely to belong to Indigenous communities and organizations. Members of these communities are also less likely to identify as Indigenous.

Chapter 6 establishes that experiencing only state-led labor extraction increased demands for *autonomy*. Using process tracing and archival data, along with experimental and natural experimental evidence Bolivia and Peru, I demonstrate that government-organized conscription of Indigenous communities to build roads and railways triggered violent and nonviolent forms of ethnic resistance. Exposure to conscription also increased communities' membership in Indigenous organizations, reshaped Indigenous institutions, and created a collective memory of exploitation that sparked a long-term increase in community demands for autonomy.

Chapter 7 demonstrates that experiencing state-led *and* rural elite extraction increased long-term demands for *integration*. Using case studies, process tracing, electoral data, and a close analysis of historical Indigenous-peasant movements, the chapter sheds light on why peasant and Indigenous demands more often coexist in Bolivia than in Peru. The findings may also explain why Indigenous mobilization has been more likely to occur at the national level in Bolivia and the local level in Peru.

Chapter 8 summarizes the book's main findings and explores the potential scope conditions of the argument. To demonstrate both the empirical purchase and the limitations of my theory, I examine two cases beyond historical labor extraction: the 1930s-era Livestock Reduction Program of the US government and the contemporary seizure of Indigenous land in the Chapare region of Bolivia. I then turn to a discussion of how institutional and structural factors may condition the willingness of communities to express demands. I conclude by exploring the expected welfare effects of autonomy, with insights that should further refine our understanding of when communities pursue it.

The study of Indigenous autonomy is arguably more timely than ever. In recent decades, international organizations, such as the International Labor Organization and the United Nations, have issued guidelines that advocate greater autonomy for native populations. Governments have adopted frameworks for recognizing Indigenous rights from Nepal to the Central African Republic. Perhaps nowhere have conversations around Indigenous autonomy been more salient than in Latin America, where autonomy-expanding provisions have increasingly been enshrined in constitutions that recognize the plurinational or pluricultural nature of contemporary nation-states. Most scholarship on Indigenous rights in the region examines cross-national variation in governments' willingness to recognize autonomy.[32] Yet, as autonomy comes to occupy an even more central place within Latin American politics, it becomes essential to understand when local-level Indigenous *communities* embrace it. This book thus moves beyond supply-side approaches to analyze subnational, demand-side variation in Indigenous autonomy.

32. This research focuses on the opportunity space provided by pluricultural constitutions and peace agreements (Van Cott 2001), the importance of strong, national-level Indigenous movements in lobbying for autonomy (Yashar 2005), the nature of the predominant political-economic ideology (e.g., neoliberalism, developmentalism), ethnic fractionalization and socioeconomic development (Holzinger et al. 2019), and the role of international organizations (Brysk 2000).

# 2

# Exploring Variation in Indigenous Community Demands

"The law grabbed us, and we grabbed the law."

—BOLIVIAN INDIGENOUS LEADER IN INTERVIEW WITH
JOSÉ ANTONIO LUCERO, 1999

THERE IS a near consensus in the academic and policy community that "adopting more rights is better" (Chilton and Versteeg 2020, 63). According to this prevailing logic, disenfranchised and marginalized groups are likely to embrace any right offered by the government because these rights can be leveraged to make demands for further entitlements. Autonomy—government recognition of long-standing ethnic political and economic institutions— appears to provide a paradigmatic case of just such a right. Some scholars even describe it as "the demand through which all other claims are fulfilled" (Van Cott 2001, 31).[1]

Yet, assuming that disenfranchised and marginalized groups prefer autonomy risks ignoring potentially complex interactions among rights. While a given right may enable the achievement of more rights, it can also crowd out others. For a group that prioritizes collective land rights, for example, the right to private property may be a worse outcome than no rights at all. Similarly, for a group that wants representation within existing state institutions, political autonomy might be viewed as a step backward.[2]

---

1. See also Díaz-Polanco (1998).

2. Lawrence (2013) finds, for example, that colonial populations in Sub-Saharan Africa did not inherently prefer independence and often pursued it only after calls for political equality failed.

This chapter demonstrates the often overlooked variation in Indigenous groups' preferences for autonomy. In Peru, just two Indigenous groups, the Wampis and the Awajun, have achieved political self-governance. In Bolivia and Ecuador, fewer than 10 percent of eligible Indigenous communities have pursued political autonomy. And about two-thirds of Indigenous communities in the Mexican state of Oaxaca have adopted Indigenous political institutions (*usos y costumbres*) at the local level, but uptake in other states has been virtually nonexistent. Each of these countries has a policy framework to recognize autonomy, but communities differ in their willingness to take on the cost of pursuing this recognition.

Communities that embrace these autonomy-increasing policies likely have an underlying preference for autonomy. The converse—i.e., that a failure to act indicates opposition to autonomy—is not necessarily true. Groups may choose not to pursue autonomy because they prefer other rights (e.g., representation within the state, private land titles) that autonomy would crowd out. Groups may also reject autonomy because they prefer stronger recognition of their long-standing institutions than the government currently offers. I therefore use this chapter to examine preferences over autonomy in anticipation of the theory and analyses presented in subsequent chapters.

I perform a nested analysis of autonomy demands. Demands for autonomy vary at the community level, but the demands of a given community may reflect the distribution of preferences among all members or only a subset of influential group members. This chapter examines preferences for autonomy at various levels of analysis below, above, and including the community. I analyze survey data to evaluate the attitudes of individual community members and leaders and assess behavioral outcomes at the community and municipal levels.

I begin by investigating support for economic and political forms of autonomy. The former includes community decisions to preserve traditional patterns of collective landholding and to seek government recognition of these communal lands; the latter involves the recognition of Indigenous political institutions (e.g., deliberative assemblies). I then analyze the reasons why communities may not pursue autonomy before assessing other types of community demands, especially for assimilation and integration.

The evidence reveals three main points. First, many Indigenous peoples value autonomy and Indigenous cultural rights. Second, not all those who want autonomy prioritize it: they may believe other, class-based rights should take precedence. Finally, there is a strategic logic that can explain opposition to autonomy: Indigenous respondents fear discrimination, especially against children, or believe Indigenous institutions reduce their material well-being.

## 2.1  Variation in Preferences for Economic Autonomy

I first analyze community preferences for economic autonomy, or government recognition of traditional, Indigenous economic institutions (collectively held land). Communal land is arguably the fundamental Indigenous institution. Yashar (1998) calls demands for land "the symbolic glue that enables communities with diverse needs (including redistribution, titling, and territorial autonomy) to mobilize behind a common cause" (36). If land-related demands vary, we might expect preferences regarding other Indigenous rights to differ as well.

The divergence in preferences over communal land has deep historical roots. In Peru, the government offered to recognize Indigenous communal land beginning in 1920. However, fewer than 20 percent of Indigenous communities sought communal land titles between 1920 and 1962. While Peru's Indigenous communities differed in their willingness to pursue economic autonomy, Bolivian Indigenous communities varied in their willingness to *defend* it. In response to an 1874 law that sought to privatize communal land, many Indigenous communities in Bolivia opposed land privatization and blocked government efforts to survey their land. However, this was not universally true, as "'acceptance' reached a high point in Cochabamba . . . [where] many Indians in the department's central valleys willingly received private titles" (Gotkowitz 2008, 33). In Chile, two early-twentieth-century Indigenous organizations, the Caupolicán Society and the Araucanian Federation, diverged in their attitudes toward economic autonomy. The former "held its main celebrations in hotels in Temuco, wearing Western formal dress, with impressive bilingual menus. Its stance in the debate over lands was clearly on the side of division into parcels" (Albó 1999, 788). The latter, meanwhile, "was much more concerned with cultural identity and tradition. . . . In terms of the territory issue, it vigorously defended the communal character of the 'reductions' or reserves" (Albó 1999, 788). And in Mexico, many Indigenous communities fought the implementation of the 1856 Lerdo Law, which sought to privatize communal Indigenous lands, but others "saw ways to use the land laws to improve their situation," including seeking private titles to defend their land against outsiders (Caplan 2009, 177).

Evidence from more contemporary periods likewise demonstrates variation in communities' embrace of economic autonomy. Figure 2.1 plots subnational variation in preferences for collectively held land in Chile, Peru, Bolivia, and Mexico. In each case, communities had the power to decide whether to operate some portion of their land as private property; the government did not uniformly impose privatization and parcelization as it had in earlier periods. Communities' responses to this opportunity demonstrate how much they valued communal land—and thus economic autonomy.

Chile provides a helpful starting point for the analysis. In 1926, an Indigenous Mapuche political organizer, Manuel Manquilef, proposed a law that would allow each Indigenous community (*reserva*) to dissolve and parcel out its communal lands. Manquilef believed that "it was only through their legal recognition as independent property owners that the Mapuche would be able to achieve equality with Chileans" (Crow 2022, 83). A revision of Manquilef's law (Law 4169), approved by the Chilean Congress in 1931, required a third of community members to approve parcelization. Most Mapuche people opposed the law. A 1931 government decree accompanying the law stated that land privatization "frequently goes against the wishes of the majority, and sometimes even of the totality of the interested community members."[3] Despite general opposition, some 800 communities opted for parcelization, which gave 13,000 families individual land plots (World Bank 2002, 219). Most of these communities were in the provinces of Malleco and Cautín, but sizable minorities in other provinces also opted for privatization. Thus, while some Mapuche viewed Manquilef as a "traitor to the race," others appear to have embraced his assimilationist vision (Crow 2022, 83).[4] The law remained in effect until 1971, when all land was parceled out. In 1993, the Chilean government implemented Law 19.253, which recognized and protected Indigenous communal lands, resulting in a break "from the integration-assimilation

---

3. Decree 266, May 20, 1931, Chile.

4. It is impossible to determine the degree to which the process of land division was voluntary, but the available evidence suggests it often was. Law 4169 required that "the Court will make sure that the exchange benefits the Indigenous people, that they give their consent freely and spontaneously, and that they meet all the previously expressed requirements" (author translation). The World Bank suggests this process was, in fact, "voluntary" (World Bank 2002, 219). After the land was divided, however, legal institutions often benefited large landowners who purchased parceled Indigenous land (Comisión Verdad Histórica y Nuevo Trato con los Pueblos Indígenas 2009, 48–49).

Percent of native communities with only communal property

0    25    50    75    100

**Bolivia (2011)**
Lowland (TCO) — 120
Highland (comunidad) — 1108
Highland (ayllu) — 31

**Chile (1971)**
Valdivia (reservas) — 478
Osorno (reservas) — 40
Malleco (reservas) — 280
Cautín (reservas) — 2041
Biobío (reservas) — 6
Arauco (reservas) — 77

**Mexico (2016)**
Yucatan (ejidos) — 711
Quintana Roo (ejidos) — 281
Puebla (ejidos) — 1024
Oaxaca (ejidos) — 792
Hidalgo (ejidos) — 979
Guerrero (ejidos) — 1022
Chiapas (ejidos) — 26
Campeche (ejidos) — 374

**Peru (2012)**
South (comunidades) — 2770
North (comunidades) — 636
Central (comunidades) — 1436

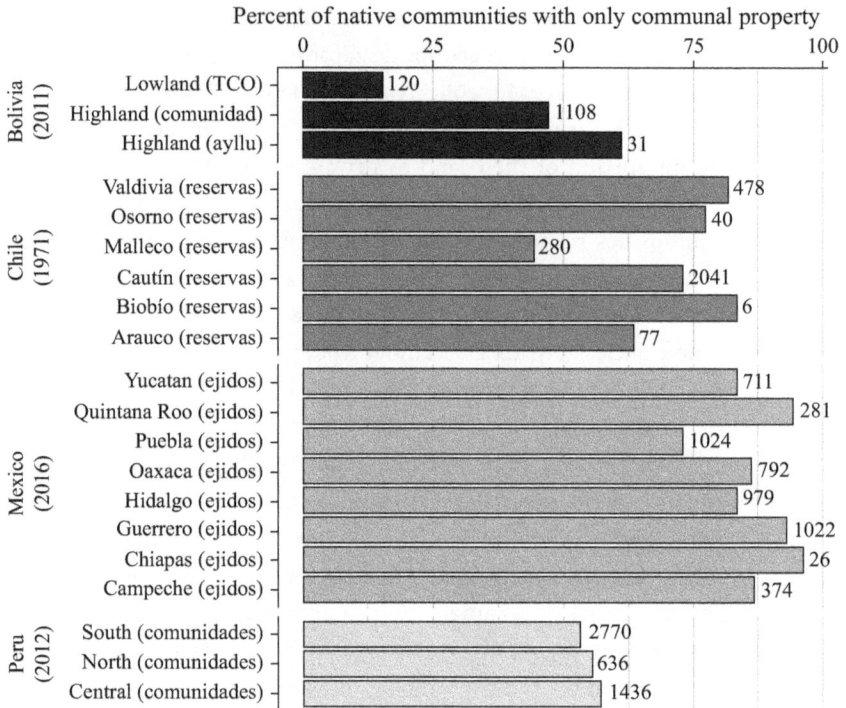

FIGURE 2.1. Private and communal land in Latin American Indigenous communities

*Note*: The graph depicts the percentage of Latin American Indigenous communities that operates all land collectively. These include Native Community Lands (TCOs), *comunidades* (communities), and *ayllus* (territorially based kinship groups) in Bolivia; *reservas* (reserves) in Chile; *ejidos* (collectively owned land) in Mexico; and *comunidades* (Indigenous-peasant communities) in Peru. I include subnational regions in Bolivia and Peru, Mexican states with at least one-third (self-identified) Indigenous population, and Chilean provinces where communal lands exist. The numbers to the side of the bars indicate how many communities are included in each category.

*Source*: Paye et al. (2011, 2013); Sistema Integral de Modernización Catastral y Registral (2016); Comisión Verdad Histórica y Nuevo Trato con los Pueblos Indígenas (2009); Instituto Nacional de Estadística e Informática (2014).

dynamics that had historically characterized state action" (Comisión Verdad Histórica y Nuevo Trato con los Pueblos Indígenas 2009, 133, author translation).

In Bolivia and Peru, Native Community Lands (*tierras comunitarias de origen*, TCOs), *comunidades* (peasant communities), and *ayllus* (territorially based kinship groups) can opt to operate at least a portion of their land as private property, leading to mixed land tenure systems. Divergence in the degree to which communities pursue this strategy provides insight into preferences over economic autonomy (i.e., greater support for autonomy should reduce privately held land) and potential divisions within communities.[5] In Peru, about 40 percent of Indigenous communities operate some of their land as private property, and almost 10 percent treat all of their land as private property. Nearly half operate all of their land collectively, which is true across Peru's regions (Figure 2.1). In Bolivia, there is substantially more cross-regional variation, with lowland TCOs being more likely to have parceled out at least some of their land than highland communities and ayllus.

In Mexico, land privatization rates have been relatively low. In 1992, the Mexican government amended Article 27 of the country's constitution to permit the privatization of collectively held land (*ejidos*). In states with a large Indigenous population (over one-third of residents), ejidos have been privatized at relatively low rates. In most of these states, over 80 percent of ejidos comprise only communal land. As in Chile, Bolivia, and Peru, many Indigenous peoples in Mexico feared that parcelization "would erode traditional customs and begin to divide people within the community," leading to land loss (Smith et al. 2009, 193). Communities often fought to achieve certification of community boundaries and sought to avoid their land being parcelled into private plots (Smith et al. 2009, 196). The notable exception is Puebla, where about 25 percent of ejidos have pursued parcelization.

The cases depicted in Figure 2.1 demonstrate key cross-community variation in preferences for economic autonomy. In Peru and Bolivia, about half of the Indigenous communities have maintained exclusively communal land.

---

5. Preserving communal land is essential to preventing "checkerboarding"—a label arising from the US case in which the interspersing of communal and private land prevents economically viable agriculture and coordinated development projects (Wilkins 2007, 118). Such land arrangements (called mixed tenure here) generally indicate divisions over preferences for autonomy.

In Mexico, around 75 percent of ejidos have preserved communal land,[6] but a sizable minority have opted to privatize their land. Likewise, in Chile, a large number of communities sought to parcel out their collectively held lands when given the opportunity. The prioritization of autonomy demands partially reflects the national-level political environment. Often, the state sets the terms of what demands are feasible or plausible. Groups may pursue the rights for which recognition is most likely—even at the expense of demanding those that are more inherently valued. Economic autonomy can be costly for the government to recognize as it creates potential barriers to expropriating Indigenous land for future infrastructure development and resource extraction.[7] Many Indigenous communities may therefore refuse economic autonomy because they believe the government is not credible in enforcing collective land titles.

### 2.1.1  Variation in Investment in Indigenous Economic Institutions

In addition to direct measures of support for economic autonomy, we can also examine the degree to which Indigenous groups value the underlying traditional economic institutions that government recognition would bolster. Such institutions are costly to preserve; they require a substantial investment of community members' time and—often—money. The *cargo* system, for example, exists throughout Latin America and requires community members to rotate through full-time service posts, including justice of the peace and organizer of religious and social festivals. During their months or even years of service in these positions, members of communities not only lose the income they would otherwise earn but also often bear the financial costs

6. This number is likely higher if we focus only on Indigenous agrarian communities, which must vote to become an ejido before they can privatize their land.

7. While autonomy is uniformly difficult to achieve, the feasibility of state action on integration demands varies by domain. For instance, cultural rights are less costly than policies that change the economic or political balance of power among ethnic groups (e.g., affirmative action and electoral reservations). Often, governments have pursued quotas over electoral reservations because the latter poses a greater threat to existing political parties (Htun 2016). Political autonomy demands that pose a threat to the state's monopoly of control over territory—e.g., self-governance, prior consultation—are generally the least likely to be addressed. Even when the state recognizes Indigenous political autonomy, it frequently erects barriers to autonomy's implementation. In Bolivia, both government officials and a leader of an important Indigenous organization told me that the national government was the key barrier to implementing political autonomy.

of the activities for which they are responsible. Several community members interviewed for this study noted that they could go bankrupt from fulfilling these responsibilities. While less time-consuming, other forms of communal labor (e.g., *tequio, faena, minka*) are also costly: community members are often required to contribute their labor to build infrastructure projects or farm collectively held land and to aid other community members who are in need.

Community members are increasingly unwilling to participate in these institutions. In a survey I conducted with over 1,000 Indigenous Bolivians, I asked respondents to estimate the likelihood that members of their community would work on an unpaid basis to produce a needed public work. Only 37 percent said members of their community were "very likely" to provide labor for such a project, while 36 percent said it was somewhat or very improbable that their neighbors would work on such a project.[8] In Mexico, unpaid community service constitutes a source of stress for many members. Toomas Gross surveyed community authorities in Oaxaca and found that 42 percent of respondents would worry if they were assigned a *cargo* with significant responsibility, while 35 percent would feel it was an obligation. Only 15.4 percent would feel pride or satisfaction.[9] Thus, the costs of participation can be high for community members, and investment in these institutions has declined in recent years.

Indigenous leaders can use a series of tools to induce participation in these potentially costly institutions. In an original survey I administered to over 300 Indigenous community presidents in Cusco, Peru, leaders frequently alluded to the importance of levying fines on nonparticipants, which ranged from US$10–30; some also mentioned that those who did not participate would lose their access to communal land and water. In one community I visited in Junín, a local official showed me the whip that was long used to punish those who did not comply with their communal labor obligations. The Mexican government conducted a study of *usos y costumbres* municipalities and documented the modal punishment for nonparticipation in the cargo system. The most common was social sanctioning (22 percent), followed by a fine (13 percent) and expulsion (5 percent). Other punishments included losing access to communal land or time in the community jail.

8. Twenty-seven percent said their community's participation in such a project was "somewhat probable."

9. I thank Toomas Gross for privately sharing this data.

Indigenous leaders increasingly struggle to implement these punishments. A key challenge has been the expansion of private landholding. Winder (2014) argues that "it has become increasingly difficult to mobilize voluntary labor. The *comunidad* has no way of applying sanctions to non-*comuneros* and to . . . *comuneros* who do not have usufructure [the right to use land belonging to someone else] of communal lands" (232). The ability to mediate access to collectively held land has traditionally served as an important source of leverage for Indigenous community leaders over their members.[10] A further challenge for Indigenous leaders has been increased community integration into external markets which has raised the opportunity cost to community members of participating in unpaid work. Several community presidents I interviewed in Peru attributed the decline in the use of communal labor to an increased expectation of payment from community members. Given the availability of outside opportunities of wage employment, many leaders have struggled to carry out collective labor events.

Indigenous elites have demonstrated varying abilities to overcome these challenges and compel members to invest in Indigenous institutions. Leaders in Mexico have been fairly successful. A survey conducted by Corres et al. (2016) in *usos y costumbres* municipalities in Oaxaca found that almost 70 percent of community members participated voluntarily in communal labor events (*tequio*), and 60 percent participated voluntarily in the cargo system. Gross's survey revealed that 81 percent of Oaxacan Indigenous leaders felt their ability to organize unpaid communal labor had increased or stayed the same in recent years.

In Peru, evidence about the recent trajectory of communal labor is more mixed. In 2017, I surveyed community presidents in Cusco, asking about the number of public goods their community produced using collective labor 20 years ago versus the previous year (i.e., in 2016). Over half (55 percent) reported that their communities produced fewer public goods with communal labor than 20 years ago. The rest noted there was no change or even *more* production of goods using communal labor. However, leaders were considerably more optimistic when I asked whether community members were more or less likely to participate in communal labor in 2016 than in 1996. The majority (59 percent) said that community members were at least as likely to participate today as they were 20 years ago; 31 percent said they were even more

10. In Appendix B, I demonstrate a strong relationship between communal landholding in Peru and the persistence of traditional labor institutions.

likely to participate today.[11] Thus, while evidence across cases often suggests a decline in the use of communal labor, there is variation across communities and countries, with many leaders and members reporting a strong persistence of traditional economic institutions.[12]

The above analysis has important implications for autonomy demands in Latin America. It provides suggestive evidence that Indigenous institutions are under some degree of threat; members in certain areas are unwilling to undertake costly investments in unpaid labor. Such contributions are critical to the survival of the Indigenous institutions that serve as the basis for autonomy claims. Yet, in many communities, Indigenous economic institutions continue to thrive. The theory I develop in this book can explain this variation.

## 2.2   Variation in Preferences for Political Autonomy

Just as communities are divided over preserving traditional economic institutions, they also hold complex and varied attitudes toward recognizing Indigenous political institutions. In contemporary Latin America, political autonomy has most commonly involved replacing subnational governments (often, municipalities) with traditional Indigenous assemblies. Mexico has arguably the strongest Indigenous autonomy framework. Since 1995, nearly 80 percent of municipalities in Oaxaca have operated under *usos y costumbres*, which substitute political party governance with communal assemblies and direct democracy.[13] Many people who live under these autonomy arrangements support their preservation and view them as superior to

11. I replicated this question but included a prime mentioning that community members increasingly expect payment for their labor. As the second and third panels of Appendix Figure OA2 show, community presidents' estimates were generally not sensitive to this new information. This may be due to the fact that the payment issue is already on the front of community presidents' minds; 70 percent of surveyed community presidents cited members' expectation to be remunerated as the central challenge to mobilizing unpaid labor.

12. Leaders also claim a remarkable ability to compel investment in Indigenous institutions. On average, Peruvian community presidents estimated that over 90 percent of members would participate in an unpaid labor event that they organized.

13. Indigenous identities alone do not explain these differences. Self-identification rates are similar across autonomous (71 percent) and non-autonomous municipalities (65 percent). Nearly 30 percent of respondents speak an Indigenous language in party-governed municipalities compared with 36 percent in *usos* municipalities.

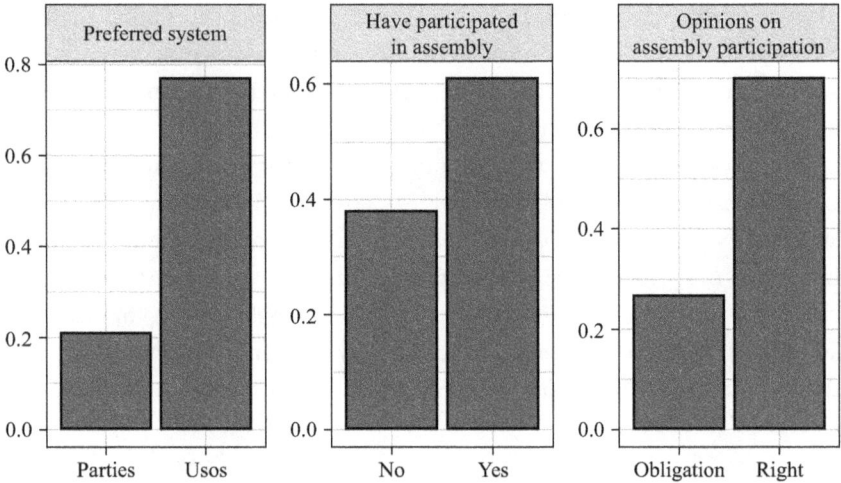

FIGURE 2.2. Attitudes toward autonomy in Oaxaca, Mexico
*Note*: The figure plots the percentage of respondents in each category. The sample includes only respondents living in autonomous, *usos y costumbres* (usos) municipalities in Oaxaca, Mexico (2016). The outcomes include responses to three questions: what is the respondent's preferred system of government, has the respondent participated in a community assembly, and does the respondent view assembly participation as a right or as an obligation. $N = 1,008$.
*Source*: Meixueiro et al. (2020).

state institutions, but not all do. A 2016 survey asked residents of autonomous, Indigenous municipalities in Oaxaca whether they supported maintaining their autonomous government or returning to governance under political parties; whether they had ever participated in their communal assembly; and whether they viewed assembly participation as a right or an obligation (Meixueiro et al. 2020).

Figure 2.2 plots variation in attitudes toward political autonomy in Mexico. While the *usos y costumbres* regime receives substantial support from survey respondents, about 20 percent would like to return to political party governance. Just under 30 percent viewed participation in the communal assembly as an obligation rather than a right, and almost 40 percent claimed they had never participated in the assembly.[14] A majority of respondents in

14. The data is only collected for *usos y costumbres* municipalities. However, the decision to adopt *usos y costumbres* is itself a potential measure of autonomy demands.

autonomous municipalities also stated that they prioritized state infrastructural investments over protections for Indigenous territories.[15]

Conflicts over autonomy in Mexico can further be observed in a comparison of two states. Oaxaca is characterized by widespread political and economic autonomy, which the evidence above suggests many Indigenous residents support. Chiapas has a similarly large Indigenous population that has articulated demands in a very different way. Recondo (2007) describes this difference, saying of Chiapas, "The discourse is closer to a classic indigenismo of the integrationist type than to the demands for recognition and autonomy developed in those years by the 'indianista' organizations" (193). He attributes this to the conflict that began in the state in 1994, arguing, "The members of the Clandestine Revolutionary Indigenous Committee would have wanted to give a 'national' scope to the uprising from the beginning, and avoid it[s] being perceived as an 'indian war,' a local ethnic conflict" (Recondo 2007, 194, author translation). As of 2023, just one municipality in Chiapas, Oxchuc, had voted to adopt *usos y costumbres*. Even in this case, however, where Indigenous peoples constitute over 98 percent of the population, support for autonomy was mixed.[16] Fifty-nine percent voted in favor of *usos y costumbres,* and 38 percent voted against it (Instituto Nacional de los Pueblos Indígenas 2019).

Support for political autonomy has likewise been uneven across Bolivian Indigenous communities. While 75 percent of Indigenous community members support political autonomy, only 26 percent are "very supportive."[17] Just under 20 percent are opposed or strongly opposed. The relatively low levels of *strong* support for autonomy may explain why less than a quarter of Bolivia's eligible Indigenous municipalities have pursued autonomous status. Even in municipalities that have adopted autonomy, attitudes remain mixed about whether its effects are positive or negative. A shortage of financial revenue

---

15. Interestingly, respondents chose to prioritize infrastructure investments even when they were given the chance to choose both options: territorial protection *and* infrastructure. See Appendix Figure OA1. Importantly, this finding does not suggest that a majority of Oaxacans disapprove of the government playing a role in protecting Indigenous territory. When respondents were asked to choose between territorial protection or resource extraction, they overwhelmingly (81 percent) chose the former. Figure OA1 therefore reveals that some Indigenous respondents may prefer government involvement in protecting Indigenous territory but will sacrifice this protection for other demands that are either more pressing or more credibly delivered by the government.

16. Ethnicity statistics are taken from the 2020 Mexican Census.

17. Author survey, 2020.

has led to public backlash against the autonomous municipal government of Charagua, Bolivia. One Indigenous leader said, "Now we have land, but what good is that if we don't have resources?"[18] Another resident echoed this sentiment: "We are worse than before. . . . I want a recall on this autonomy" (Stauffer 2018). This underscores an important point of this book; demands for autonomy can fail at any stage of the process. Indigenous groups may struggle to mobilize to make an initial demand for autonomy's adoption; they may choose not to complete the requirements for autonomy's implementation; and, once it is implemented, they may decide to return to the previous status quo of state institutions. Framed in this way, sustained demands for autonomy present a somewhat surprising outcome.[19]

## 2.3   Potential Risks of Autonomy

Communities choose to support or oppose autonomy for multiple reasons. Autonomy can promote the persistence of Indigenous cultures and institutions, resolve potential conflicts with outside actors, and provide the tools (e.g., language skills, land tenure security) needed to improve community welfare. However, autonomy can also fundamentally transform Indigenous institutions by—perhaps paradoxically—inviting greater government regulation. Some of these interventions, which are facilitated and justified by the process of state recognition, nominally promote democracy and inclusion. Governments have stepped in to force deliberative Indigenous assemblies to include women or to require that community posts be decided through free and fair elections. In Peru, for example, the national government requires Indigenous and peasant communities to demonstrate, among other tasks, that their *junta directiva* (directive assembly) includes at least 30 percent women, that community presidents serve no more than two-year terms in office, and that elections to the *junta* have multiple lists of candidates.[20]

Of course, even well-intentioned efforts by the state may have undesirable effects. Imposing term limits on community leaders in Peru, for example, may result in more democratic local government but can lead to frequent turnover of officials—making it difficult for leaders to build the networks and resources to govern effectively. In Bolivia, autonomous Indigenous municipalities have

---

18. See Stauffer (2018).
19. I return to this point in the conclusion.
20. See Superintendencia Nacional de los Registros Públicos (2016).

created governing statutes to delineate their local political institutions, but the government must approve them. This can provide needed oversight, but it can also impede Indigenous governments' independence. Such interference has been regularly observed elsewhere. For example, political parties in Mexico often violate prohibitions on meddling in local elections in autonomous Indigenous municipalities (Eisenstadt 2011).[21]

In addition to harboring fears of increased interference, some communities are deeply skeptical of the state's ability to provide autonomy in a way that benefits Indigenous peoples rather than the government. Silvia Rivera Cusicanqui maintains, for example, that state efforts to recognize Indigenous cultural rights "have been the concealing mechanism par excellence for new forms of colonization" (Cusicanqui 2012, 99–100). Hale likewise argues:

> Who, for example, makes the fine distinctions that determine when an initiative is needed for 'external protection' of an oppressed group's cultural rights, and when that initiative has 'gone too far' into the realm of 'internal restrictions'? The answer, implicitly at least, is 'the state.' And yet, this notion of the state as impartial arbiter of the conflict between individual and group rights is deeply suspect, since in nearly every important question of cultural rights the state is also a key protagonist in that conflict. Feminist theorists have perhaps most effectively drawn attention to this contradiction, given the irony and incongruence of a patriarchal state intervening on behalf of individual women's rights in the face of the male-dominated prerogatives of the community. (Hale 2002, 493)

The state has also meddled in Indigenous political institutions. In the 1930s, for example, Peruvian President Óscar Benavides directed the Ministry of Public Health, Labor, and Social Security to appoint the governing body of recognized Indigenous communities (Davies 1974, 127). Furthermore, because autonomy requires collaboration with the government to ensure protections are enforced, communities are incentivized to select leaders with strong ties to state officials. This strategy can promote productive cooperation in some cases (Baldwin 2015; Falleti and Riofrancos 2018), but co-optation or nefarious collusion in others. This presents a fundamental paradox

---

21. Extending beyond Latin America, Native reservations in the United States were given the opportunity to adopt autonomy statutes in the 1930s. Yet, the US government circulated a model piece of legislation indicating how much—and what kind—of autonomy the government would allow; most tribes adopted constitutions that closely reflected this model.

for Indigenous communities: community leaders who can best advocate for autonomy—through linkages to the state—may be the greatest threat to its legitimate exercise.

Governments can also discourage preferences for autonomy by blocking its implementation. In Bolivia, many majority-Indigenous municipalities have faced key logistical and bureaucratic challenges to achieving autonomous status. Government agencies have refused to support municipalities' pursuit of autonomy because it would replace local mayors who are aligned with the incumbent with potentially nonaligned Indigenous officials.[22] Thus, in some cases, preferences for autonomy are shaped by its particular institutional form.[23] In other cases, Indigenous communities oppose the very concept of autonomy, preferring instead either assimilation or integration. The remainder of this chapter discusses theoretical and empirical differences among these three demands.

## 2.4 Autonomy, Integration, or (and?) Assimilation

Indigenous peoples can demand many rights, which I group into three broad categories: autonomy, integration, and assimilation (Table 2.1). I exclude demands for secession and independence, which have often motivated instances of conflict in multiethnic societies but are extraordinarily rare in Latin America. The absence of these demands can be linked to three factors. First, the relative dispersion of Indigenous populations complicates collective action and prevents the formation of a clear, contiguous territory around which a viable independent state might form.[24] A second factor involves the strategic advantage of seeking rights within an existing nation-state. As discussed in Chapter 1, nation-states can provide public goods (e.g., national defense) that would be prohibitively expensive for small Indigenous communities to provide independently. A final factor relates to the limited benefits

22. Interview with Bolivian official in Vice-Ministry of Autonomy, July 2023.

23. While many respondents to my 2020 survey of Indigenous Bolivians reported that they desired political autonomy, they were hesitant to fully embrace the institutional form it has taken in their country. I asked how important it was for their community to achieve government recognition of traditional, Indigenous authorities and political institutions. While 66 percent said that this was "very important," only 26 percent were "very supportive" of their community adopting the political autonomy arrangements offered by the government.

24. See "Why Latin America has no serious separatist movements," *The Economist*, November 23, 2017.

TABLE 2.1. Autonomy, integration, and assimilation: Definitions and examples

| Autonomy | Integration | Assimilation |
|---|---|---|
| *Indigenous cultures and identities preserved within Indigenous institutions* | *Indigenous cultures and identities preserved within state institutions* | *Indigenous cultures and identities not preserved (and often eliminated)* |
| **Examples:** | | |
| - Political autonomy<br>- Communal landholding | - Electoral reservations/quotas for Indigenous groups<br>- Bilingual education<br>- Multicultural constitutions<br>- Affirmative action programs | - Class-based rights<br>- Private property<br>- Spanish-only education |

that independence would provide. Many instances of secession are motivated by a desire to obtain control over resources contained on a group's land but are exploited by those who do not belong to the group. With the exception of a small number of communities in the Amazon and the Andes, most communities lack resources that would animate such a push—which may be necessarily violent—for secession. Yet, even for resource-rich communities, other demands may allow groups to obtain greater control over resources without the potential perils of secession.

Autonomy demands generally prioritize recognizing or restoring communal land and granting local self-governance rights. They involve the recognition of Indigenous identities and institutions. Assimilation demands involve nonethnically differentiated rights that emphasize other (e.g., class) identities that cross-cut ethnic groups and generally undermine ethnic institutions and identities (e.g., Spanish-only education and private landholding). Integration demands occupy a middle ground between autonomy and assimilation: they often involve recognizing Indigenous identities and cultural rights within the framework of existing state and market institutions. Examples include multicultural constitutions, bilingual education, anti-discrimination policies, ethnic quotas and electoral reservations, and affirmative action programs.

Preferences for autonomy, assimilation, and integration are not necessarily mutually exclusive. Communities may prefer all three to the status quo but assign different weights to the benefits each provides. They can—and often do—articulate demands for packages of rights that cross-cut my three categories. For example, Chile's 1993 Indigenous law, which Indigenous communities helped author, included provisions for both recognition of Indigenous communal land (autonomy) and bilingual education (integration). Even where communities simultaneously make multiple demands, they often prioritize certain ones over others. For example, at the turn of the twentieth century, Indigenous community members in Bolivia viewed private land titles as the only way to sustain access to land and thus to their communal institutions; as Gotkowitz (2008) observes, "the acceptance of individual titles did not necessarily equal the recognition of private property" (34).

To demonstrate the importance of this issue prioritization, I analyze data from Mexico's 2017 National Discrimination Survey. Over 87 percent of the 3,000 Indigenous respondents stated that it was an "advantage" for Indigenous communities to preserve their customs and traditions. Yet, when asked to rank several issues in order of importance, only 11 percent said that a loss of political and cultural institutions was the main problem facing Indigenous communities today; 20 percent said poverty was the biggest issue, followed by a lack of basic services (19 percent), unemployment (17 percent), inadequate social programs (14 percent), and resource extraction (13 percent). Only 5 percent of respondents cited insecure land access.

Differences in priorities are even starker regarding issues that correspond more closely to autonomy, integration, and assimilation. In my 2020 survey of Indigenous Bolivians, I asked respondents to indicate how important particular issues were for members of their community. These included: children receiving bilingual education (measure of cultural integration), children receiving education only in Spanish (measure of assimilation), guaranteed representation of Indigenous peoples in local governments (measure of political integration), recognition of Indigenous political authorities (measure of political autonomy), and recognition of communal land (measure of economic autonomy).

Figure 2.3 depicts two key trends in Indigenous groups' demands in Bolivia. First, respondents who do not speak Indigenous languages but otherwise self-identify as Indigenous have remarkably similar preferences to those who speak an Indigenous language, with two notable exceptions: political autonomy and Indigenous representation. Indigenous-language speakers value political autonomy and mandated ethnic representation more than those who do not speak an Indigenous language. Second, support for autonomy—as measured

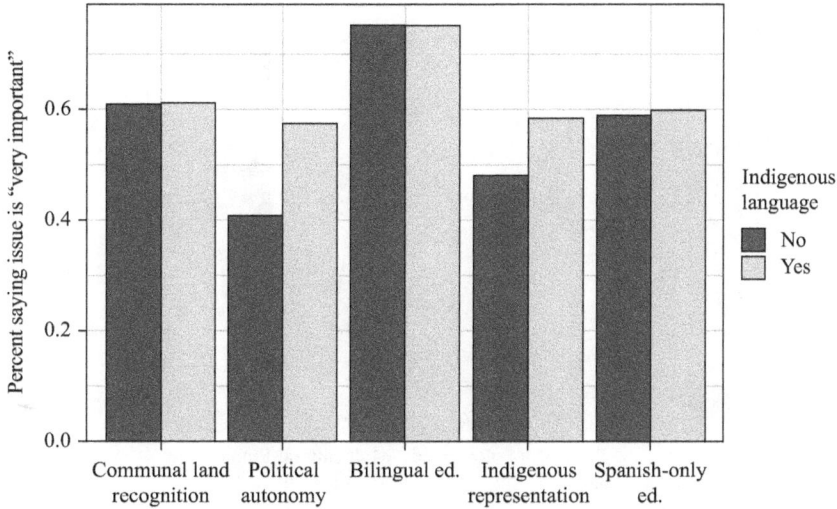

FIGURE 2.3. Demands for autonomy, integration, and assimilation in Bolivia
*Note*: The figure illustrates the percentage of self-identified Indigenous respondents who identify each demand as "very important." Expected satisficers—i.e., those who responded with the highest possible value for each item—have been removed. $N = 765$.
*Source*: 2020 author survey of Indigenous Bolivians.

by communal land titles—and assimilation sit at similar levels. The policy that is preferred by an overwhelming majority is an integrationist one: bilingual education.

The Bolivian evidence suggests that preferences over autonomy, integration, and assimilation are complex and not mutually exclusive. As discussed above, some communities may want autonomy but ultimately reject it either because they prefer another outcome or because they view it as too costly or impossible to achieve.

As in Bolivia, Indigenous groups in Chile have expressed divergent preferences over autonomy, assimilation, and integration. The Center for Intercultural and Indigenous Studies (CIIR) surveyed 1,400 self-identified Indigenous Chileans in 2018. The survey asked respondents to identify their support for various issues, including the return of Indigenous land, the recognition of Indigenous political authorities, reserved seats for Indigenous peoples in the Chilean legislature, employment, and constitutional recognition of Chile as a multi-cultural country. The results are disaggregated by Northern Andean Pueblos, which include Aimara, Quechua, Likan Antai, and Colla Peoples on

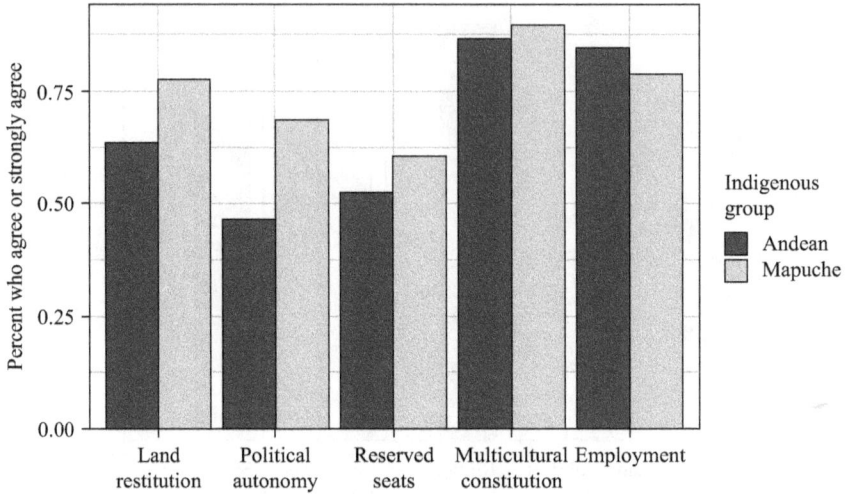

FIGURE 2.4. Demands for autonomy, integration, and assimilation in Chile
*Note*: The figure displays the percentage of self-identified Indigenous respondents who agree or strongly agree that the issues listed are important for Indigenous communities. Results disaggregated by Northern Andean (Andean) and Mapuche respondents. $N = 1,415$.
*Source*: 2018 CIIR Longitudinal Study of Intercultural Relations.

the one hand, and Mapuche Peoples of Central and Southern Chile on the other.

Figure 2.4 demonstrates that around 80 percent of Indigenous Chileans support cultural rights (integration) and employment (integration/assimilation). Policies that involve recognizing ethnic political and economic rights, including those related to autonomy (restitution of land, recognition of Indigenous political institutions) and political integration (reserved seats in the legislature) are more divisive. The Mapuche are generally more supportive of both autonomy and integration policies than Andean Indigenous respondents in Chile. Yet, there are clear divisions over autonomy and political integration, even within the Mapuche people; while a majority support these policies, a sizeable minority does not. For Andean Indigenous peoples, autonomy demands are generally subordinated to cultural integration and class-based concerns—in this case, employment.

The drafting of a new Chilean constitution has sharpened divisions around autonomy. The initial version of the Constitution in 2022 promoted integration. It recognized Chile as a plurinational country and extended cultural rights alongside a broader set of left-leaning, class-based guarantees. Some Indigenous peoples enthusiastically supported these cultural rights. Julio Hotus, a member of the Pascua Council of Elders, said he thought the new constitution promised "a new life for the country. . . . For us, the Rapanui, it is the opportunity of the century" (Cozzaglio and Abramovic 2022). Others claimed the constitution did not go far enough and should recognize autonomy. Víctor Queipul, chief of the Temucuicui community, rejected the constitution and demanded territorial authority, asserting, "We want to rebuild ourselves as a Mapuche Nation, not otherwise" (Cozzaglio and Abramovic 2022).

In addition to differentiating among the three types of demands, I also distinguish between rights that promote and reinforce Indigenous identities and cultures (integration and autonomy) and those that do not (assimilation). This distinction can be clearly observed in Peru. Some Indigenous leaders believe long-standing cultural practices may be a barrier to community progress. An Indigenous community leader from Cusco told me, "No one here wants to be *runakuna* [Quechua speakers] . . . [because] there is discrimination."[25] The leader then explained that his community did not, in fact, want to give up their language but wanted the outside world to see that they were not only *runakuna*. When I asked him how this might be achieved, he mentioned that the community needed to send more students to universities in Cusco and Lima and open their community to tourism. He then said, "Our only option is to adapt. That's what we have always done." Other leaders, however, noted that more investment was needed in Indigenous institutions, presumably as an alternative to state-sanctioned development. One leader told me, "Our land is the only thing that protects us. Our community is the only thing that protects us. Without that, we would have disappeared a long time ago."[26] When I asked what the responsibility of the government was to his community, he responded, "What it has never done. Leave us alone until we need them."

Similar variation emerged in a Peruvian Ministry of Culture survey of over 1,600 Andean and Amazonian self-identified Indigenous respondents. Figure 2.5 displays responses to three questions designed to measure attitudes toward Indigenous cultures and institutions. Respondents were asked to indicate the degree to which they agreed with three statements: children should avoid

25. Author interview, Urubamba, 2017.
26. Author interview, Apurímac, 2016.

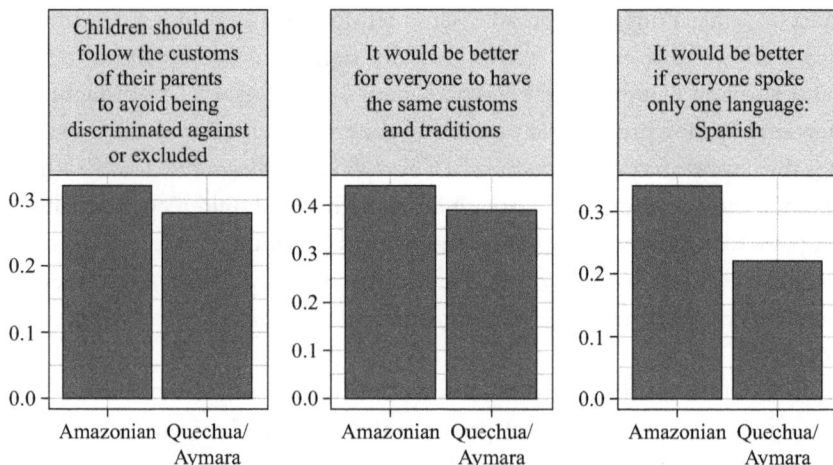

FIGURE 2.5. Attitudes toward assimilation and integration in Peru
*Note*: The figure plots the percentage of self-identified Indigenous respondents who agree with each statement. Quechua/Aymara respondents tend to be from the highlands, while Amazonian respondents are from the lowlands. $N = 1,750$.
*Source*: Ministry of Culture 2017.

adopting their parents' traditions to prevent discrimination; it would be better for everyone to have the same cultures and traditions; and it would be better for everyone to speak only Spanish. Most disagreed with or felt neutral about these statements. However, a sizable minority of highland and—especially— lowland Indigenous peoples expressed some support for them. This may be because of the particular marginalization of Amazonian (lowland) Indigenous cultures, even relative to those of the Andean (highland) Quechua and Aymara peoples. The cost of maintaining Indigenous institutions and cultures might, therefore, be viewed as higher—i.e., more discrimination—in the lowlands than in the highlands.

## 2.5   Conclusion

The book's first two chapters have discussed several critical axes of variation in Indigenous demands for autonomy. Chapter 1 demonstrated variation in the degree to which Indigenous groups have taken up political and economic autonomy in the Americas. The beginning of this chapter built on these insights to establish there is also variation in the privatization of communal land (economic autonomy) in four Latin American countries: Chile,

Bolivia, Peru, and Mexico. The chapter then evaluated more fine-grained data on community attitudes, examining variation in preferences for the Indigenous institutions that serve as the basis for autonomy claims. It concluded by disentangling the book's main outcome variable: demands for autonomy, integration, and assimilation.

The results outlined in this chapter motivate the theoretical and empirical exercise that follows. Community members vary in both their inherent preferences over autonomy—some want it, while others prefer assimilation or integration—and the degree to which they are willing to prioritize autonomy over other demands (e.g., employment, Spanish-only education). The strength of Indigenous institutions profoundly shapes communities' preferences for autonomy—and their willingness to act on behalf of these preferences.

The sociocultural and political economy approaches I discussed in Chapter 1 cannot account for the variation outlined in this chapter. Sociocultural theories assert that autonomy arises as a demand among ethnic groups that seek to reestablish honor and dignity in the wake of discrimination. The Chilean Mapuche, however, broadly share a history of discrimination and still internally disagree over the desirability of autonomy (Figure 2.4). Furthermore, Indigenous respondents disagree over whether discrimination is best addressed through assimilation or through autonomy (Figure 2.5). Political economy approaches, which argue that autonomy demands arise from a desire to secure access to valuable resources, likewise fall short. Nearly all Latin American Indigenous communities reside on poor-quality agricultural land. Since autonomy offers little material benefit (due to low resource rents), political economy theories would predict it to be demanded at low rates. Yet, even communities in highland Peru, Bolivia, and Mexico—where resources are particularly scarce—make autonomy demands.[27] Likewise, if demands for autonomy are driven by a desire to control resources, communities in the Amazon, which have more mineral and oil wealth, should be most likely to claim autonomy rights. Yet, they tend to value ethnic rights less than resource-poor highland groups (Figure 2.5).

In the following chapter, I introduce a theory to explain the variation discussed thus far. I argue that exposure to different forms of past labor extraction reshaped Indigenous communities, either strengthening or weakening their

---

27. For most Indigenous communities, especially in the highlands, fertile land was generally taken in the colonial and immediate post-independence periods, as I discuss in Chapter 4.

long-standing ethnic institutions. Where resistance to extraction occurred through ethnic identities and institutions, communities have been more likely to demand Indigenous autonomy subsequently. Conversely, where unions and left parties played a more central role in mobilizing resistance, demands for integration and assimilation have been more common. This theory sheds new light on the historical foundations of contemporary Indigenous demands.

# 3

# Explaining Indigenous
# Community Demands

Nowadays they call us peasants; those of us who are Aymara workers, miners,
professionals and intellectuals have been stripped of our personality as the
AYMARA people.

—JUAN CONDORI URUCHI, BOLIVIA, 1976

Indian people have become extremely wary of promises made by the federal
government. The past has shown them that even the most innocent-looking
proposal is often fraught with implications the sum total of which is loss of
land.

—VINE DELORIA, *CUSTER DIED FOR YOUR SINS*

THIS CHAPTER develops the book's central argument, which explains variation in Indigenous community demands for autonomy, assimilation, and integration. The primary explanatory variable of interest is extraction, which involves non-Indigenous actors appropriating Indigenous land, labor, and capital. I analyze two forms of extraction, which are distinguished by the actor that perpetrates them. The first is *state-led* extraction, which typically triggered enduring community-level investments in Indigenous institutions and, therefore, long-term demands for autonomy. The second is *rural elite* extraction, which occurred through the expansion of large estates and debt peonage arrangements; it drove Indigenous peasants to turn to class-based institutions (e.g., labor unions and left parties) rather than Indigenous institutions, and thus encouraged assimilation. Communities that experienced both forms of extraction—by states *and* rural elites—demanded integration, simultaneously articulating both class and ethnic claims but privileging the former over the latter. The chapter builds on the argument outlined in Figure 3.1.

I begin by examining the preferences of the primary actors in my argument: Indigenous community members, Indigenous elites, rural sector unions, and left parties. I then conceptualize different forms of extraction and justify my focus on one particular extractive type and period: the mobilization of unpaid Indigenous *labor* following independence. The remainder of the chapter develops my argument, theorizing how state-led and rural elite extraction shapes Indigenous communities' long-term demands, which arise through distinct mechanisms of persistence.

## 3.1 The Actors and Their Interests

Much of the prior research on autonomy highlights the importance of regional- and national-level Indigenous organizations in shaping communities' demand-making behavior. I build on this important work but focus on a much more local unit of analysis: the Indigenous community. For centuries, the community has been the primary level of social, political, and economic organization and identity for native peoples in Latin America. Each roughly the size of a village or a small town, these physical communities are primarily known as *comunidades,* but also as *ayllus* (Andean South America) or *calpulli* (Mexico). Historically, many of these communities comprised a local council of elders, a rotating president, and a deliberative community assembly in which only adult male community members were allowed to participate. Social institutions of reciprocity provided insurance against risk, and economic activity revolved around subsistence and often collective agriculture. The community president served an executive function during his—as it was almost always a man—relatively brief tenure in office, while the council of elders played an oversight role in guiding the community's long-term vision.[1] Distinct communities emerged during the pre-colonial period based on kinship groups; cooperation among communities—even those that spoke a common language—could never be assumed.

Because of the great diversity within and across communities, it is difficult to define a single set of preferences that would accurately reflect the goals

1. Many of these institutions remain in place in Indigenous and peasant communities.

| Historical cause | → | Proximate cause | → | Mechanism | → | Outcome |
|---|---|---|---|---|---|---|
| Mode of extraction | → | Community investment decisions | → | Nature of long-term mobilization | → | Autonomy, assimilation, or integration demands |

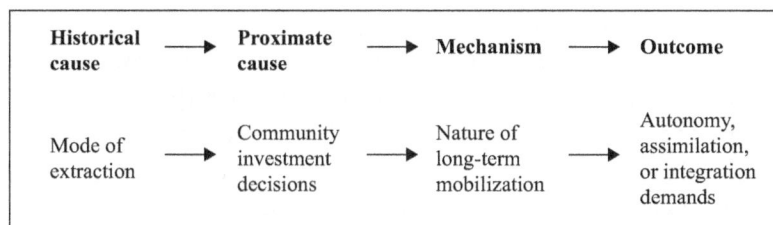

FIGURE 3.1. Theory: Extraction and Indigenous demands

and desires of all Indigenous community members. I, therefore, leave the preferences of Indigenous community members intentionally broad and assume that members make decisions based on two factors. First, they seek to preserve their community for future generations either by strengthening the traditional economic, political, and social institutions that bind it together or by promoting individual-level entitlements that increase quality of life and economic opportunities, thus discouraging out-migration. The former can best be achieved through autonomy, while the latter might be obtained through autonomy, integration, or assimilation. The second factor that shapes decision-making is the constraints under which Indigenous community members operate. Communities have traditionally been located in remote areas, often isolated from transportation infrastructure, communication networks, and schools. Especially in the past, community members depended greatly on Indigenous and non-Indigenous elites for information about threats (and how to address them). Elites could then use—and, in some cases, manipulate—this information to promote demands that reflected their interests.

Two primary groups of elites have historically mobilized Indigenous communities: Indigenous authorities through traditional, ethnic institutions and non-Indigenous leaders through class-based organizations (e.g., unions and left parties).[2] The Indigenous leaders I interviewed and surveyed for this book generally expressed an interest in maximizing their community's welfare while maintaining their own power.[3] Leaders usually reflect the preferences of their

2. Violent and non-consensual mobilization—such as participation in the armies of regional political and economic elites (e.g., *caudillos*) in the nineteenth century or military conscription at the turn of the twentieth century—is beyond the scope of this study.

3. These goals are often linked: if leaders failed to protect their community members, they could lose their political position.

community members, especially in Latin America, where communal assemblies select leaders. They also play a crucial role in shaping their members' demands for rights. Like ethnic entrepreneurs described in work on India (Chandra 2004) and Sub-Saharan Africa (Posner 2005), Indigenous leaders can determine the salience of local identities and thus the types of rights their communities can claim. They have greater access to outside information, which enables them to know rights available to their community.[4] They can faithfully (or selectively) communicate this information to shape members' preferences and behaviors.

Indigenous leaders have generally preferred autonomy because it protects the Indigenous institutions from which they derive their power. For example, communal land creates a territorial space over which leaders can exercise authority. As Yashar (2005) argues, "The legal registration of communities and granting of community-based property created a legally defined, state-sanctioned, geographic area that allowed for the growth and/or maintenance of politically autonomous local enclaves, Indigenous culture, and political practices" (63). Self-governance and sovereignty claims are difficult—if not impossible—to make without a territorial base. Privately held land can be bought or sold, threatening the community's territorial cohesion. For example, private land titles on reservations in the United States have led to a distinctive "checkerboarding" pattern in which non-tribal members bought land from tribal members, leading to out-migration and reduced group solidarity.[5]

Collectively held land regimes also give community leaders leverage over their members. Under these arrangements, individual members do not have a legal right to a particular plot of land. Instead, community authorities mediate access to communal land, a power they can use to encourage compliance with their dictates. For example, if community members do not participate in collective labor institutions to build or repair public works, the leader can withdraw their access to communal land. Thus, Indigenous leaders generally prefer autonomy because it reinforces the institutions from which they derive their power.

Where traditional leaders are unavailable, unproven, or ineffective, Indigenous community members have sought allies from outside the community,

---

4. Rank-and-file community members were sometimes unaware of different rights that might be claimed. This sentiment arises clearly in Elisabeth Wood's interview with a peasant laborer in El Salvador, who said, "We didn't even know about rights" (Wood 2003, 202).

5. See, e.g., Bureau of Indian Affairs (n.d.).

including labor unions and left parties. In the early to mid-twentieth century in Latin America, Indigenous peasants served as an essential base for revolutionary movements and parties that claimed to represent popular sector interests. These included Mexico's Institutional Revolutionary Party (*Partido Revlucionario Institucional*, PRI) and Bolivia's Revolutionary Nationalist Movement (*Movimiento Nacionalista Revolucionario*, MNR). In their efforts to construct broad, worker-peasant coalitions, left parties and allied labor unions emphasized the importance of class-based identities, viewing ethnicity as a source of division that could prevent the popular sectors from unifying. As such, these organizations generally preferred assimilation or integration policies to autonomy.

The relative power of labor unions, left parties, and traditional Indigenous leaders varied across communities. In this chapter, I argue that labor coercion shaped each actor's ability to mobilize community members to make demands on the state, which in turn determined the long-term likelihood of autonomy, assimilation, and integration demands. The next section explains why I focus on coercive labor institutions, particularly those that arose at the turn of the twentieth century.

## 3.2 The Importance of Labor Extraction

Spanish colonialism exposed Indigenous communities to various forms of extraction—which I define as any effort by rural elites or the central state to take Indigenous labor and natural and financial wealth on either a temporary or a permanent basis. Pre-colonial institutions facilitated these extractive efforts; the Spanish appropriated the language and norms around these practices to justify their coercive labor practices. For instance, the Inca empire required subjects to pay tribute and provide unpaid labor on public and private works. The colonial-era *mita*, through which the Spanish mobilized Indigenous labor to work without pay in mines, was adapted from these pre-colonial practices; *mit'a* is a Quechua word that referred to voluntary service contributions to the Inca empire. Extraction continued, and perhaps worsened, during the post-independence period.

I categorize extractive efforts by colonial and post-independence regimes in Latin America along two dimensions: the extent of disruption and the degree of Indigenous elite co-optation (Table 3.1). The first dimension considers how harmful these institutions were to Indigenous communities' short- and long-term welfare. Less harmful forms of extraction included head taxes,

TABLE 3.1. Typology of extraction

| | | Degree of Indigenous elite co-optation | |
| | | Lower | Higher |
|---|---|---|---|
| Extent of disruption | Lower | **State-imposed head taxes (post-independence)** Examples: Indigenous head tax | **State-imposed head taxes (colonial)** Examples: Indian tribute |
| | Higher | **State-led labor extraction (post-independence)** Examples: Road conscription, military conscription | **Rural-elite extraction** Examples: Expansion of large estates & debt peonage; colonial-era *encomienda* system **State-led labor extraction (colonial)** Examples: Mita |

such as the notorious colonial and postcolonial Indian tribute. These contributions of money, livestock, and agricultural produce were generally less invasive and did not remove individuals from their communities. They also allowed communities to justify preserving their communal land; colonial-era "tributary pacts" granted communities autonomy and certain land rights in exchange for tribute payments (Platt 1982). As such, some Indigenous peoples viewed the tribute as necessary for preserving their ethnic rights. Indigenous communities in Peru, for example, protested against eliminating the tribute based on the belief that "the community which we had enjoyed for several centuries . . . *had been correlative to the tribute* and that [with] it[s] being abolished, so also was [our community] abolished" (Thurner 1997, 113, emphasis in original). In 1858, communities in Ecuador "rose up violently and demanded the return of the tribute system" following its abolition (O'Connor 2007, 49).

Labor coercion, by contrast, had more pernicious and disruptive effects and often did not provide any reciprocal benefit to contributing communities. Coercive labor practices involved central states and rural elites removing individuals from their communities for extended periods, forcing them to engage in backbreaking labor. This type of extraction had enduring, negative consequences for the economic welfare and human capital of affected communities (Dell 2010). *Rural elites*, who were often large landowners, attempted to atomize community members by assigning them to small plots of unproductive land with corresponding debt obligations. This practice of debt peonage was particularly disruptive since it often endured for generations. Those who did not provide sufficient labor to the landowner lost their rights to the land. The division and individualization of land resulted in the dissolution of many Indigenous communities. A notable example is the colonial-era *encomienda*, in which landowners received Crown-backed access to unpaid Indigenous labor. *State* efforts to conscript Indigenous labor, in contrast, were often short-term; conscripts typically worked two to four weeks a year and then returned to their communities. Despite differences in their duration, both forms of labor extraction were ultimately harmful to Indigenous community welfare and were frequently met with resistance.

The second dimension of my typology is the extent to which extractive practices co-opted Indigenous elites. During the colonial period, Indigenous leaders, often known as *caciques* or *kurakas*, mobilized labor for state officials and rural elites (Dell 2010; Albiez-Wieck 2022, 93) and collected tribute (Platt 1982). Some served as administrators and foremen on large estates, maintaining order among community members in exchange for better access to land or less time working on the hacienda "demesne," or land on an estate reserved for the owner's use.[6]

Beginning in the late colonial period, governments reduced their dependence on Indigenous leaders for extraction. After the Tupac Amaru rebellion of 1780–1782, the Spanish Crown sought to systematically weaken Indigenous leaders in Andean South America to prevent them from organizing future rebellions (Jacobsen 1993, 96–97). The state's skepticism and fear of Indigenous leaders continued into the post-independence period, especially in Peru and Ecuador, where governments developed new methods of collecting tribute directly (Larson 2004, 106). The state also relied less on traditional ethnic authorities for assistance in conscripting Indigenous labor. Rather than working with caciques or kurakas, government bureaucrats mobilized workers directly for infrastructure projects.

While states bypassed Indigenous leaders in the late colonial and early post-independence periods, many rural elites continued to find it more cost-effective to collude with local, ethnic authorities to gain access to unpaid Indigenous labor.[7] These efforts involved both bribery and threats.

---

6. See, e.g., Mayer (1995, 184); Klein (1993, 148); Jacobsen (1993, 295); Paige (1978, 345).

7. That these forms of extraction were more disruptive also incentivized brokering agreements with Indigenous leaders to keep workers from fleeing or rebelling.

Landowners who failed to co-opt Indigenous leaders sometimes took Indigenous land (and labor) by force (see Chapter 7).

This book focuses on instances of disruptive extraction, which are those cases in which states and rural elites exploited unpaid Indigenous labor. Because of their adverse effects on community welfare, these instances of extraction should have had the most enduring effects. They were also the most likely to spark coordinated resistance by affected communities. Tilly (1978) argues, "any mobilization at all is more costly to the poor and powerless; only a threat to the little they have is likely to move them to mobilize" (75). For Indigenous community members, who tended to be very poor, extraction drained household resources, including land, labor, and material wealth (e.g., livestock, agricultural produce). The cost of inaction was high, and the *experience* of extraction generated a shared sense of grievance against the perpetrator (Mayer 1995, 58). Community members thus commonly mobilized collectively to defend against extraction; the form this resistance took varied based on the actor responsible for exploitation.

I focus on two types of extraction: state-led and rural elite extraction. State-led extraction—particularly in the post-independence period—bypassed Indigenous institutions and authorities. As such, it presented a clearer choice between an extractive state and non-extractive Indigenous institutions; the latter became an active tool for mobilizing resistance to extraction in which Indigenous communities could (and often did) invest. Rural elite extraction, in contrast, more often involved Indigenous elite collaboration with extractors. This collaboration reduced community members' trust in Indigenous leaders and led them to instead seek alliances with outside actors who could more credibly mobilize resistance to extraction: labor unions and left parties.

I focus on the turn of the twentieth century for three main reasons. First, this was when labor conscription and hacienda expansion were arguably most prevalent across the cases I study. Second, comparing across types of extraction within the same period reduces the influence of potential time-varying confounders. Finally, this period marked the beginning of the sustained mobilization of Indigenous communities through unions, left parties, and—to a lesser degree—Indigenous organizations. Therefore, resistance to labor coercion could be effectively institutionalized through popular sector organizations for the first time. The following section develops the first part of my argument: state-led labor extraction increased long-term autonomy demands.

## 3.3 State-Led Extraction and Autonomy Demands

Immediately after obtaining independence in the 1820s, governments in Latin America struggled to consolidate their power, define a national identity, and establish independent, productive economies. Between 1850 and 1950, post-colonial nation-states focused on "defining and forming/actualizing national community by extending citizenship and integrating national economies into a global capitalist economy" (Nugent and Fallaw 2020, ix). To expand their internal markets and export sector and increase their penetration into areas with historically low state capacity, governments invested in transportation infrastructure, particularly roads and railways (Summerhill 2006).

Most of these "liberal" governments were in debt from the wars of independence and struggled to establish non-colonial forms of taxation. They turned to foreign capital to purchase the materials for infrastructure projects, but labor, the costliest input, presented a greater challenge. State officials could not offer sufficiently high wages to recruit workers to remote, challenging worksites. They, therefore, reintroduced the colonial-era practice of using unpaid labor to produce infrastructure projects. In countries with large Indigenous populations, governments implemented new laws that forced Indigenous, working-age males to work without pay to build roads and railways.[8] Labor drafts for infrastructure were implemented in Bolivia (Schurz 1921, 88), Guatemala (Bulmer-Thomas 1987, 72), Mexico (Smith 2020; Vaughan and Lewis 2006, 227), and Peru (Basadre 2014, 197).

Many of these laws drew heavily on the legacy of the colonial-era mining *mita*, which required Indigenous men to provide unpaid labor in distant mines to extract wealth for the Spanish Crown. Like the *mita*, the labor drafts exploited uncompensated Indigenous workers to enable government activities. Both instances of labor conscription physically harmed workers, reduced the material wealth of Indigenous communities, and reinforced long-standing inequalities between Indigenous and non-Indigenous groups. Labor drafts in the post-independence period had such a disproportionate impact on Indigenous populations that these programs were often referred to as a modern *mita* (Contreras and Zuloaga 2014, 225; Mariátegui

8. During this time, governments also conscripted Indigenous men to serve in the military and deliver the mail.

1988, 74). However, the *mita* co-opted Indigenous elites, who were responsible for mobilizing workers (Dell 2010). Post-independence labor conscription instead relied on government bureaucrats posted to Indigenous areas (Chapters 4 and 5).

I argue that this state-led extraction constituted a transformative experience for affected communities in three ways.[9] First, it was associated with a particular historical moment (the turn-of-the-twentieth century) when many governments used native groups' labor to build massive infrastructure projects. Following the Great Depression, government revenue and incentives to build infrastructure sharply declined, reducing the demand for conscription. Therefore, the period of labor conscription was temporally delimited. Second, conscription affected a large portion of the Indigenous population.[10] In Bolivia and Peru, for example, all males of working age (18–60 years old) were eligible to be drafted, but these efforts overwhelmingly targeted Indigenous communities.[11] Nearly every household in affected communities experienced labor conscription, and observers often argue that this period of labor conscription harmed Indigenous communities even more than the notorious extractive practices of the colonial era.[12] Furthermore, as men were absent from communities, conscription also deeply affected women, increasing their roles in community and household leadership and defense (O'Connor 2007, 77–82). These experiences thus presented a moment of "significant change" for Indigenous communities. Finally, communities' experiences of labor conscription varied geographically; those closer to work sites were more deeply affected than those farther away. As a result, distinct trajectories emerged—because of exposure to conscription—that endured across time. In the next section, I argue that Indigenous communities met conscription with resistance; they invested in Indigenous institutions that provided the basis for future autonomy demands.

9. As such, labor conscription is analogous to what Collier and Collier (2002) define as a critical juncture: "A period of significant change, which occurs in distinct ways in different countries (or other units of analysis) and which is hypothesized to produce distinct legacies" (29).

10. In theory, labor conscription laws applied to a country's entire adult male population, but the wealthier (often non-Indigenous peoples) could pay a fine instead of serving.

11. Archival materials suggest around 40 percent and 35 percent of the community population in Peru and Bolivia, respectively, was eligible for road conscription in the early 1900s.

12. See, e.g., Urgente (2019).

### 3.3.1 *From Mobilizing Against Conscription to Mobilizing for Autonomy*

Community leaders have historically been responsible for organizing collective action among their members by offering inducements or making threats.[13] Yet, not all leaders have been able to mobilize their communities to make demands on the state. For example, a 1969 survey of community leaders in three Peruvian departments—Cusco, Junín, and Pasco—found that 36 percent felt they could not influence policy, and only 12 percent reported they could influence policy without outside help (Handelman 1974, 272). Nearly half the respondents said that they and their communities could "never" exert pressure on the government (Handelman 1974, 272). In a 2017 survey I conducted in Cusco, over two-thirds of Indigenous community presidents said they were "not at all" sure their community could obtain government assistance when needed. Since I assume that community leaders prefer autonomy to other outcomes, understanding why some can mobilize their members to make demands on the state while others cannot is essential to explaining variation in autonomy demands.

I argue that state-led extraction—and especially communities' response to it through Indigenous institutions and authorities—made communities more likely to demand autonomy in the future (Figure 3.2). Government participation in (and coordination of) extraction often reduced communities' trust in the state in the short term, which reduced the viability of paths to inclusion through state-sanctioned institutions (i.e., assimilation and integration). This was particularly true for the post-independence period, when governments generally refused to co-opt Indigenous elites into extraction, creating a clear dichotomy between extractive state institutions on the one hand, and the Indigenous institutions that could resist them on the other. In these cases, Indigenous institutions gained legitimacy at the expense of the state, and community members invested in them accordingly, particularly to resist state-led extraction.

This investment in Indigenous institutions, originally to resist state-led extraction, endured through three key mechanisms that promoted long-term autonomy demands. First, mobilizing to resist extraction redefined Indigenous institutions. Historically, communities had been organized in a relatively

---

13. As discussed above, threats can include revoking access to communal land, beatings, and banishment. One community leader showed me the wooden stick traditionally used to flog those who did not participate (Author interview, Jauja, May 2017).

| Historical cause | → | Proximate cause | → | Mechanism | → | Outcome |
|---|---|---|---|---|---|---|
| Mode of extraction | → | Community investment decisions | → | Nature of long-term mobilization | → | Autonomy, assimilation, or integration demands |
| State-led extraction | → | Investment in Indigenous institutions | → | Mobilization along ethnic lines | → | Autonomy demands |

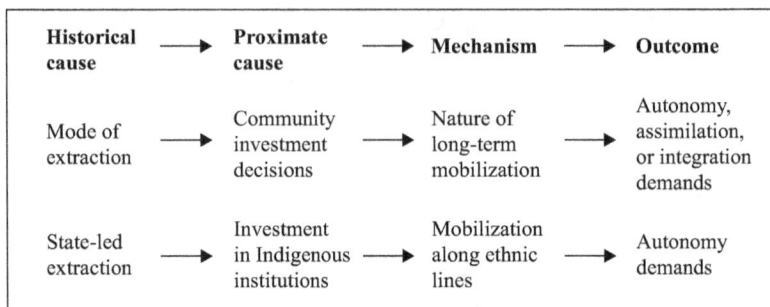

FIGURE 3.2. Theory: State-led extraction increases autonomy demands

horizontal way; members rotated through leadership roles. Labor conscription encouraged leaders to take on new and more powerful roles within their communities to organize collective resistance. Bolivian and Peruvian Indigenous community leaders adopted the titles of *cacique* (*chief*) and "colonel," respectively, which signaled the increasingly vertical structure of power relations within communities (Gotkowitz 2008; Heilman 2010b). This hierarchical structure endured. Gotkowitz (2008) elaborates how Bolivian *caciques* "created their own institutions, and sought official recognition of their titles" (87).[14] While the title of colonel vanished in Peru, leaders remained able to coerce members into collective action (Heilman 2010b). As these leaders' authority strengthened, they endeavored to promote both the ethnic *identities* that bound their communities together and the ethnic *institutions* that helped legitimize their claims to authority.

Second, stronger Indigenous institutions and identities led communities to develop deeper ties to Indigenous *organizations*, which further reinforced ethnic identities and institutions; many of these groups evolved into contemporary pro-Indigenous rights organizations. Peruvian Indigenous leaders formed local branches of the Tahuantinsuyo Pro-Indigenous Rights Committee, which organized communities to resist road conscription and demand government respect for Indigenous institutions (de la Cadena 2000, 82–99).[15] In response to conscription, Bolivian Indigenous community leaders founded the Oldest Autonomous Mayors, which declared that "Indians could no longer

14. Irurozqui (2000) observes that *caciques* sought "to strengthen . . . their organizations in the face of an adverse climate" (105).

15. In Huanta, the Committee's local branch was accused of "stirring up the area's Indians" to resist conscription (Heilman 2010a, 65).

be subjected to 'forced' labor" (Ari 2014, 102). As in Peru, these organizations reinforced demands for "specific ethnic programs . . . [which] all demanded the Indianization of the collectorships" (Platt 1987, 304). This mobilization around ethnic identity proved self-reinforcing and thus endured in the face of twentieth-century challenges, including market integration and the rise of peasant unions—both of which threatened to undermine community institutions.[16] Arias (1990), for example, argues of Guatemalan Indigenous groups, "Where a dominated group maintains its own ethnic-cultural identity, that very identity easily becomes a force for the mobilization of that group" (230).

Finally, state-led extraction generated a sustained grievance against the government as well as a collective memory of the role of Indigenous institutions as both a substitute for the state and a source of resistance to it. Since state-led extraction, including labor conscription, only targeted Indigenous peoples, paths to inclusion in the state (e.g., integration or assimilation) did not seem credible. When communities could not trust state institutions to represent their interests, ethnic institutions offered a potentially attractive and necessary alternative.

Together, these three mechanisms of persistence increased the salience of ethnic identities and generated enduring preferences for autonomy. Preserving Indigenous institutions and leaders served as the basis for autonomy claims: autonomy is unnecessary if communities have no ethnic institutions to recognize. Furthermore, connections to Indigenous organizations reinforced ethnic identities and helped crowd out the influence of unions, which often mobilized communities along class lines. Collective memory also helped promote and sustain ethnic autonomy demands. Rappaport (1990) observes that "knowledge of the past is . . . central to efforts at strengthening a communal identity, indispensable in the maintenance of autonomy in the face of European domination" (11–12).[17] Furthermore, the memory of past ethnic resistance to the government may have offered an important model for future mobilization against the state (Tarrow 2011, 29–30).

16. The 1969 survey in Peru (referenced above) highlights the importance of these linkages with external allies in facilitating effective mobilization.

17. Collective memory can, therefore, facilitate Indigenous mobilization and protest, which in turn reinforce collective memory and, more broadly, an Indigenous consciousness (Zubrzycki and Woźny 2020, 178–179). Irurozqui (2000) analyzes Bolivian Indigenous uprisings in response to labor conscription in the early twentieth century and remarks on the lasting "impact the rebellions had on Indian national and political consciousness," creating an Indigenous identity that facilitated long-term mobilization for ethnic rights (87).

State-led extraction shaped not only preferences for autonomy but also community members' incentives and capacity to engage in costly mobilization on its behalf. Incumbents at the subnational and national levels have often resisted autonomy and have long sought to establish control over peripheral areas, where state presence and security have been historically weak (Mazzuca 2021; O'Donnell 1993; Soifer 2015). While offering autonomy to locally legitimate Indigenous leaders may promote order and good governance,[18] it is generally viewed as a second-best option for incumbents—who have preferred direct forms of rule that assimilation might more effectively achieve. As such, even when national governments have adopted policies that offer autonomy, they have frequently erected financial and bureaucratic obstacles to obtaining it that result in an uneven and generally low level of implementation. Decade-long waitlists, prohibitively expensive registration fees, and impenetrable bureaucratic paperwork have all threatened to dampen community members' enthusiasm for autonomy.

The three mechanisms of persistence that arise from resistance to conscription can help Indigenous communities overcome these barriers and mobilize to demand autonomy. Strong Indigenous institutions can facilitate the collective action needed to encourage community members to contribute time and money to achieve autonomy.[19] Leaders can also draw on the collective memory of conscription to organize protests and marches for autonomy— demanding that the government atone for past wrongs.[20] Memory of these grievances can encourage communities to invest in preserving historical documents (e.g., colonial-era land titles, nineteenth-century legal judgments) that are essential to community survival and that bolster Indigenous rights claims (Medrano 2011, 289). Finally, Indigenous organizations can provide financial and legal resources, which reduce the cost of achieving autonomy and make communities more likely to mobilize to demand it.

Communities that experienced state-led extraction have been more likely to demand autonomy in the contemporary period. This was particularly true for labor conscription, which was the most systematic, enduring, and widespread example of state-led extraction in the twentieth century. Earlier

18. See, e.g., Baldwin (2013) and Falleti and Riofrancos (2018).

19. For example, where communal landholding institutions persist, those who do not participate in efforts to gain autonomy may be denied land rights.

20. The memory of resistance to conscription can also provide a roadmap for future mobilization.

experiences with state-led extraction, including the Indian head tax, could have triggered similar reactions. Yet, these effects may have been fleeting due to the absence of the theorized mechanisms of persistence for conscription. Unlike many prior forms of extraction, Indigenous elites were generally not co-opted into conscription in the early twentieth century and therefore played an important role in organizing responses to it; the collective mobilization they organized—through Indigenous institutions—made communities more likely to demand autonomy.

## 3.4   Rural Elite Extraction and Assimilation Demands

Just as the period between 1850 and 1950 resulted in a massive expansion of state infrastructure through the mobilization of unpaid Indigenous labor, this period also presented new opportunities for rural elites to take native groups' land and labor. In the early colonial period, the Spanish Crown seized productive Indigenous land and redistributed it to European settlers, reset-tling Indigenous communities into concentrated *reducciones* (reductions), where colonizers could more easily monitor them and extract their wealth. However, during the remainder of the colonial era—and, in some cases, after independence—governments offered protection for Indigenous lands against non-Indigenous landowners. The colonial-era Indian tribute, a prin-cipal source of revenue for the Spanish Crown, demonstrates this logic. While post-independence governments had hoped to abolish the tribute to sever ties with the colonial era, they often maintained it due to a lack of alterna-tive revenue sources. For instance, in 1830s Ecuador, the tribute accounted for 35 percent of national revenue and half to two-thirds of district-level rev-enue in the highlands (Van Aken 1981, 450). In Bolivia, the importance of the tribute rose from 45 percent of total revenues in 1832 to 56 percent in 1846 (Klein 1992, 114). In Peru, the Indian tribute accounted for over a quar-ter of government income between 1839 and 1845 (Bonilla 1985, 544–545). To encourage Indigenous communities to pay their tax obligations, colonial and post-independence governments entered into the aforementioned trib-utary pacts with Indigenous communities (Caplan 2009, 19; Platt 1982). If a large landowner attempted to encroach on a community's land, representa-tives of that community could seek recourse through courts or bureaucratic agencies. Furthermore, landowners, who often received a share of the tribute, had an incentive to avoid overextraction and the community out-migration or rebellion it might trigger.

The tributary pact—and thus government protections for Indigenous land rights—rapidly eroded in the mid-nineteenth century. A boom in primary product exports allowed governments to reduce their dependence on the tribute. In Ecuador, the mid-century cacao export boom significantly increased customs revenues, which rose to 35 percent of total revenue by the late 1850s; the tribute fell to just over 8 percent of government income in that decade (Van Aken 1981, 447–450). In Peru, a boom in guano, a fertilizer produced by seabirds, reduced the relative importance of the tribute, leading to its abolition in 1854 (Bonilla 1985, 252). And in Bolivia, the nineteenth-century growth of silver exports decreased the importance of the tribute, which fell to only 10 percent of national income by 1886 (Grieshaber 1977, 221). By 1900, all governments in the region had formally abolished the Indian tribute.

The export boom also boosted large landowners' demand for productive land and rural labor. Liberal governments of the late nineteenth century offered limited opposition to rural elites' expansionist goals; they were eager to promote economic growth and no longer had an incentive to protect Indigenous land. Large-scale land reforms divided and privatized Indigenous communal land; these included the Ley Lerdo in Mexico (1856), the Ley de Exvinculación de Tierras in Bolivia (1874), as well as similar laws in Peru, El Salvador, Guatemala, and Nicaragua.[21]

Landowners exploited these laws to purchase or seize Indigenous communal land—particularly to access the Indigenous labor tied to it. This resulted in an enormous erosion of Indigenous communal lands and an increased concentration of land in the hands of a small number of often non-Indigenous landowners. Indigenous communities in Bolivia contained about half of the country's land and rural population in 1880, but by 1930, these communities contained "less than a third of both" (Klein 1992, 152). In Mexico, Indigenous communities lost their right to exist under the Ley Lerdo (Lerdo Law), enabling a massive expansion of large estates; by 1910, 4 million Indigenous people had no land title, and many of them worked for the 834 landowners who controlled 90 percent of the country's cultivated land (Ewen 2016, 84).

I argue that this period of hacienda expansion—from roughly 1870 to 1930—fundamentally reshaped Indigenous communities in three ways that correspond to a critical juncture (Figure 3.3). First, this period of hacienda expansion was associated with a unique and clearly delineated historical moment, fueled mainly by primary product export booms. It thus differed

---

21. See, e.g., Gotkowitz (2008, 40). See also the Dawes Act of 1887 in the United States.

| Historical cause | → | Proximate cause | → | Mechanism | → | Outcome |
|---|---|---|---|---|---|---|
| Mode of extraction | → | Community investment decisions | → | Nature of long-term mobilization | → | Autonomy, assimilation, or integration demands |
| Rural elite extraction | → | Investment in labor organizations | → | Mobilization along class lines | → | Assimilation demands |

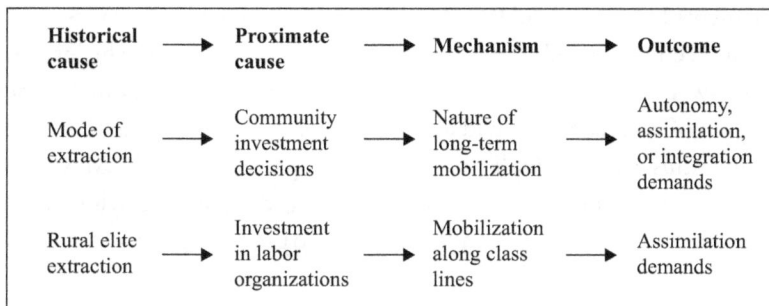

FIGURE 3.3. Theory: Rural elite extraction increases assimilation demands

from prior periods; Bernstein et al. (1992) argue that "from 1870, Latin America experienced an expansion of export agriculture, not least on the *hacienda*, that was qualitatively different from, as well as much greater than, earlier phases of commercialization" (37). Following the Great Depression and the subsequent period of import substitution industrialization, however, investment in agriculture declined considerably, reducing the returns to labor-intensive agriculture and slowing hacienda expansion once again.

Second, hacienda expansion at the turn of the twentieth century provided a moment of significant change. Large landowners seized Indigenous land, trapping many community members in exploitative relationships of debt peonage: they labored for the landowner in exchange for permission to live and work on the lands they traditionally occupied. The transition from subsistence—and in a few cases market-oriented—production to debt peonage arrangements fundamentally transformed the nature of production and work in Indigenous communities. Previously, risk came mainly from nature, other communities, or non-Indigenous outsiders, who could threaten the community's productive capacity. Now, danger came from the abusive practices of landowners, who exploited laborers and could kick workers off the estate. Despite the greater precarity of work in these communities, their social bonds were generally not disrupted; political and social hierarchies often remained intact in these "captive communities" (Albó 1999, 772; Grieshaber 1979, 120; Favre 1976, 130–131).

Finally, hacienda expansion was unevenly experienced across geographic space. A community's exposure to land seizure by large landowners depended on the value of labor and land in the surrounding area. Communities in areas conducive to producing booming primary products were especially vulnerable to land seizures. For example, Indigenous communities in Peru's southern

departments lost more land than those in the central regions because the former produced sheep and alpaca for wool—an increasingly valuable export in
the early twentieth century ( Jacobsen 1993).[22] The same was true in the northern region of Bolivia, which had a similar geography and climate to southern
Peru and thus was favorable to sheep and alpaca grazing. In Mexico, the
most vigorous assaults on communal land emerged in Morelos, where Indigenous communities possessed lands conducive to producing sugar (Grieshaber
1979, 118).

In this section, I argue that these experiences with rural elite extraction shaped Indigenous demands in distinct ways from state-led extraction.
Whereas the latter provoked a collective reinvestment in Indigenous institutions, the former triggered community-level investments in non-Indigenous,
class-based labor unions and left political parties. These organizations' raison
d'être was often to develop a broad, cross-ethnic alliance based on class identities. Close linkages to these organizations transformed community member
preferences, promoting demands for assimilation over autonomy.

### 3.4.1   From Indigenous Communities to Peasant Communities

I argue that large estate owners' encroachment onto native lands fundamentally reshaped community members' ties to ethnic institutions. Historically,
communities maintained a moral economy organized around subsistence
agriculture in which social insurance institutions (e.g., reciprocity, redistribution) protected community households against economic volatility.[23] For
example, if the head of a household fell ill, other community members would
help harvest his crops. By the early twentieth century, some communities,
albeit relatively few, had embraced the market economy, with some members
selling their agricultural products and textiles in external markets.

However, large landowners' capture of Indigenous community land fundamentally disrupted both moral and market economies. While production
previously benefited either an individual or the community, debt peonage
relationships privileged the needs and desires of landowners. When seizing
Indigenous lands, landowners particularly sought to capture rural labor, which
was scarcer than land. Landowners thus had an incentive to keep community members tied to captured lands through debt peonage arrangements

---

22. Sheep wool exports nearly tripled between 1840 and 1917 ( Jacobsen 1993, 173–174).
23. See, e.g., Polanyi (1944); Scott (1977); Paige (1978); Thompson (1971).

that promised "tenants" usufruct rights to a plot of land in exchange for either providing a portion of that land's products to the landowner or working on a plot of land operated by the landowner. These relationships were profoundly hierarchical, exploitative, abusive, and precarious. Debt peonage arrangements, therefore, created a base of community members who could be mobilized around a common grievance of exploitation. In the case of state-led extraction, this resistance occurred along ethnic lines and through Indigenous institutions.

Yet, rural elite extraction often undermined these Indigenous institutions. Indigenous leaders generally faced prohibitively high barriers to mobilizing against hacienda owners. While community leaders continued to fulfill many traditional functions (e.g., organizing festivities), the hacienda owner could quickly replace them if they threatened unrest. Landlords often intervened in and manipulated Indigenous institutions to serve their own goals, selecting and replacing Indigenous leaders at will.[24] In the early phases of hacienda expansion, some Indigenous leaders actively colluded with landowners to obtain better quality land and supervisory positions (Jacobsen 1993, 295). As such, rural elite extraction frequently blurred the line between extractive and Indigenous institutions and, thereby, discredited the latter.

Debt peonage also weakened Indigenous institutions by transforming the demands of community members in ways that diverged from long-standing claims for Indigenous rights. The exploitative and ongoing relationship between landlords and peons increased the salience of demands for basic worker protections; such demands did not exist previously when labor was relatively free. At the turn of the century, Indigenous leaders had limited expertise in articulating or lobbying for these rights and thus struggled to mobilize collective resistance to hacienda owners. The early period of hacienda expansion (c. 1870 to c. 1930) was therefore characterized by something of a paradox: while community members had many grievances against landowners, there were few community-based channels through which these demands could be expressed. As Albó (1999) observed, "[debt peonage] tended to generate in its victims an ambiguous attitude, filially submissive and at the same time rebellious" (769).

In the first decades of the twentieth century, new organizations, including labor unions and political parties, arose to faithfully represent the demands arising from peons on the large estates. As early as the 1920s and 1930s, rural sector unions emerged in the countryside to mobilize Indigenous

24. See, e.g., Carter (1965, 43).

communities. In Peru, these included the Regional Indian Workers Federa-tion, created in 1923, and the General Federation of Yanaconas, established in 1924 (Albó 1999, 780). The first peasant union in Bolivia emerged in 1936 in Cochabamba, and the Juan Montalvo Union, which later evolved into the Ecuadorian Federation of Indians, became Ecuador's first peasant union when it was established in 1926 (Albó 1999, 796–801). In 1931, the Mexican Peasant Confederation (CCM) was formed to connect the diverse regional peasant unions created since the turn of the century (de la Peña 1998, 320). The power of rural sector unions steadily expanded in the ensuing decades. By 1954, there was a peasant union "in every major village and in many smaller aldeas in Guatemala," and the *campesino* (peasant) league had become "the largest organization in the country" (Handy 1994, 170).

Left parties also expanded their presence during this time, often draw-ing on support from hacienda workers. The diffusion of Marxism that pro-voked the emergence of unions also inspired intellectuals and urban elites to form communist and socialist political parties. José Carlos Mariátegui, a noted Peruvian intellectual during the 1920s, founded the Communist Party of Peru; he believed that traditional Indigenous institutions were fundamen-tally communist and, as such, native peoples should be the principal base of the country's communist revolution (Mariátegui 1988). Ecuador's Commu-nist Party, founded in 1931, similarly mobilized Indigenous communities in the countryside to create a broad "worker-peasant bloc" (Becker 2008, 35). Social-ist and communist parties also gained strength in Chile in the 1950s, when Salvador Allende's Popular Socialist Party adopted the motto "the unity of the Mapuches [a Chilean Indigenous ethnic group] and the poor Chileans" (Albó 1999, 821). In Bolivia, the 1940s witnessed the rise of the MNR, which mobi-lized Indigenous peasants in the countryside and eventually seized power in 1952 (Gotkowitz 2008).

Non-Marxist left parties also experienced a degree of success in mobiliz-ing Indigenous peasants during the mid-twentieth century. The Party of the Guatemalan Revolution, an explicitly non-Communist, left party that orga-nized Indigenous and non-Indigenous peasants, won an overwhelming share of the rural vote in the early 1950s (Handy 1994, 171). In Mexico, the National Revolutionary Party under President Lázaro Cárdenas (1934–1940) mobilized Indigenous peasants, who it considered essential members of a nascent and "very fragile coalition" (Dawson 2020, 96).

Rural unions and left parties shared the goal of building a worker-peasant alliance to facilitate pro-labor policies, a Marxist revolution, or both; the linkages between these organizations were often strong, and in many cases the delineation between them was not abundantly clear. Whether mobilizing together or separately, these non-Indigenous organizations required a large, popular sector base to achieve their goals. Hacienda workers represented just such a population, which had a well-defined but latent grievance. Unions and left parties sought to mobilize these workers around the exploitative and abusive conditions of debt peonage—and create a class consciousness among peasants that would serve the organizations' ideological objectives.

Mobilizing around class was not simply a sincere desire of left parties and unions but also a strategic decision. The urban-rural cleavage frequently overlapped with an ethnic divide between *mestizos* (those of mixed European and Indigenous descent), who were more likely to reside in urban areas, and Indigenous peoples, who generally lived in rural areas. Downplaying ethnicity and emphasizing a common class goal allowed unions and parties to paper over potential internal divisions. This generally involved lobbying for class-based rights and, in rural areas, peasant rights.

Unions and left parties became effective allies of Indigenous community members who were trapped on haciendas and dissatisfied with Indigenous institutions. Unlike traditional, ethnic institutions, class-based organizations had leadership structures that operated independently of the landlord. Local union leaders, who either emerged from communities or came from nearby towns or cities, could thus credibly mobilize on behalf of the hacienda peasants' interests. Labor organizations and left parties also had a ready-made language, arising from Marx, that advocated for the most salient rights to exploited peasants: worker protections and land ownership as opposed to labor exploitation and land tenancy.[25] Many peasants were illiterate—large landowners often sought to keep them this way—and generally had limited contact with outsiders. Thus, class-based organizations defined a set of rights that peasants could claim and feasibly obtain to address their central demands. Using these advantages, unions and left parties considered haciendas prime targets for electoral, contentious, and sometimes violent mobilization.

Thus, rural elite extraction determined where rural sector unions and left parties would mobilize. These organizations were more likely to target Indigenous peasants on haciendas because of the work-related nature of peasant

---

25. In line with the assumptions of community member demands discussed above, these concessions would improve community welfare and bolster the strength of the communal unit. For example, peasants frequently demanded the restoration of collectively held land.

concerns, the delegitimization of Indigenous institutions, and favorable structural conditions that facilitated class-based mobilization. Mobilization was less likely to occur in Indigenous communities that remained "free," where Indigenous institutions and authorities remained influential, and workers' rights were relatively less salient.[26]

The organizational efforts of unions and left parties had enduring effects on Indigenous community mobilization and demands; as Handelman (1974) observes, peasant unions "had never previously existed in the highlands. They offered the peasantry an opportunity for more enduring participation in the political system" (6). The effects of this initial mobilization endured through two key mechanisms of persistence.

First, Indigenous communities gained government-provided benefits from their linkages with unions. In the mid-twentieth century, left parties and corporatist regimes acquired national power throughout Latin America—from Bolivia to Mexico to Argentina to Brazil. Cultivating ties with unions was both an ideological goal of these governments and a strategic way to maintain political power. Union membership became a key channel through which affiliated communities could access state resources.

Second, unions' relative success in achieving their goals vis-à-vis *private* actors promoted communities' continued mobilization with rural labor organizations. In the mid-twentieth century, many union-organized strikes convinced landlords to address labor-related demands, including higher wages, shorter workdays, better working conditions, and an end to unpaid labor. These successes encouraged Indigenous peasants to continue their union affiliation.

Rural sector unions and the left parties to which they were tied played a central role in mobilizing Indigenous communities to demand class-based rights. The success of this mobilization—for the two reasons listed above—resulted in electoral victories for left parties and empowered rural sector unions, which further increased ties between Indigenous communities and class-based organizations. These linkages, however, undermined ties to ethnic identities and institutions and made communities less likely to demand autonomy.

Class-based institutions instead promoted demands for assimilation, an outcome that often served the interests of both labor organizations and the

26. In free communities that experienced state-led labor conscription, an eight-hour work day, a wage, or better working conditions did not reflect their central demand: an end to conscription.

left parties to which they were tied.[27] These demands partially arose from government efforts to reward—through policy and rhetoric—class-based mobilization. As Yashar (1998) observes, "reforms obliged Indians to define themselves as peasants, particularly if they hoped to gain access to state resources. Official political discourse promoted assimilation into mestizo culture and extended resources to rural citizens insofar as they identified and organized as peasants" (33). The MNR in Bolivia, for example, attempted to replace traditional Indigenous institutions with affiliated rural sector unions (Gotkowitz 2008, 281). In Mexico, the hegemonic PRI government made deliberate—and generally successful—efforts in the mid-twentieth century to repress ethnic mobilization (Mallon 1992, 49). And in Peru, the leftist military government (1968–1975) used the term *campesino* (peasant) in its rhetoric and policy to reduce the salience of ethnicity. As Héctor Bejár, an official in the Peruvian military government, explained, "In that period structuralism existed as a great worldwide trend of the anthropologists . . . and there was a Latin American structuralist current that placed a lot of emphasis on the economy: 'They are not Indians; what shall we call them? Campesinos. Because their role is to be in the countryside and produce in the countryside.'"[28] These rhetorical shifts signaled governments' desire to reward mobilization along class lines and discourage—or even punish—mobilization along ethnic lines.

One of the chief ways governments encouraged peasant identities was through large-scale land reforms, which disproportionately benefited hacienda communities—over non-hacienda ("free") ones. In the 1930s, the Mexican government required each beneficiary of the agrarian reform to join the National Campesino Confederation (CNC), a peasant league (Lord 1965, 10). In many cases, unions were directly or indirectly responsible for implementing agrarian reform, which increased their power vis-à-vis the government, peasants, and large landowners. Rural sector unions in Bolivia "became the most important actors in the implementation of the [1953] agrarian reform" adopted by the MNR (Soliz 2021). Local union bosses in Venezuela served "as brokers for their peasant clients in dealing with the many government agencies and programs involved in the land reform program" (Powell

---

27. In recent years, the power of left parties and rural unions has declined in many of the cases examined in this book, which has led to a resurgence in ethnic identification (Carter 2024b). To the extent this has occurred, it may constitute the "end of the legacy" as described by Collier and Collier (2002, 30–31).

28. As quoted in Cant (2012, 33).

1971, 142). Guatemala's rural unions were vital in educating peasants about the country's 1951 land reform (Gleijeses 1989). And in Chile, unions used the threat of land reform to pressure hacienda owners to improve working conditions (Alexander 1972, 17). Thus, land reform tended to privilege mobilization with class-based actors—both the political parties that pushed for land reform and the unions that implemented and benefited from it. Hacienda workers stood to gain the most from land reform, which increased their dependence on left parties and unions.[29] Union mobilization was less likely in "free" communities. Albó (1987) observes that in Bolivia, "in the regions dominated by the communities rather than by the haciendas, this dependent relationship [between rural Indigenous communities and the MNR], although present, did not penetrate as deeply. . . . The struggle to regain land barely came into play in the communities, which meant that the MNR's 'benevolent paternalism' was embodied in less benefits" (385). Thus, the enduring ties between Indigenous communities on haciendas and class-based organizations (unions, left parties) promoted demands for assimilation.

## 3.5   The Hybrid Case of Integration Demands

Class and ethnic mobilization are not mutually exclusive.[30] Many Indigenous communities and their leaders pursued class-based demands alongside

29. A potential exception to these trends is Peru, where the left military government actively sought to weaken rural unions, despite having implemented a land reform (Lowenthal 2015, 9).

30. The complementarity or substitutability of these rights depends essentially on the domain: land presents the most opportunities for conflict. Unions and left parties often articulated mixed messages on land. On the one hand, private property helped undermine potentially competing ethnic identities and marked a step toward the goal of promoting small, family farms (Ackerman 2021, 61–63). On the other hand, collective land was thought to increase group solidarity, allowing for easier mobilization of Indigenous and peasant communities. Different left and corporatist governments thus developed divergent strategies. In Mexico, land was allocated as collectively held *ejidos*, which contained a substantial amount of de facto private property; an estimated 96 percent of *ejido* land was farmed as private parcels in 1950 (Ackerman 2021, 53). In Peru, land was allocated as cooperatives with state-appointed managers; peasants—who had been unionized prior to the land reform—were dissatisfied with the cooperative system and often lobbied for parcelization. As Hunefeldt (2010, 115–117) notes, demands for parcelization did not necessarily reflect an inherent desire for private land but rather a viable solution to problems associated with cooperatives and their management. The Bolivian land reform redistributed all land as individually owned, private parcels. Yet, even the partial privatization of communal land could pose a threat to communities. Mayer (1995) argues that in Peru, "by 1987

those for "symbolic" Indigenous rights. This most often occurred within unions, which sometimes adopted cultural symbols, Indigenous languages, and even the names of prominent, historical Indigenous leaders, while prioritizing demands for higher wages, better working conditions, and an end to landowner abuses. Although few Indigenous rights were secured in the short term, these movements did not suppress Indigenous identities; instead, they permitted (and, in some cases, celebrated) them. This led to demands for *integration*: Indigenous communities pursued inclusion through state-sanctioned institutions (rather than Indigenous ones) while maintaining their ethnic identities.

This section argues that these integration demands were most likely to arise in communities that experienced both state-led and rural elite extraction. The theory posits that these forms of extraction led to investments in both Indigenous and class-based institutions. While communities were eager to adopt work-related, peasant demands advocated by unions, they were skeptical of full-scale assimilation due to their negative experiences with government-led extraction. In such cases, Indigenous communities pressed unions and left parties to incorporate demands for ethnic rights alongside other, often privileged demands for class-based rights. However, they were rarely able to convince union leaders to include demands for the most costly ethnic rights that would protect their long-standing Indigenous institutions through autonomy.

### 3.5.1   To Form or Transform an Organization?

Before delving into the effects of multiple forms of extraction, it is crucial to understand the way that organizations form and change, and how insiders and outsiders influence these processes. This understanding is particularly important when investigating integration demands, which often arose when Indigenous leaders had sufficient power to transform non-Indigenous organizations. I provide here a brief overview of how this process can unfold.

Indigenous leaders, by assumption (see above), prefer autonomy to integration or assimilation. Such leaders can (and do) organize collective mobilization that involves only their community, but these communities are often small, containing fewer than 1,000 people. Mobilization is most successful when community leaders can coordinate collective action across

---

the parcelization and differentiation of peasant lands caused great problems for the stability of the community" (365).

multiple communities. Organizations play a crucial role in facilitating this inter-community cooperation. They incorporate multiple groups into a single institutional structure that can coordinate protests, strikes, or even violent action. Importantly, organizations provide a set of defined leaders and intermediaries who can negotiate with the government and private actors to secure desired concessions. Because the quest for rights is a long-term, iterated game, organizations are essential for coordinating sustained political and social mobilization.

Organizations adopt agendas that are reflective of their key stakeholders. The initial stakeholders—and thus "agenda setters"—are those who are present at the time the organization is founded.[31] There is often limited dissent at these initial moments as the organizational founders unite around a common preference for certain policies.[32] Over time, an organization's goals can and often will shift. These changes can occur in response to structural (e.g., changing composition of the economy) or institutional (e.g., democratization) changes.

In the cases of assimilation described above, class-based organizations unilaterally determined which rights and claims they would advocate. For integration, however, Indigenous communities and their leaders played a role in shaping and shifting the demands of the organizations to which they belonged. I describe these processes using the language of Streeck and Thelen (2005). Some organizations chose *layering*, which involved adding Indigenous rights to existing demands for class-based rights (e.g., higher wages, better working conditions) within unions and left parties. In the 1970s, for example, the Central of Agricultural Workers and Peasants (CIOAC) in Chiapas, Mexico lobbied for not only "credit and product commercialization" but also for "Indian rights and autonomy" (Mattiace 2003, 32). Similarly, the Peruvian Regional Indigenous-Worker Federation (Federación Indígena Obrera Regional Peruana) lobbied for communal land rights alongside demands for greater protection for workers on haciendas.

31. As Ahlquist and Levi (2013) observe, "sustained political mobilization requires an ideologically motivated founding leadership cohort who devises organizational rules that facilitate both industrial success and coordinated expectations about the leaders' political objectives" (6).

32. If a group of individuals, likely relatively small, has overcome collective action problems to form an organization, it is likely that all its menbers are firmly dedicated to a set of clear principles.

| Insider dominance: | Layering: | Displacement: |
|---|---|---|
| Only class rights through unions/left parties | Indigenous rights added to class-based agenda | Indigenous rights replace class-based rights |

*Least preferred*       **Fusion:**            **Innovation:**       *Most preferred*

|  | Fusion: | Innovation: |  |
|---|---|---|---|
|  | New, "hybrid" class-ethnic demands | Only Indigenous rights through ethnic orgs. |  |

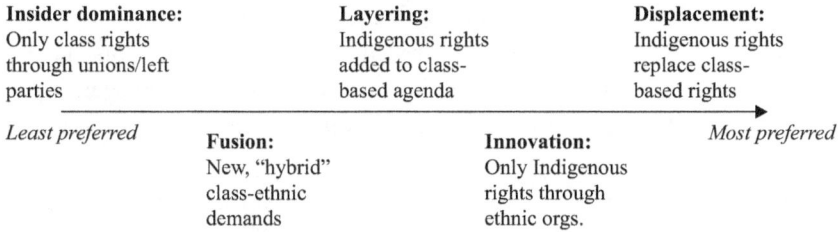

FIGURE 3.4. Indigenous leader preferences over organizational strategies

In other cases, unions and parties used a *fusion* approach, creating new demands out of existing class and ethnic rights. For example, bilingual education merges union demands for literacy expansion with native peoples' demands to preserve Indigenous languages. Food sovereignty combines Indigenous demands for local autonomy and respect for native culture with the productionist concerns of peasant unions.[33] Another example of fusion is mixed land tenure, where communities can operate some portion of their land privately and another portion as common agricultural or pasture land (Chapter 2).[34]

In rare cases, Indigenous leaders could achieve *displacement*—replacing class-based demands with ethnic rights within the existing structure of a union or political party. This had the benefit of providing an existing organizational infrastructure for demand-making on the national government or private actors, while allowing Indigenous leaders to take the lead in agenda setting. Indigenous leaders could also *innovate*, forming ethnic-based organizations that lobbied solely for Indigenous rights. Such an approach allowed for the faithful expression of Indigenous leader preferences but required a costly investment in establishing a new organization. These different outcomes are outlined in Figure 3.4.

Leaders of rural unions and left parties generally wanted to recruit as many members as possible while maintaining control over their organization's agenda. This desire for control reflected either a goal of preserving power

33. The UN Declaration on Peasant Rights defines food sovereignty as "the right to participate in decision-making processes on food and agriculture policy and the right to healthy and adequate food produced through ecologically sound and sustainable methods that respect their cultures" (United Nations 2008, 10).

34. In Peru, for example, just under a third of Indigenous communities operate under mixed land tenure regimes, and over half do in Bolivia.

or a commitment to pursuing an ideological motive—which, in this case, involved mobilization around a class-based identity for labor rights. Therefore, leaders of unions and left parties only compromised on their agenda and power within the organization when it was the only way to mobilize a new constituency.

The incumbent agenda setters of class-based organizations thus held opposing preferences to those of Indigenous elites. They generally preferred insider dominance, which allowed them to maintain control over the message and mission of their organization. Any organizational adaptation—through fusion or layering—could broaden the potential membership base and respond to changing institutional and structural conditions. Yet, these changes could also generate new challenges. Layering may have reduced the coherence of the organizational mission and further divided organizational resources across a broader range of policy advocacy activities; fusion risked alienating all constituents by endeavoring to meet some of their demands but failing to fully satisfy any constituency. Innovation mainly had negative implications for incumbent agenda setters as it generated alternative social organizations that could compete for political and social influence. Displacement was the least preferred outcome because it could lead to the abandonment of policies that motivated the participation of critical activists and members, which could erode the organization's base and oust the incumbent agenda setters.

The framework depicted in Figure 3.4 sheds light on how demands for integration emerge. I begin with the observation that Indigenous leaders have a collective action endowment—their ability to organize their community members—which increases with the strength of Indigenous institutions. For reasons discussed above, this endowment should be higher for communities that experienced state-led labor conscription. Leaders with a higher collective action endowment can adopt two strategies to make *sustained* demands on the state. First, they can form their own ethnic organizations, drawing on existing networks and connections with leaders of other Indigenous communities (innovation). These organizations generally articulate demands for ethnic rights (autonomy). Sometimes, these organizations have a national structure, which is similar to that of a union. For example, the Tahuantinsuyo Pro-Indigenous Rights Committee of 1920s Peru had a national leadership base with provincial and municipal chapters staffed by Indigenous elites. Bolivia's Oldest Autonomous Mayors (AMP) had a similar organizational structure. However, organizations are costly to establish. They require an initial investment in time to coordinate various stakeholders who are aligned in their support of a given issue. They may also require a financial investment to establish a physical base (e.g., offices, meeting space), hire personnel, or register with the government. Furthermore, ethnic organizations may not always fully represent the demands of community members, who may prioritize class-based claims. In many cases, it is easier and more cost-effective to pursue a second strategy: joining an existing class-based organization.

Two factors shaped the likelihood of alliances between Indigenous community leaders and class-based organizations. First, the strength of Indigenous leaders and institutions proved important. Indigenous authorities who had a demonstrated ability to collectively mobilize their community members were more attractive allies for unions; in exchange for their cooperation, these leaders could use their leverage to pressure unions and left parties to adopt demands for Indigenous rights through fusion, layering, or displacement. A second factor involved the grassroots pressure from community members on Indigenous leaders to address class-based concerns, which could best be represented through unions and left parties.

Both conditions—powerful Indigenous leaders and grassroots demands for workers' rights—were most likely to be met in communities that experienced both state-led and rural elite extraction. As I argue above, communities that experienced labor conscription mobilized collectively to resist it, often through Indigenous institutions and authorities; Indigenous leaders' ability to mobilize their communities was a skill highly valued by unions and left parties. Likewise, a failure to bring these communities into the fold could result in organizational innovation by Indigenous leaders, leading to the formation of competing organizations, due to the work-related nature of their demands. Communities that experienced rural elite extraction were also natural allies of class-based organizations. As I argued above, communities that experienced hacienda expansion and subsequent debt peonage were more likely to respond to class-based appeals.

Yet, communities that experienced both forms of extraction did not simply join unions and embrace their assimilationist goals. The relative strength and leverage of Indigenous leaders and institutions, arising from experiences of labor conscription, allowed communities to achieve concessions from class-based organizations. These included leadership positions for community leaders within unions and left parties, the use of Indigenous languages and symbols at organization meetings, and the creation of unions at the community (rather than the hacienda or municipality) level. I argue that these symbolic demands resulted in few concrete policy changes in the

| Historical cause → | Proximate cause → | Mechanism → | Outcome |
|---|---|---|---|
| Mode of extraction → | Community investment decisions → | Nature of long-term mobilization → | Autonomy, assimilation, or integration demands |
| State-led and rural-elite extraction → | Investment in labor organizations and Indigenous institutions → | Mobilization along class lines with symbolic ethnic content → | Integration demands |

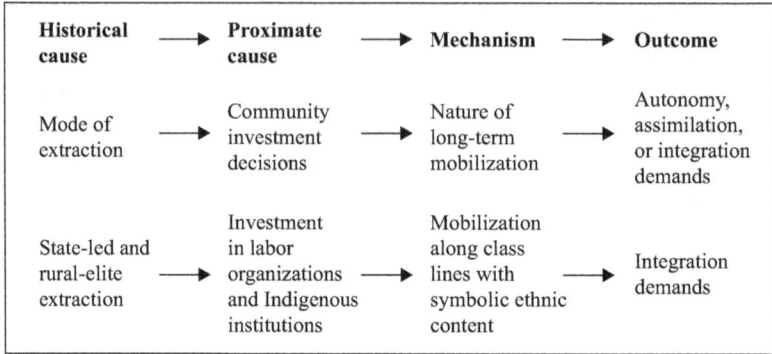

FIGURE 3.5. Theory: Both forms of extraction increase integration demands

short term; however, they helped preserve an Indigenous identity despite a climate—especially in the mid-twentieth century—increasingly opposed to ethnic mobilization (Figure 3.5). In communities that lost land to large estates but did not experience state-led labor conscription, rural sector unions and left parties were more effective at suppressing ethnic mobilization and demands for Indigenous rights and sidelining traditional ethnic authorities. For example, the Cochabamba region in Bolivia experienced limited labor conscription and high levels of hacienda expansion. Peasant unions are now much stronger there—and Indigenous organizations much weaker—than in most neighboring departments (see Chapter 5).

Sequencing has significant implications for integration demands. The timing of extraction can unfold in various ways and create paths that I label "extractive sequences" (depicted in Figure 3.6). The nature of the competition between rural elites and the state over Indigenous labor shapes these sequences. Communities that experienced rural elite extraction were less likely to be affected later by state-led labor conscription, largely due to the scarcity of rural labor. Landowners—through bribes or resistance—refused to allow the government to force Indigenous laborers to work on roads and railways. Egan (2019), for example, finds that Indigenous hacienda workers were less likely to participate in the Bolivian government's road conscription program (Prestación Vial) because "hacendados [hacienda owners] either negotiated [workers'] non-attendance, turned a blind eye to worker evasion of the call, or resisted the state on this issue" (127). The same was true in Peru, where hacienda owners often protected Indigenous labor from unpaid work on government roads (Heilman 2010a, 68).

Early rural elite extraction
*Hacienda expansion in Bolivia (pre-1888) & Peru (pre-1920)*
— *Yes* → **Assimilation (a)**

*No* → State-led extraction *Labor conscription in Bolivia (1888-c.1950) & Peru (1920-1930)*

— *Yes* → Later rural elite extraction *Hacienda expansion in Bolivia (c. 1900-c. 1950) & Peru (1930-c. 1967)*
  — *No* → **Autonomy (b)**
  — *Yes* → **Integration (c)**
  — *No* → **No demand (d)**
  — *Yes* → **Assimilation (a)**

— *No* → Later rural elite extraction *Hacienda expansion in Bolivia (c. 1900-c. 1950) & Peru (1930-c. 1967)*

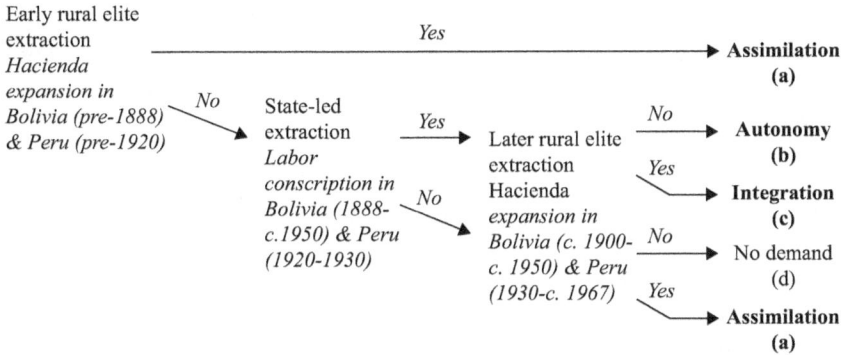

FIGURE 3.6. Extractive sequences and their effects for Indigenous demand-making

Following the logic outlined above, experiencing only *rural elite* extraction generally led to long-term demands for assimilation: path (a) in Figure 3.6. Communities that experienced only *state-led* extraction have been more likely to demand autonomy: path (b).[35]

I argue that path (c)—labor conscription first and then hacienda expansion—increased demands for integration. Indigenous leaders used the mobilization capacity developed through labor conscription to resist subsequent co-optation by rural elites. In these cases, Indigenous leaders and institutions remained strong, even in the face of hacienda expansion. Yet, for the reasons described above, communities often found it necessary to form alliances with class-based organizations to represent their increasingly complex constellation of demands, which included both ethnic and class claims. As such, Indigenous communities did not simply adopt union and left party demands for assimilation. They and their leaders used their mobilizational strength as leverage to extract concessions (recognition of ethnic identities) from class-based organizations. Ultimately, this shifted the demands

35. Labor conscription could have reduced the likelihood that communities experienced later debt peonage on large estates, though in a less deterministic way than what is outlined in path (a). As I discuss in Chapter 6, conscription encouraged Indigenous leaders to invest in their ability to mobilize collective resistance among their community members. Because this increase in community leaders' mobilizational strength was enduring, we should also expect that communities affected by conscription would have been better positioned to resist future hacienda expansion. In some cases, leaders of these communities did, in fact, successfully mobilize to stop the encroachment of large estates on communal land.

of these organizations—and the communities that mobilized with them—toward integration. As such, the path outlined in Figure 3.5 was likely to emerge only when communities experienced state-led extraction *before* rural elite extraction.

## 3.6   Conclusion

This chapter has outlined the book's theoretical framework. I have focused on two pivotal experiences that occurred around the turn of the twentieth century. The first was state-led labor conscription, which empowered Indigenous community leaders to mobilize their communities for autonomy. The second was the expansion of large estates around the same time period; exposure to this form of extraction increased the power of rural sector unions and left parties, leading to demands for class-based rights and, often, assimilation.

I have also argued in this chapter that exposure to one form of extraction can affect the likelihood of being exposed to the other. The timing of exposure to each form of extraction is theoretically important and empirically informative. For example, state-led conscription made rural elite extraction more likely; the expansion of railroads into a country's interior increased the incentives for landowners in those areas to invest in expanding their landholdings and thus economic production (Henderson 1997). This suggests a compatibility between these two forms of extraction when labor conscription occurs first. Ultimately, this sequencing led to demands for integration, as powerful Indigenous leaders formed alliances with unions and left parties to produce demands that included class and ethnic components. Where hacienda expansion instead preceded state-led labor conscription, there was less compatibility between these two forms of extraction. Indigenous communities captured by large estates before the onset of state-led labor conscription had some "protection" from being conscripted since landowners were not eager to lose their workers to a distant government road or railway construction project (Heilman 2010b, 517). The relationship—and temporal interdependence—between these two forms of extraction has key implications for my theory, which I discuss further in Chapter 7.

I argue that the forms of extraction theorized in this chapter are crucial for understanding later forms of Indigenous mobilization and demand-making. Yet, native communities have also faced other types of extraction by states and rural elites both before and after the periods I study. The identity of the extractor is not enough to hypothesize the potential long-term legacies of these events. We must also consider the historical moment in which extraction occurred, which provides insight into whether extraction bypassed or incorporated Indigenous elites (Table 3.1). Any disruptive extraction that bypassed Indigenous elites generally provoked investment in ethnic identities and institutions. Where extractive efforts instead co-opted Indigenous leaders, the expected effects depend on a further variable: the alternatives that community members had to resist. My study period featured both ethnic and class-based organizations that could mobilize community members.

My theory constitutes the first systematic effort to understand Indigenous groups' responses to extraction. Scholars have examined extraction's important, harmful welfare effects in Latin America (Dell 2010; Mahoney 2010).[36] Yet, these accounts largely neglect the widespread acts of defiance and opposition by Indigenous communities. This book attempts to fill this gap by analyzing how extraction motivated communities to resist in distinct ways and how these acts of defiance and opposition shaped contemporary Indigenous demand-making. In the remaining chapters, I test my theory using evidence from the cases of Peru and Bolivia.

36. See also Lee and Schultz (2012) for a discussion of the effects of labor extraction in Sub-Saharan Africa.

# 4

# Varieties of Labor Extraction in Bolivia and Peru

"This exceptional condition of the Indian has kept him subject and resigned to the degrading exercise of *free services*, an abuse contrary to freedom and equality as citizens, and used in favor of the political official, . . . the elites, and even their friends."

—HERACLIO FERNÁNDEZ, PREFECT OF
APURÍMAC (PERU), 1912

AT THE turn of the twentieth century, rural elites and central states increasingly sought to exploit Indigenous workers. Large landowners took advantage of booming primary product export markets by capturing rural, Indigenous labor through land seizures and debt peonage arrangements. Meanwhile, central states increasingly mobilized unpaid Indigenous labor to work on large infrastructure projects—especially railroads and highways, which national political leaders considered indispensable for state consolidation, economic growth, and enhancing their countries' international reputations.

The previous chapter developed a theory to explain the divergent effects of state-led and rural elite extraction. This chapter describes these two distinct forms of extraction in the primary empirical cases of Peru and Bolivia. It explains why, where, and how extraction occurred. The analysis thus highlights empirical variation along the book's primary independent variable of interest: the level and type of labor extraction communities faced.

## 4.1   Rural Elite Extraction in Peru and Bolivia

A defining trait of extraction in colonial Latin America involved the creation of reciprocal pacts through which representatives of the Spanish Crown
recognized Indigenous communal lands and local self-governance in exchange
for continued payment of a discriminatory head tax called the Indian tribute.[1]
If a boundary dispute arose with a large landowner (*hacendado*), communities' status as tributaries helped them to defend their territory successfully. If
communities lost their land, they would struggle to produce enough to meet
their tribute obligations. As such, the Crown sought to limit extraction by
other actors. Over-extraction could lead to outmigration or rebellion, either
of which threatened the Crown's interest. Post-independence governments
likewise had a reason to keep individuals in fixed communities that could
easily be monitored and taxed.[2] Lacking the capacity and resources to adopt
alternative forms of revenue collection or update existing ones, post-colonial
governments benefited from a stable tax base.

The rise of alternative sources of income in the early post-independence
period allowed central governments to gradually transition away from the
Indian tribute as a primary source of revenue. In Bolivia, the tribute fell from
41 percent of government revenue in 1852 to just 8 percent in 1869 (Grieshaber
1977, 292–293). Its importance continued to decrease following the implementation of a mineral tax and a silver boom in the 1870s and 1880s. In Peru, the
Indian tribute accounted for over a quarter of government revenue between
1839 and 1845, but it represented a substantially smaller proportion after the
guano boom of the early 1850s (Bonilla 1985, 244). In Peru and Bolivia, the
Indian tribute was formally abolished in 1854 and 1874, respectively.[3] It is no
coincidence that this occurred near the passage of two of the most harmful pieces of legislation for Indigenous communities: the 1852 Peruvian Civil
Code and Bolivia's 1874 *Ley de Exvinculación*. These laws, which removed protections for Indigenous communal lands, triggered an expansion of rural elite
estates (*haciendas*) in both countries.

1. See, e.g., Platt (1982).

2. Land seizures by non-Indigenous elites could lead Indigenous peoples to flee their communities, making it more difficult to locate subjects for tribute collection. During the Republican period, tribute collection shifted from the community to the individual level, generating
new logistical advantages to having taxpayers located in known communities (Jacobsen 1997,
137).

3. Importantly, however, the tribute did not immediately end in either case.

Rural elites generally seized Indigenous communal land to gain control of Indigenous workers; the land itself had limited agricultural value.[4] Large landowners used favorable policy frameworks to purchase or seize Indigenous land. Community members were allowed to live and work on a small plot of the land in exchange for providing labor service to the landowner. Often, this involved working on the landlord's farm for a set amount of days each week. Theoretically, the landowner paid an indentured servant's taxes and ensured he had enough time to farm his own plot for subsistence. In reality, these relationships were frequently coercive and abusive. Communities campaigned consistently throughout the early twentieth century to end these exploitative relationships of debt peonage, which were variously labeled *pongueaje* (Bolivia), *yanaconaje* (Peru), *terraje* (Colombia), *huasipungo* (Ecuador), and *inquilinaje* (Chile).[5]

Despite the exploitation associated with debt peonage, affected communities generally remained intact in what Albó (1999) calls a "captive community organized within the bounds of the hacienda" (772). Traditional Indigenous elites held onto power, although the landlord could overrule or even replace them (Drzewieniecki 1996, 150). This section provides an overview of the expansion of large estates at the turn of the twentieth century; some communities were exposed to hacienda encroachment—and thus debt peonage—while others were not.

### 4.1.1   Peru, 1852–1920

Flush with cash from its main export (guano), which accounted for nearly 40 percent of government revenue by 1852 (Figure 4.1), the Peruvian government began its attack on long-standing Indigenous land rights (Hunt 1984, 72). The 1852 Civil Code effectively outlawed inalienable, collectively held land. Two years later, the government repealed the Indian tribute, further reducing state incentives to protect community land (Larson 1996, 623–624). The end of both de jure and de facto protections for Indigenous land resulted in renewed attacks by rural elites. As Bonilla (1985) observes, "with the abolition of the tribute the landowners increasingly sought to appropriate the land belonging to the Indians, as a way of maintaining access to Indian labour and control over

---

4. As Langer (1989) observes, "In areas such as the Andes and Mesoamerica, where large concentrations of Indians survived in communities dating back to the early colonial period, the elites realized that they first had to destroy the Indians' land base to obtain their labor" (2).

5. See, e.g., Albó (1999, 769).

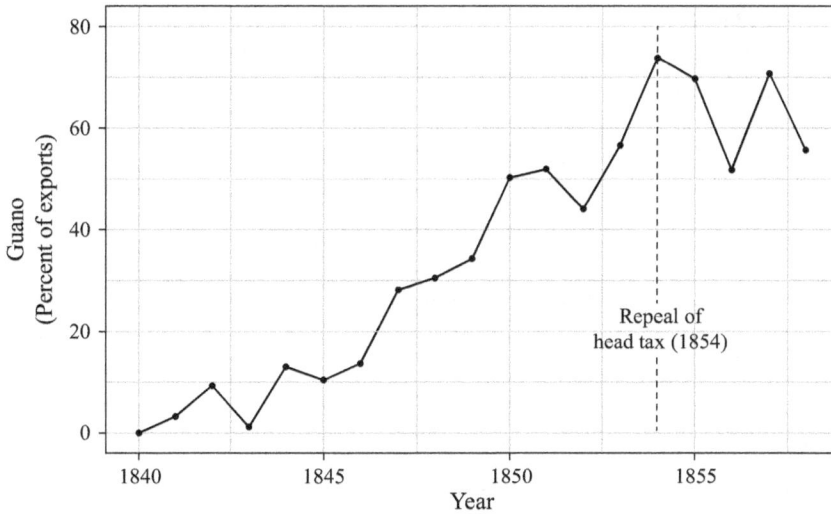

FIGURE 4.1. Growth of guano exports in Peru in the mid-nineteenth century
*Note:* Data collected from Hunt (1973, 64).

its availability, and the state no longer had an incentive to protect the Indian community from the encroachment of the hacienda" (552).[6]

Landowners used several strategies to take Indigenous land after these laws were passed. For example, they loaned community members money for food and other items and seized their land when they were unable to repay this debt (Jacobsen 1993, 229). The loans were often secured via contracts that Indigenous peasants were unable to read (due to illiteracy or lack of knowledge of Spanish); local notaries, acting as landlords' agents, endorsed these agreements (Jacobsen 1993, 230). Large estate owners could also use the legal system to claim rights to Indigenous land. Lawsuits challenging rural elite efforts to seize Indigenous land often endured for many years, creating an unsustainable financial hardship for affected communities. As Jacobsen (1993) observes:

> Of every hundred cases over land brought before courts in the department of Puno in 1893, only five were concluded within the year. Many suits dragged on for years or even generations. Often the litigants decided to abandon the judicial struggle and settle out of court. The economically weaker party had been exhausted by the high cost of litigation and was now

6. See Appendix Figures OA3 and OA4.

willing to accept the terms of the stronger party. In the context of hacienda expansion strategies, such cases constituted the continuation of economic means of land acquisition within the judicial arena. (235)

Certain communities in the southern highlands were more vulnerable to land loss than others. Some were located at altitudes conducive to producing high-quality wool. Others were close to railheads of the new Southern Railway, which linked wool-producing provinces to the commercial centers of Cusco and Arequipa.[7] Periodic declines in wool prices often exacerbated the pressure on Indigenous land and labor. Drinot (2000) observes, "As landowners' incomes from wool fell, the impetus to overexploit the *hacienda's colonos* [tenants] grew," particularly through the "extract[ion] of greater free labour services" (161–162).

Beyond the southern highlands, including in regions of central Peru suitable for wool production, land and workers were also absorbed into large estates (Long and Roberts 1984, 30–34). In northern Peru, particularly in Cajamarca, landowners encroached on Indigenous land to increase foodstuff production for the country's growing urban population (Taylor 1984). Labor was particularly valued: "For the landlords [in Cajamarca], control over peasant labor was the basic source of wealth. . . . The greater the hacienda's control over peasant labor, the more feasible it was to expand production on the demesne when market conditions warranted doing so" (Deere 1990, 31–32).

The timing of rural elite extraction differentiated southern Peru from the rest of the highland region: the expansion of large estates generally happened later in the south. The War of the Pacific with Chile (1879–1883) had a relatively limited impact on land tenure relations in the southern highlands but had a much stronger impact in the north and—especially—central Peru, where the War had the short-term effect of reversing hacienda expansion (Manrique 1988, 86, 116).[8] Despite this brief reversal, the expansion of

7. Unlike other primary product exports, wool was generally sold domestically, which helped make Cusco and Arequipa important, regional economic hubs.

8. Peruvian General Andrés Avelino Cáceres led a campaign of Indigenous peasants against landowners who were accused of collaborating with Chilean forces. In a circular to Indigenous peasants, Cáceres wrote, "Despite the sanctity of the cause we defend, there is no shortage of perverted Peruvians who, making common cause with the Chileans, offer to serve as spies, or guide them along lost paths, or supply them with cattle, grain, money, and other resources to help them in their evil work of devastation. . . . It is necessary for you all to persecute and denounce these traitors in order to impose the punishment that their infamous behavior deserves" (Manrique 1988, 43, fn. 6, author translation).

TABLE 4.1. Growth of haciendas in Peruvian highlands, by region, 1876–1940

| | | Number of haciendas | | |
|---|---|---|---|---|
| | | 1876 | 1940 | Growth rate |
| North | Ancash | 196 | 1,344 | 686% |
| | Cajamarca | 335 | 1,253 | 374% |
| | La Libertad | 204 | 458 | 225% |
| | **Total** | 735 | 3,055 | 416% |
| Central | Huánuco | 85 | 571 | 671% |
| | Junín | 319 | 721 | 226% |
| | **Total** | 404 | 1,292 | 319% |
| South | Apurímac | 180 | 531 | 295% |
| | Ayacucho | 225 | 967 | 430% |
| | Cusco | 692 | 1,718 | 250% |
| | Huancavelica | 352 | 720 | 205% |
| | Puno | 723 | 1,691 | 233% |
| | **Total** | 2,172 | 5,697 | 259% |

*Source*: Macera (1976) and Perez (1972).

haciendas seems to have recovered by the 1890s,[9] to have been accelerated by the wool boom of the First World War, and to have culminated in central Peru experiencing similar levels of hacienda expansion to that of the south.

Table 4.1 demonstrates the growth of haciendas throughout the Peruvian highlands between 1876 and 1940. The data suggests a remarkable expansion in the number of large estates, a fairly consistent increase across different regions of Peru. Much of this expansion, as suggested earlier, occurred in areas favorable to sheep, alpaca, and cattle herding; highland regions of Cusco and Puno were especially conducive to high-quality wool production. Owners of large estates had—in prior eras—seized much of the land in the fertile, lower-lying Andean valleys, which were more suitable for agriculture.

The growth of large estates resulted in higher levels of debt peonage. In Peru, the chief institution of debt peonage was known as *yanaconaje*, and the workers were called *yanaconas* or, in some cases, *colonos* (tenants).

9. See, e.g., Smith (1991, 77).

The institution of *yanaconaje* dates from pre-colonial times and was originally used to denote a servant to officials of the Inca Empire (Matos Mar 1976, 22).[10] During the colonial period, *yanaconaje* was associated with labor tenancy on large estates—through which an individual worked for a landlord in exchange for access to land and basic guarantees of subsistence. Indigenous community members became *yanaconas* in one of two ways. In some cases, Indigenous communities were forced into *yanaconaje* when large estate owners seized their land. In other cases, Indigenous individuals fled to haciendas to escape tributary obligations, coerced labor in distant mines (i.e., *mita*), or forced purchases of unnecessary goods (i.e., *reparto*) by colonial officials (Jacobsen 1993, 84). Becoming a *yanacona* could protect community members from these obligations.

After Peru became independent, Indigenous community members often entered the *yanacona* class by force. As legal frameworks became more permissive and internal economic markets expanded, the owners of large estates expanded their territory to address persistent labor shortages and expand their wealth. Matos Mar (1976) explains that landowners could not afford to cultivate their territories without the practice of *yanaconaje*, which "allowed them to use labor and work instruments without the need for greater capital" (72, author translation). Hacienda laborers frequently worked in inhumane conditions: "peasants who did not comply with their charges were punished, being subjected to the stocks. Widows were forced to work under the whip to cover the debts of their husbands or children" (Escárzaga Nicté 1999, 157, author translation).

The prevalence of *yanaconaje* varied considerably across Peru (Figure 4.2). In the coastal areas, home to large sugar and cotton plantations, *yanacona* labor was widespread. The practice of *yanaconaje* was also prevalent in the northern and southern highlands, especially in the wool-producing areas of Cusco and Puno. Despite the turn-of-the-twentieth-century growth of haciendas in central Peru, *yanaconaje* was less common in this region, and independent peasant farmers comprised a large share of the rural, non-hacienda population. Outside of the wool-producting estates, the non-hacienda rural population of southern Peru was more likely to reside in relatively remote Indigenous communities.

10. In the Quechua Indigenous language, *yana* means "slave" and *kuna* means people.

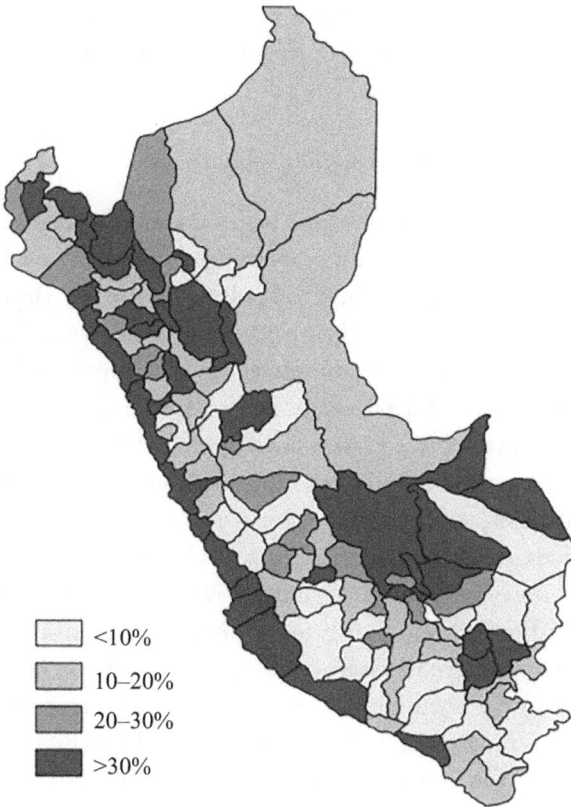

FIGURE 4.2. Rural population on haciendas in Peru (1940)
*Note*: Statistics reflect the proportion of the rural population residing on large estates (*haciendas*).
*Source*: Perez (1972).

Many long-standing Indigenous institutions and cultural practices survived hacienda expansion in late nineteenth and early twentieth century Peru. In the department of Ancash, Indigenous communities that were "controlled by the large haciendas, . . . managed to maintain their ways of production and organization" (Escárzaga Nicté 1999, 156, author translation). Manrique (1988) argues that the communities captured onto haciendas "in many cases are more unified . . . than traditional *comunidades campesinas* [peasant communities]" (97, author translation). According to Favre (1976), "a traditional culture [is] very much alive in haciendas" (130, author translation); he argues it was precisely the maintenance of long-standing institutions and cultural practices that helped landowners maintain their control (131). Landowners sometimes paid for communities' traditional festivals to initiate and maintain relationships of debt peonage.

### 4.1.2   Bolivia, 1866–1920

Attacks on Bolivian communities' land began under President Mariano Melgarejo, who declared the parcelization of Indigenous communal land in 1866. After the land was divided, members had only 60 days to pay a legally required fee, or they would lose access to their land (Soliz 2021, 22–23). This triggered an "unprecedented process of communal land expropriation" (Gotkowitz 2008, 20). Government officials auctioned off the land of 356 communities to private buyers in the three years following Melgarejo's decree (Grieshaber 1977, 21). In 1871, a constitutional assembly declared this law—and all others associated with Melgarejo's term in office—null, promising a return of stolen communal lands (Rodríguez Ostria 2014, 324). Yet, this respite was short-lived, and the Bolivian government quickly reverted to and expanded upon Melgarejo's land privatization program. In 1874, the administration of President Tomás Frías proposed and secured the passage of the Ley de Exvinculación that "[abolished] the community as a juridical, taxpaying, and landholding unit" and once again divided Indigenous communal lands into private parcels (Larson 1996, 667). A period of massive expansion of large estates followed, which was rivaled only by "the period of the establishment of landed estates in the seventeenth century . . . in the amount of land that came under the control of haciendas and plantations" (Langer 1989, 2). Rivera Cusicanqui (1978) argues that the law "set loose the most important process of communal land expropriation in the history of the Republic" (105). A small group of landowners accounted for most of this expansion. Between 1880 and 1920, rural elites in La Paz purchased over 12,000 plots of land. Fifty individuals alone were responsible for nearly 40 percent of these purchases (Grieshaber 1990, 78). Benedicto Goitia, for instance, bought 798 plots, accounting for 6 percent of all land purchases in La Paz over this 40-year period (Grieshaber 1990, 77–78). Most buyers were "members of the growing altiplano commercial and landowning elite" (Jackson 1994, 85).[11]

11. Appendix Figure OA5, for example, shows the careers of the individuals who bought land in La Paz in the 40 years after the passage of the Ley de Exvinculación. Most were already large landowners, with others holding prestigious positions as lawyers, businessmen, military officials, or mine owners.

Much of the land purchased—either legally or fraudulently—during this period belonged to Indigenous communities. The number of Indigenous peoples living in traditional communities thus declined drastically between 1854 and 1900, from an estimated 585,000 to fewer than 250,000 in Bolivia's five largest departments (Oruro, Chuquisaca, La Paz, Potosí, and Cochabamba). This change cannot be fully attributed to urbanization, as Bolivia's population was still two-thirds rural in the mid-twentieth century (Soliz 2021, 19).[12] The share of land possessed by Indigenous communities also fell dramatically during this time: from two-thirds of the country's cultivable land in the early nineteenth century to just 26 percent in 1950 (Soliz 2021, 19). Perhaps surprisingly, Indigenous communities persisted as units despite losing land and people; between 1851 and 1950, the number of communities actually increased—from 3,210 to 3,642 (Bonilla 1985, 101).

Not all communities were equally affected by the assault on land and labor that followed Melgarejo's 1874 law, as Figure 4.3 demonstrates. For example, while some provinces in Cochabamba lost nearly their entire Indigenous community population, others more than tripled in size. Even in La Paz, which is generally regarded as the department most affected by hacienda expansion during this period, some provinces lost nearly all their community population, while others lost substantially less.

In addition to variation in their population decline, Bolivian communities also varied in the amount of land they lost at the turn of the twentieth century. Figure 4.4 plots the percentage of parcels of Indigenous communal land purchased by non-Indigenous individuals in the department of La Paz. Examining this data, communities in some provinces—Cercado, Larecaja, Omasuyos, and Pacajes—lost a significant portion of their land, while others—including Muñecas, Caupolicán, and Yungas—lost very little. Data from 75 districts in La Paz demonstrates even greater variation: while some communities lost nearly all of their land, many others lost only a tiny portion, if any at all.[13] Extending beyond La Paz, Cusicanqui (1990) observes that the communities in northern Potosí were generally able to resist hacienda expansion and even achieved an end to parcelization in 1902 (103).[14]

---

12. Nevertheless, some of these reductions in population could be related to out-migration for reasons unrelated to land seizures or disease. A significant epidemic swept through Bolivia in the late 1870s, for example (Jackson 1994, 18).

13. See Online Appendix Figure OA6.

14. On this latter point, see Platt (1987, 318).

Percent change in community population

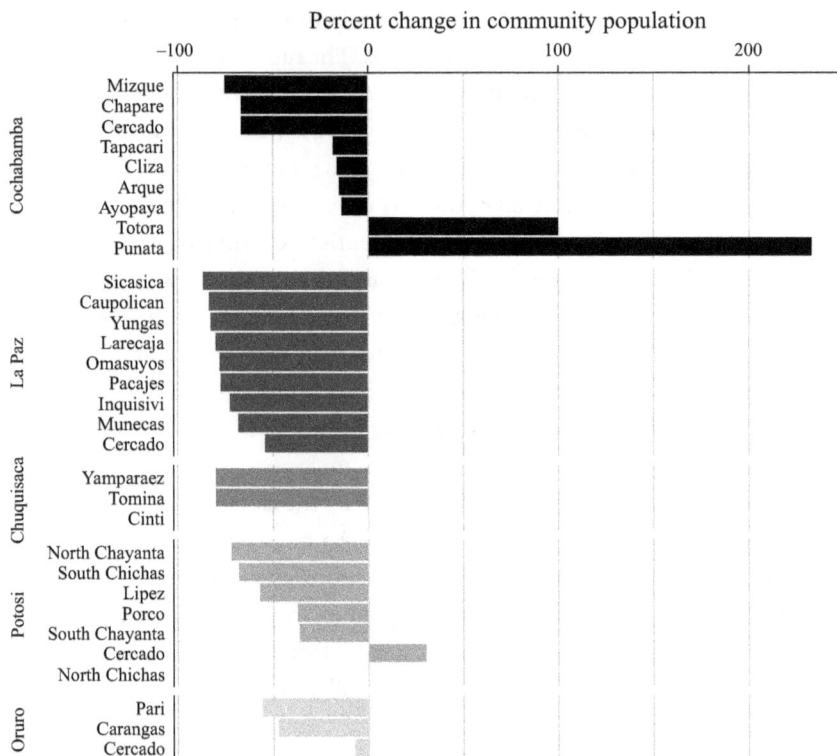

FIGURE 4.3. Provincial-level change in community population (1854–1900, Bolivia)
*Note*: Estimated population based on tributary and taxation data.
*Source*: McBride (1921).

As in Peru, the capture of Indigenous land by non-Indigenous individuals represented both a profound disruption and a continuity of traditional practices. Many families continued to farm the same land plots for generations, and bonds among community members remained mostly unchanged. Communities that preserved their long-standing political and social institutions even after being captured onto haciendas are thus known as "captive communities" (Albó 1999, 772). Yet, large landowners' theft of traditional communal lands was also deeply transformative. While community members preserved their access to land, they lost control over their labor. Indigenous laborers became debt peons, or *colonos*, to retain access to their land. In his discussion of Bolivia's debt peonage system (*pongueaje*), Reyeros (1949) describes the *colono* as "an integral part of the soil. He passes from owner to owner like the land" (12). Gotkowitz (2008) details how *colonos* worked on the demesne

Communal land plots

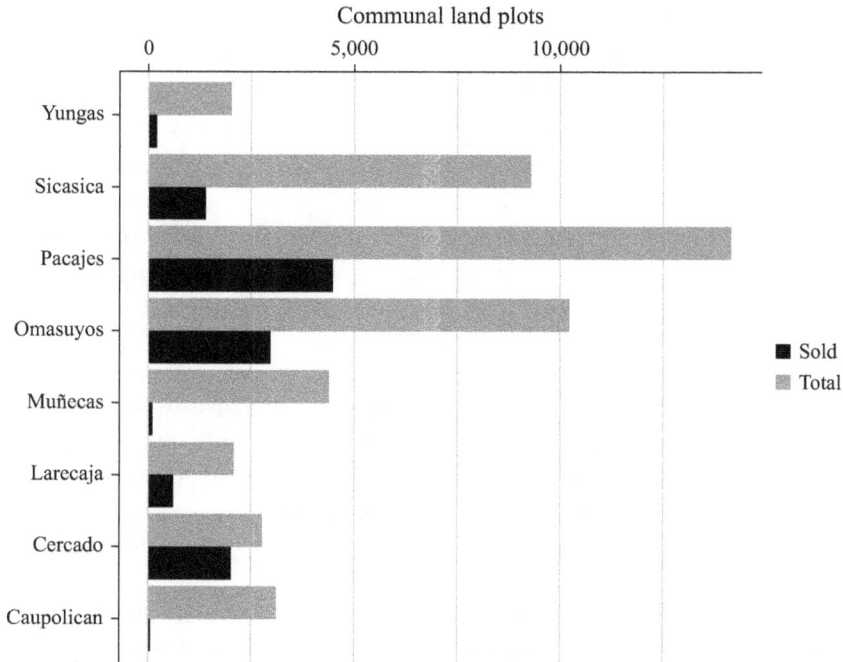

FIGURE 4.4. Purchases of Indigenous communal land in La Paz, Bolivia (1877). The graph documents purchases of Indigenous land by non-Indigenous individuals.
*Note*: Data collected from department of La Paz, Bolivia.
*Source*: Grieshaber (1990).

or paid the estate owner in cash or in kind to retain access to a small land plot; *colonos* also had more extensive responsibilities, including "transporting crops to markets or mills, repairing irrigation ditches, caring for the owners' livestock, spinning (*hilado*), making *muko* (*mukeo*), running errands or delivering messages (*cacha*), and completing terms of domestic service" (136).

These extensive responsibilities created an enormous burden for workers on large estates. As Gotkowitz (2008) notes, "When colonos did not complete the required labor, owners or administrators punished them by confiscating their clothing or tools, which were only returned once the work was doubly fulfilled. Landlords with multiple properties further penalized wayward workers by making them toil on estates far from the property where they lived" (138). Smith (1977) observes that on one hacienda, an administrator "threatened colonos with a pistol if they disobeyed his orders," exclaiming, "How much do you think you are worth? You are only worth 100 bolivianos" (242). Postero (2017) discusses precisely how the transition of Indigenous community members into landless peasants further deepened inequalities, arguing, "While many mounted vigorous resistance, many others were integrated into this system in a position of deep disadvantage" (45). Beginning in the late nineteenth century, intellectuals and politicians began challenging these exploitative practices and lobbying to abolish the debt peonage system in Bolivia.

Yet, the exploitative labor arrangements on haciendas remained unchanged until the mid-twentieth century. Advocates of *pongueaje* argued that working as a tenant on a large estate was preferable to living in a traditional community. *La Reforma*, a newspaper in La Paz, argued in 1871,

> The condition of the Indian tenant is by all means superior to the comunario [community member] condition because the only master he has to obey is the owner. The latter for his own convenience has to treat him well and become his protector so that he will not desert the farm which is worth nothing without tenants.[15]

Landlords often followed this line of paternalistic reasoning in justifying the continued use of coercive labor institutions. One *hacendado* bragged that "he had created a school on the hacienda, hired a teacher for peasant children, and bought medicine for the [workers]" (Soliz 2021, 32). Yet, these grand claims belied a harsher and more abusive reality that would come to light through peasant movements and uprisings on large estates in the early twentieth century. I examine the nature of these movements in the next chapter.

## 4.2   State-Led Extraction in Peru and Bolivia

Between 1870 and 1930, governments throughout Latin America sought to invest in transportation infrastructure to expand internal markets and the export sector (Summerhill 2006). Many countries—particularly those with large Indigenous populations, such as Peru (Mallon 2014, 233), Ecuador (Baud 2007, 86), Guatemala (McCreery 1994, 302), Bolivia (Schurz 1921, 88), and Mexico (Vaughan and Lewis 2006, 227)—introduced laws conscripting working-age males to build roads and railways without pay. Indigenous males were the overwhelming—and often sole—targets of government efforts to mobilize unpaid labor. Unlike more sustained forms of coerced labor that were likely to break up communities (such as indentured servitude or slavery), this

15. Cited in Rodríguez Ostria (1980, 61).

labor extraction was generally short-term. Indigenous workers often returned to their communities once their service was done, leaving communities intact.

### 4.2.1   Peru, 1920–1930

Latin America's most notable example of post-independence labor conscription occurred in Peru under President Augusto Leguía (1919–1930), who built the country's first major highway based on the route of the abandoned collection of pre-colonial roads known as the Qhapaq Ñan, or Inca Road (Chaplin 2015, 65).[16] To build his highway, Leguía proposed the *Ley de Conscripción Vial*, or Road Conscription Law, which required Indigenous men of working age to provide unpaid labor to build roads (Basadre 2014, 207; Davies 1974, 84).[17] However, archival documents from the departments of Ayacucho, Lima, and Ancash suggest that the government conscripted men as young as 16 and as old as 70 to work on the roads (Dirección de Vías de Comunicación 1928). Unlike previous instances of state-led extraction, such as the colonial-era mining mita or "Indian tribute," Leguía's law did not enlist the cooperation of Indigenous leaders; instead, *juntas viales*, or provincial-level commissions appointed by the national government, were responsible for mobilizing Indigenous laborers.[18] For ten years, *juntas viales* traveled to Indigenous communities in their provinces to mobilize workers to build roads. The government enlisted provincial police to ensure community members complied with their obligations.[19]

Abuses abounded under the road conscription program. *Juntas viales* forced Indigenous laborers to work far more than was their obligation—sometimes for months at a time—without providing food, shelter, clothing, or even certificates proving they had fulfilled their duty, without which they could be forced to serve again (Basadre 2014, 197; Calisto 1993, 174–175; Mallon 2014, 233). Stein (1980, 61) notes, "Indians were forced to leave their homes and travel many miles over difficult terrain to the construction sites. . . . Generally the workers received little if any food and no medical attention; deaths among the 'conscriptos' were not uncommon."

16. The Inca Road was not a single road but a collection of roads.

17. The government defined the universe of conscripts using military conscription rolls.

18. Provinces are Peru's second-level administrative tier.

19. Yet, landowners in Peru often opposed road conscription because it threatened their access to cheap Indigenous labor (Heilman 2010b, 517).

For reasons I discuss below, not all communities were eligible for con-scription. In the early 1920s, the government mandated that working-age men in many communities register in the provincial *padrón vial*, or road-building registry. Provincial governments then circulated *convocatorias* (announce-ments) revealing which communities would work on a project—e.g., building a bridge, repairing a road (Meza Bazán 1999, 148–149). *Juntas viales* arrived to march workers to the construction sites. Individuals were often conscripted multiple times, and the practice only ended with the termination of the road conscription program in 1930.

In eligible communities, many working-age men labored on the roads. For example, according to evidence from Pomabamba's *padrón vial*, over 16,480 workers—which constituted most of the 19,000 Indigenous males docu-mented in the 1940 Census—had built almost 100 km of roads in the province by 1929 (Dirección de Vías de Comunicación 1928, 249). In the province of Lima, 44,800 workers were conscripted in the first half of 1928 alone (Direc-ción de Vías de Comunicación 1928, 217); the 1940 Census calculates that just over 67,000 Indigenous males resided in the province. In the province of Pal-lasca, about half of the 1940 Indigenous male population worked on a single project in 1928 (Dirección de Vías de Comunicación 1928, 100).

Because labor conscription occurred annually or biannually between 1920 and 1930, communities often worked on multiple projects. Araujo Antonio (1991) estimates that eligible conscripts worked 30 to 40 days a year through-out the 10-year program (50). A community in the province of Canta had to help build four different bridges between February 1929 and April 1930 (Meza Bazán 1999, 149). Not all communities worked on every project; in the first half of 1928, communities in a few districts in Pallasca sent more than two-thirds of their conscripts to work (Cabana, Tauca, and Llapo) while others sent fewer than 30 percent of their conscripts (Yupán and Cajamala).[20] However, even if a community avoided conscription in one period, there is no evidence that it also avoided it in future periods.

Labor conscription did not uniformly affect all areas of Peru. As discussed above, Leguía's road-building program traced the ancient Qhapaq Ñan road network.[21] To confirm this, I perform a statistical analysis of the relationship

20. See Dirección de Vías de Comunicación (1928, 99).
21. Built before the arrival of the Spanish in the sixteenth century, the central part of the Qhapaq Ñan traversed the spine of the Andes from present-day Chile to Colombia. It linked the otherwise isolated parts of the Inca empire, allowing the emperor to exert effective control from Cusco. The Spanish had little use for the Inca Road, which primarily ran north to south; they

between the path of the Qhapaq Ñan and the route of Leguía's road, which yields a strong, significant, and positive relationship. This suggests that the 1920s road was, in fact, built atop the ancient one.[22]

Proximity to the Qhapaq Ñan, however, was not the only factor that created variation in exposure to labor conscription. The Road Conscription Law required laborers to work on only the road sections built in the province where they lived. As the Law stated, "Conscripts will be taken, except in exceptional cases, from the same [municipality], and cannot be taken from one province to work in another." This requirement served a logistical purpose: transporting Indigenous workers to distant work sites was costly, and, thus, government officials preferred to keep workers in their own municipality— and certainly in their own province. Furthermore, *juntas viales* were in charge of labor mobilization, and their jurisdiction stopped at provincial borders. There was also a political reason not to take laborers to other provinces. Provincial officials and the landlords they represented were protective of Indigenous laborers within their jurisdiction because "if [they] were out building highways for the president, they were not toiling in their landlords' fields" (Heilman 2010a, 66).[23]

Residents of provinces that the ancient Qhapaq Ñan passed through (shaded light gray in Figure 4.5) were, therefore, more likely to be conscripted. While proximity to infrastructure likely helped determine the probability of conscription, an individual's location in particular districts or provinces was just as, if not more, determinative of the likelihood that community members would be forced to work on roads.

### 4.2.2 Bolivia, c. 1890–c. 1950

Bolivian labor conscription lasted longer than in Peru and covered more government projects than road building. The government forced Indigenous communities to serve in the military (Shesko 2020) and deliver the

---

instead preferred east-west routes, which allowed them to transport mineral resources from the Andes to Pacific ports. By the seventeenth century, the Inca Road had fallen into disuse, with its location largely unknown. Using historical documents and a team of archaeologists, Leguía reconstructed the Qhapaq Ñan route.

22. Appendix Table OA2 shows the close ties between the ancient road and Leguía's, using an OLS regression of a binary indicator of provincial-level presence of the Qhapaq Ñan on a binary indicator of provincial-level presence of Leguía's road ($F = 12$ and $F = 16$).

23. Documents from the period suggest that the *juntas* did not recruit community members to work in other provinces (Dunn 1925, 79; International Labour Office 1929, 137–138).

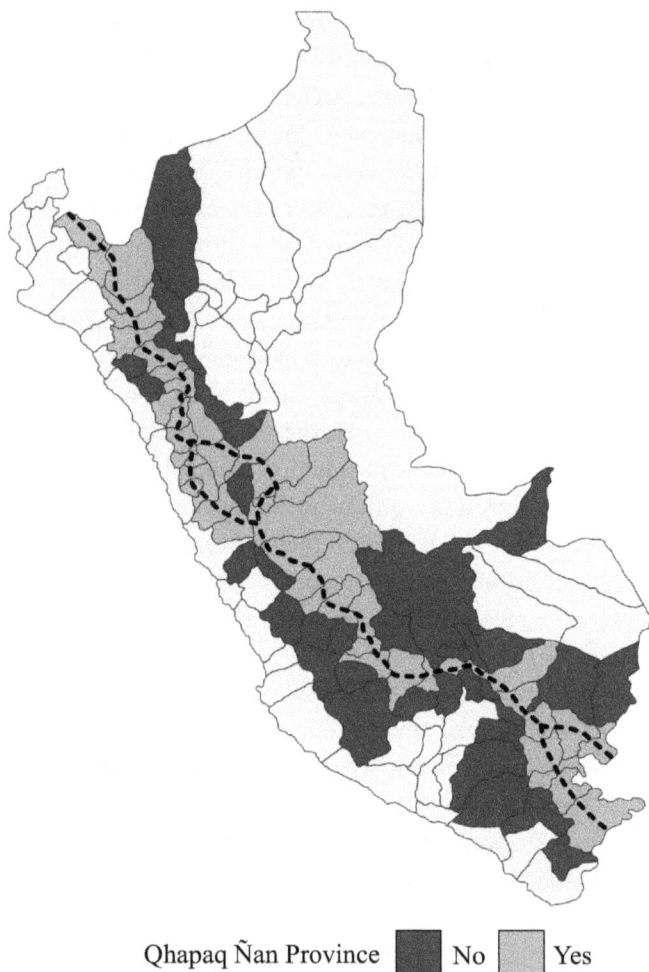

FIGURE 4.5. Qhapaq Ñan provinces in the Peruvian highlands
*Note*: The map depicts the central sierra route of the Qhapaq Ñan along with adjacent "control" provinces in the mountainous sierra. White provinces are not included in the study group. Dashed line indicates Qhapaq Ñan as known in the 1920s and 1930s. The map plots 1940 provincial borders.
*Source*: Regal (1936).

mail through the *postillonaje* system. The longest and most enduring type of labor conscription was the *prestación vial*, an infrastructure-building program launched by an 1888 law that endured until the 1950s.

Like Leguía's program, the *prestación vial* effectively constituted a tax that individuals could pay either with their labor or in cash. Due to a lack of financial resources, however, Indigenous people disproportionately paid the tax with their labor. The Annual Report of the Prefect of Potosí, for example, demonstrates that the tax was most likely to be collected in cash in parts of Potosí with a small Indigenous population, such as Porco ($\approx$ 10 percent Indigenous population) and the city of Potosí ($\approx$ 20 percent).[24] Conversely, where collection rates in labor were high, the Indigenous population was also larger, such as in Charcas ($\approx$ 68 percent) and Chayanta ($\approx$ 93 percent).[25] Thus, like the road conscription program in Peru, the *prestación vial*—in its most nefarious practices of exploiting labor—often targeted Indigenous community members who did not have the cash to pay their way out of participation and thus had to contribute labor.

Figure 4.6 provides evidence that the *prestación vial* targeted Indigenous communities. I first compare the number of Indigenous males in each department (as documented by the 1900 Census) with the number of men enrolled in the 1908 *Padrón Vial* (conscription roll). The figure displays a strong correlation ($r = 0.9$) between a department's male Indigenous population and the number of men in the conscription rolls. This strong relationship suggests that Indigenous groups were the most likely to be targeted by the conscription program.[26] Sometimes, government documents admitted to this ethnic targeting. The Prefect of Oruro wrote in his annual report in 1911, "As all inhabitants of [the province of] Carangas belong to the indigenous race, they comply with the obligation imposed on them by the esteemed Ley de Prestación Vial, with their personal labor" (Prefecto de Oruro 1911, author translation).

Road conscription ultimately affected a large share of Bolivia's population, which was majority Indigenous: nearly a fifth of Bolivians were registered for the *prestación vial*.[27] Furthermore, because conscription started at the turn of the twentieth century and continued for over 50 years, several generations of Indigenous Bolivians were affected.

Yet, exposure to labor conscription varied significantly across regions. Proximity to infrastructure projects shaped exposure to conscription. One of the key laws governing the program, the Ley de 9 de diciembre de 1905 (Law of

24. See Prefecto de Potosí 1916.

25. Data on the Indigenous population is taken from the 1900 Census. See Appendix Table OA3.

26. La Paz is a clear outlier—the number of conscripts far exceeds the Indigenous population, at least as documented by the 1900 Census. This may have been because census takers often categorized Indigenous migrants to cities, like La Paz, as *mestizos*, or mixed race (Gotkowitz 2008, 294, fn.18); thus, those classified as Indigenous for road conscription may not have been categorized in the same way for the census.

27. See Appendix Table OA4.

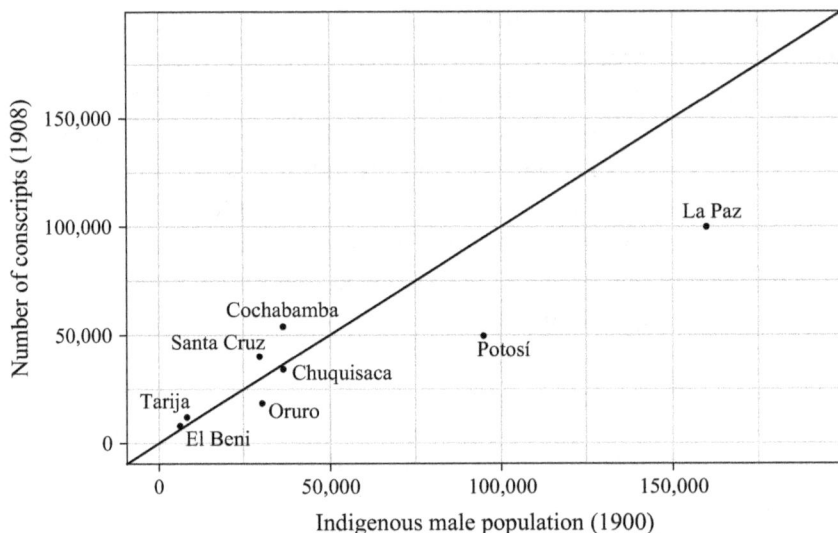

FIGURE 4.6. Prestación Vial and Indigenous population in Bolivian departments
Note: 45-degree line plotted.
Sources: Ministerio de Gobierno y Fomento (1908); Oficina Nacional de Inmigración, Estadistica y Progpaganda Geográfica (1904).

December 9, 1905), stated that workers "cannot be obligated to travel distances that exceed three leagues [≈15 km] from their home" (author translation). Idiosyncratic factors also shaped which communities experienced conscription. Until the early twentieth century, there was no standardized way to collect and update information on eligibility. This gave subnational authorities considerable discretion over conscription. In many cases, corrupt local officials collected the *prestación vial* tax in cash instead of labor, using the program to enrich themselves rather than for its intended purpose of road-building; in 1913, the Liberal government passed a law that punished local officials who failed to organize road-building projects (Egan 2019, 121–122).

The Bolivian government—for reasons that remain unclear—declared certain regions exempt from organizing labor brigades altogether. In October 1915, for example, the department of Cochabamba was released from labor contributions under the road conscription law; all working-age male residents of Cochabamba would have to instead pay the law in cash at the rate of 1 *boliviano* (Chapter 5). Thus, multiple factors—some idiosyncratic and some systematic—shaped the likelihood that Indigenous communities in Bolivia would be drafted to work on infrastructure projects without pay.

Variation in Indigenous communities' exposure to labor conscription emerges through an analysis of the department of Oruro—the area of Bolivia for which the most comprehensive data on labor conscription is available (Figure 4.7). For several of Oruro's provinces, there exists documentation of the percentage of conscripts in each canton and vice-canton who were Indigenous, white, and *mestizo*. Comparing this data with the total number of Indigenous men—documented in the 1900 Census—yields a measure of "over-extraction," or the extent to which Indigenous men account for a larger percentage of conscripts than their population share. Figure 4.7 demonstrates that most cantons and vice-cantons in Oruro exhibited over-extraction, but there is variation. In Poopó, Indigenous conscripts accounted for 92 percent of all conscripts, but Indigenous men constituted just 59 percent of the population, indicating an over-extraction rate of about 33 percent. The over-extraction rate was around ten percent in many other cantons and vice-cantons. In a few municipalities, Indigenous men appear to have been conscripted at levels far *below* their share of the population. For instance, in Antequera (at the far right of the figure), Indigenous men accounted for 76 percent of the population but only 17 percent of conscripts.

This section has outlined the prevalence of labor conscription programs in Peru and Bolivia at the turn of the twentieth century. Conscription affected large numbers of Indigenous men, but these effects were unevenly experienced across communities in both countries. The timing of extraction, a central issue for this book, also varied considerably. In the analyses employed in the subsequent chapters, I use causal and descriptive approaches to explain how this variation in exposure to extraction shaped later demand-making by Indigenous communities.

## 4.3   Case Studies in Extractive Sequences

The following chapters investigate the legacies of the three extractive paths that arise from experiencing only rural elite extraction, only state-led extraction, or both forms of extraction. The first path emerges in places that experienced early hacienda expansion, while the second appears in areas subjected only to government-organized labor conscription. The final path occurs when communities experienced early labor conscription followed by hacienda expansion.[28]

28. These sequences were discussed in detail in Chapter 3 (Figure 3.6).

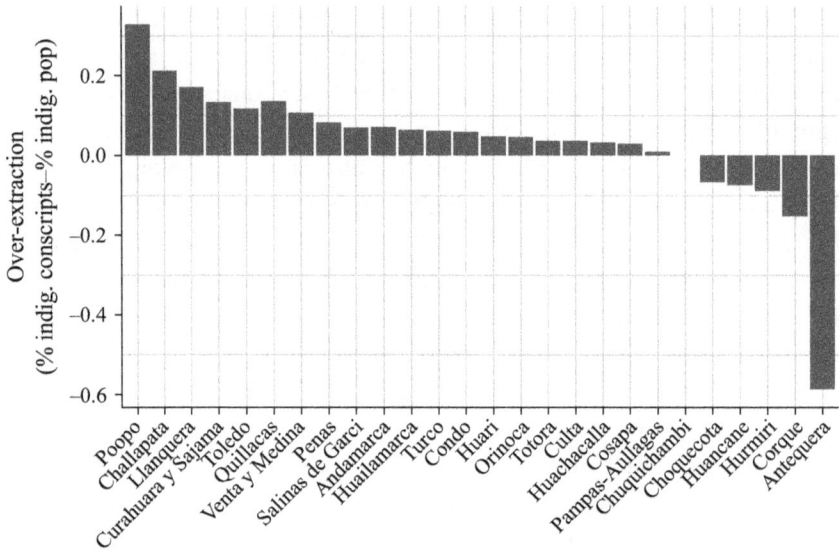

FIGURE 4.7. Over-extraction in Oruro, Bolivia (1909)
*Note*: Data coded at the canton and vice-canton level.
*Sources*: Prefectura y Comandancia General (1909); Oficina Nacional de Inmigración, Estadistica y Progpaganda Geográfica (1904).

Many of the tests of my hypotheses rely on fine-grained quantitative data documenting extractive experiences at the community, provincial, and municipal levels. However, I also conduct a series of qualitative case studies of Peruvian and Bolivian regions, which bolster the quantitative evidence and provide independent insights into key hypothesized mechanisms. Figure 4.8 depicts the cases and how they relate to the above-mentioned three paths. The first path is most likely to emerge in fertile regions, which were the areas of earliest hacienda expansion. These include Paucartambo, La Convención, and Paruro in the Peruvian department of Cusco and the valleys of Cochabamba in Bolivia. These regions experienced a substantial expansion of large estates and only limited—if any—exposure to state-led labor conscription.[29] The second path includes cases that experienced only state-led extraction; this was common in many parts of the southern Peruvian highlands, including the provinces of Quispicanchi, Canas, and Canchis in Cusco, as well as in the northern region of the Bolivian department of Potosí. In each case, hacienda

29. See Table 7.4.

| Early rural elite extraction | | | | *Yes* | | | Cochabamba, Bolivia<br>La Convención, Paruro,<br>& Paucartambo, Peru<br>(a) |

*Hacienda expansion in Bolivia (pre-1888) & Peru (pre-1920)* — *No* → State-led extraction — *Yes* → Later rural elite extraction — *No* → N. Potosí, Bolivia Quispicanchi, Canas, & Canchis, Peru (b)

*Labor conscription in Bolivia (1888–c.1950) & Peru (1920–1930)*

*Hacienda expansion in Bolivia (c.1900–c.1950) & Peru (1930–c.1967)* — *Yes* → La Paz, Oruro, & S. Potosí, Bolivia Cusco, Peru (c)

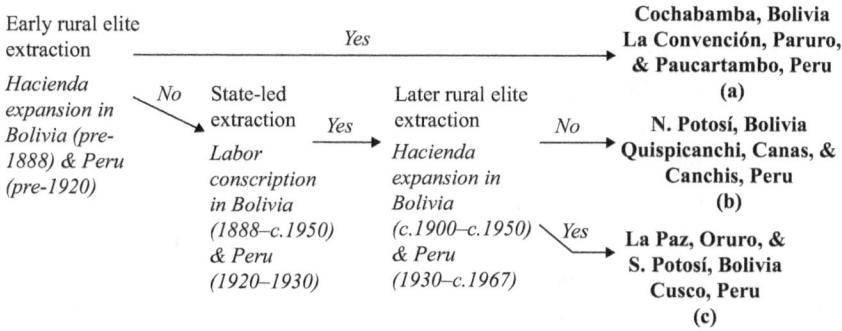

FIGURE 4.8. Extractive sequences in Peru and Bolivia

expansion was late or small-scale,[30] and exposure to state-led labor conscription was substantial. The final path includes communities in regions that experienced high levels of state-led extraction, followed by rural elite extraction. These cases include much of the Bolivian highlands (i.e., La Paz, Oruro, and Southern Potosí), as well as the capital of Cusco in the Peruvian department of the same name. Summary statistics for each of these variables are described in Chapter 7 (Tables 7.1 and 7.4).

In the following chapters, I will establish that these cases generally conform to my argument's predictions. They also shed light on broader, national-level differences between the two countries. Path (a), corresponding to assimilation, has been common in Peru and Bolivia. Path (b), which generally leads to demands for autonomy, has been more likely in Peru, while path (c), corresponding to integration, has been more prevalent in Bolivia.[31]

## 4.4 Conclusion

This chapter has provided an overview of the extractive experiences faced by Bolivian and Peruvian Indigenous communities at the turn of the twentieth century, which included a severe threat of having their labor permanently

30. See, e.g., Mörner (1975, 20) for a comparison of hacienda size in Quispicanchi, Paruro, and Paucartambo.

31. In Peru, path (c) was rare because hacienda expansion generally occurred *before* labor conscription, which began in earnest in the 1920s. As Stern (1993) observes, "by the 1920s, the great landed estates [in Peru] had locked their iron grip over lands controlled by indigenous communities during much of the nineteenth century" (328). As such, communities were less likely to experience both forms of extraction in Peru than in Bolivia.

seized by estate owners and a central state that sought to conscript their labor for large-scale infrastructure projects. The competition over Indigenous labor, which was not unique to but was particularly severe during this period, had enduring consequences.

I have detailed why these forms of labor extraction emerged at this time— primarily due to both state attempts to project power in new ways and governments' and rural elites' responses to expanding internal and external markets. The data suggests that these modes of extraction deeply affected Indigenous communities in distinct ways. The growth of haciendas reduced Indigenous community land and increased the prevalence of debt peonage; state-led labor conscription forced large numbers of Indigenous individuals to work on roads and railways, often repeatedly over years and even decades. Yet, Peruvian and Bolivian Indigenous communities varied in their exposure to these different forms of extraction: some experienced both, while others were subjected to only one.

The following chapters examine how variation in extraction shaped mobilization by Peruvian and Bolivian Indigenous communities. Chapter 5 demonstrates how rural elite extraction in Cochabamba and several provinces in the Cusco department of Peru frequently led to demands for assimilation. Chapter 6 analyzes how state-led extraction, somewhat surprisingly, increased communities' likelihood of demanding autonomy. This path has been more commonly observed in Peru than in Bolivia. Chapter 7 examines the combined effects of extraction, focusing on the Bolivian highland areas of Oruro and La Paz. Here, communities often experienced both state-led and rural elite extraction, leading to demands for integration. This path is rare in Peru, although the province of Cusco has been a notable exception.

# 5

# Explaining Assimilation Demands

The Indians were rebaptized as peasants; and their old communities (including the haciendas now distributed and parceled out among its peons) were transformed into "agrarian unions."

—XAVIER ALBÓ, 1992

The Indian struggle, with all its richness, is only one part of the entire Peruvian revolution. It exists, but there is no reason to exaggerate its importance.

—HUGO BLANCO, PERUVIAN PEASANT ORGANIZER, 1972

THE RAPID expansion of haciendas at the turn of the twentieth century—discussed at length in the preceding chapter—profoundly transformed Indigenous groups in Latin America in the short and long terms. After losing their access to collectively held land, many Indigenous individuals became debt peons, working under abusive labor conditions for a landlord in exchange for usufruct access to a small plot of land. Landowners discouraged resistance to their abusive practices in direct and indirect ways. They co-opted traditional Indigenous elites, rewarding collaborators with privileged positions as supervisors and more productive land. They limited access to tools, including education and literacy, that would have empowered peasants to articulate their demands beyond the hacienda (Cotler 1970; McClintock 1981, 76). Landlords replaced collective landholding with individually farmed plots and created individualized debt obligations, which jointly threatened to undermine long-standing patterns of communal solidarity. They also discouraged collective

Early rural elite
extraction
                                                    **Cochabamba, Bolivia**
*Hacienda*                        *Yes*             **La Convención, Paruro,**
*expansion in*          ─────────────────────────▶  **& Paucartambo, Peru**
*Bolivia (pre-*                                          **(a)**
*1888) & Peru*
*(pre-1920)*

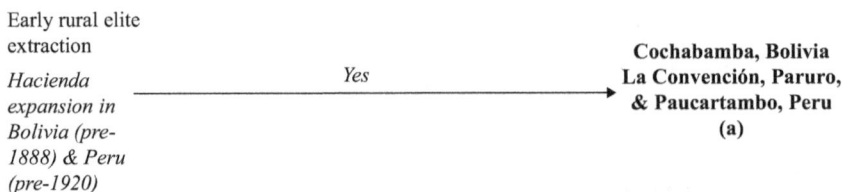

FIGURE 5.1. Extractive sequences in Peru and Bolivia: Early hacienda expansion

action by providing incentives (e.g., relief of individual debt) or threatening corporal punishment.[1]

Facing a collective action problem—and declining trust in Indigenous institutions that landowners had co-opted or otherwise disrupted—Indigenous peasants trapped on haciendas welcomed the emergence of class-based organizations. Unions and left parties could articulate peasants' most pressing concerns related to labor, land, and education; in return, these organizations demanded peasants abandon their ethnic identities to pursue the class struggle.

This chapter analyzes how rural elite extraction in Peru and Bolivia promoted Indigenous demands for assimilation. It demonstrates that early hacienda expansion increased mobilization through unions in both countries. Ruling left parties co-opted these labor organizations in 1950s Bolivia and 1960s–1970s Peru by requiring union members to identify as peasants—thereby abandoning their ethnic identities—to access agrarian reform. These efforts reduced community member investments in Indigenous institutions and identities, which have served as the basis for autonomy demands—as I discuss further in Chapter 6. I conduct quantitative analyses of archival data for each case. I also perform a qualitative analysis of three provinces in Cusco, Peru, along with the Bolivian department of Cochabamba (Figure 5.1).

## 5.1  Hacienda Expansion and Assimilation in Peru

The previous chapter detailed the massive expansion of haciendas at the turn of the twentieth century in Peru. Much of this hacienda growth occurred in the

---

1. While collective mobilization was undermined on the estates, communal units often persisted. Soliz (2014) observes of Bolivia, "legally abolished communities did not disappear—rather they continued to exist without legal standing, hence as 'ex-communities.' Some . . . communities were taken over and incorporated into expanding hacienda estates. The members of an ex-community called themselves ex-comunarios [ex-community members]" (298, fn. 4).

southern highlands, where a wool boom transformed local economies. Before the late nineteenth century, landowners had more highly valued the lower altitude Andean valleys, whose "relatively mild climate, generally fertile soil, and abundant water favor[ed] agriculture" (Orlove 2014, 66).

The advent of steam technology, railways, and an emerging wool trade increased the appeal of higher-altitude land, which was conducive to alpaca herding.[2] Innovations in transport facilitated the movement of wool to European markets and motivated an aggressive expansion of large landowners into historically Indigenous highland areas.[3] Cueto describes how destructive the growing demand for wool became for communities in the southern department of Puno:

> Most of the peasants in Puno lived in communities with a long history, controlled their land, sold their produce and had a high degree of political autonomy. The communities coexisted side by side with great landed estates which were in the hands of no more than a few individuals, just like in other parts of southern Peru. The favourable conditions present in the wool market made many landowners expand their holdings at the expense of communal lands. Some Indian holdings were literally assaulted and absorbed by the great *haciendas*. (Cueto 2017, 49)

Forced land sales accounted for much of the hacienda expansion during this period. As haciendas expanded, landowners captured skilled Indigenous herders who had raised alpaca for generations. Workers were forced to provide wool in exchange for continued access to land. Bourricaud (1967) observes, "the hacendado is constantly in conflict with his indigenous herders; by granting land or produce he retains a means of exploiting his labor" (148, author translation). Leaving the estates also presented substantial costs to community members, as workers were "slaves" to the hacienda; if they fled, they would

---

2. The most favorable conditions for alpaca production arise between 4,000 and 5,200 meters (about 13,000–17,000 feet) above sea level. Orlove notes, "At lower altitudes, especially below 3400 meters, external parasites such as lice and mange make the wool short and uneven and reduce yields. . . . The alpacas must also eat the dry, tough grasses found at high altitude, since their teeth continue to grow through maturity and thus need a degree of wear" (Orlove 2014, 207).

3. Jacobsen (1993) observes, "Land purchases by hacendados [hacienda owners] followed export market conditions for wool as the single most important product of the altiplano livestock estates closely enough to reflect cyclical swings of wool prices and export volumes" (209).

"lose part of their animals and belongings" (Martínez Arellano 1960, 16, author translation).

Landowners often tied Indigenous labor to the land by striking cooperative agreements with Indigenous community leaders. Jacobsen notes, "The day-to-day functioning of the estate rested on the smooth cooperation of a hierarchy of Indian supervisory officers mediating between owner or administrator and the colonos" (Jacobsen 1993, 295). Paige (1978) similarly observes, "In Peruvian hacienda villages, the *varayoc* [traditional Indigenous leaders] were under the control of the foreman and were responsible for determining when work obligations had been satisfied, who was to work in the master's house, and who would be called for obligatory unpaid labor on public works" (345). He goes on to assert, "Community solidarity was therefore imposed from above rather than originating within the class of cultivators themselves and reflected the conservative interests of the oligarchy and the outside authorities it represented" (Paige 1978, 345). Edwards and Jones argue that the co-optation of Indigenous leaders was widespread:

> The leadership structure that the anthropologists found in Vicos was typical of that in hacienda communities generally. . . . Direct supervision of work on the hacienda had been handled by six Indian foremen, elderly men who had previously occupied important positions in the community's governmental and religious subsystems and who were traditionally appointed by the patron to represent his interests.[4] (Edwards and Jones 2019, 179)

Even where Indigenous leaders avoided cooptation, hacienda owners' ties to the police and military successfully discouraged many grassroots efforts to resist. The government supported large landowners against any opposition from Indigenous groups (Langer 2018, 170). Cueto (2017) describes "a series of Indian revolts between 1900 and 1920 . . . put down by force with the help of the gendarmerie and the army" (49). In a 1969 survey of community leaders in three Peruvian departments—Cusco, Junín, and Pasco—Handelman (1974) found that "virtually all village leaders believed that in almost any landlord-community conflict, the government would intervene on behalf of the *hacendado*" (179). Handelman's survey also indicates low levels of efficacy among surveyed community leaders. When asked about the prospects of

---

4. Vicos is a highland hacienda in northern Peru that was the site of extensive anthropological research in the 1950s and 1960s.

pressuring the government, leaders responded with quotes that included the following:

- "Certainly not! How could we do that?"
- "Oh, no, we would get thrown in jail if we tried that."
- "[Exerting pressure] would be a very dangerous thing to do."[5]

The exploitative conditions of debt peonage generated a new set of grievances among community members, including low pay, abusive treatment, and a lack of access to schools (Handelman 1974, 41–42).

When Indigenous institutions and leaders failed to organize effective resistance to hacienda exploitation and articulate new demands, community members turned instead to class-based organizations. Unions were the most common allies and were especially likely to mobilize Indigenous communities on large estates. To test the claim that unions were most likely to mobilize peasants on large estates, I develop measures of rural elite extraction (hacienda presence) and the prevalence of class-based organizations (union presence).

I measure *union presence* using data from Melgar Bao (1988), which contains the location of Indigenous and peasant organizations from 1920 to 1931. I coded each organization as peasant ($n = 90$), Indigenous ($n = 54$), or hybrid ($n = 26$). Peasant organizations included Societies for Peasant Defense, Rural Anarchist Cultural Societies, and Farm Workers Societies; Indigenous organizations were the committees and subcommittees of the Tahuantinsuyo Pro-Indigenous Rights Committee (discussed in the next chapter); and hybrid organizations were Peasant-Indigenous Federations (discussed further in Chapter 7).

I measure *hacienda presence* using the percentage of the rural population living on large estates in 1876 and 1940—the two years for which national-level data is available. Even though it occurs temporally after the dependent variable (union presence), I believe the 1940 population measure is a more reliable proxy for the 1920 hacienda population for three reasons. First, as discussed above, large estates expanded massively from 1876 to 1940, with much of this growth occurring between 1880 and 1920; thus, the 1940 measure is likely closer to the true hacienda population in the 1920s than the 1876 measure is. Second, the 1940 Census was more accurate than the one taken in 1876; Deere (1990) says that the former was "the first reliable enumeration of

5. All quotes from Handelman (1974, 221).

TABLE 5.1. Rural elite extraction, unions, and Indigenous organizations

| | Dependent variable | | | |
|---|---|---|---|---|
| | Peasant organizations | | Indigenous organizations | |
| | (1) | (2) | (3) | (4) |
| 1876 hacienda pop. | 1.065* | | −0.242 | |
| | (0.541) | | (0.653) | |
| 1940 hacienda pop. | | 1.873*** | | −0.352 |
| | | (0.578) | | (0.697) |
| Constant | 0.343 | 0.161 | 0.591** | 0.539** |
| | (0.214) | (0.180) | (0.258) | (0.217) |
| Observations | 95 | 110 | 95 | 110 |
| $R^2$ | 0.040 | 0.089 | 0.001 | 0.002 |

Note: $*p < 0.1$; $**p < 0.05$; $***p < 0.01$. The dependent variable indicates the number of each type of organization. The independent variable is the percent of rural population residing on haciendas. All data recorded at the provincial level. Results are from an Ordinary Least Squares (OLS) regression.
Sources: Perez (1972); Macera (1976); and Melgar Bao (1988).

Peruvian sociodemographic characteristics carried out on the basis of a house-to-house accounting" (330–331). Finally, there is no reason to believe union mobilization should have increased the presence of haciendas (i.e., reverse causation). If anything, hacienda owners should have been *less* likely to expand into—or more likely to move out of—areas where communities had already unionized. Therefore, the 1940 measure should not overstate the relationship between hacienda presence and union mobilization, but may understate it.

I use the number of peasant organizations to measure union presence and compare this to the percentage of the rural population living on haciendas in 1876 and 1940 (a measure of rural elite extraction). The analysis in Table 5.1 demonstrates a strong association between union presence and the hacienda population. Both the 1876 and, especially, the 1940 measures of hacienda strength are positively associated with union presence. Neither measure is robustly correlated with the presence of Indigenous organizations, suggesting that hacienda growth is associated with a specific type of mobilization: along class-based lines and through unions.

It is unclear which came first: did unions create the demand for peasant rights among hacienda peons, or did they mobilize individuals who already wanted peasant rights? The data suggests that the latter is more likely: the servile relations between peasants and landowners generated demands for

better treatment and an end to exploitation, independently of union mobilization. Indeed, hacienda peons, or *colonos*, sometimes organized revolts
independently (i.e., without union assistance). As Jacobsen observes,

> often in contact with the broad movement of community peasants sweep-
> ing the southern highlands, the colonos nevertheless pursued their own
> agenda. They protested against limits on huaccho [livestock belonging to
> peasants] flocks, steep fees for hacienda pastures, forced breeding programs
> designed to change the quality and color of their huacchos, and restrictions
> on the sale of their livestock products. "Unionist" demands, typical for rural
> workers, were not absent but secondary. (Jacobsen 1993, 320–321)

Thus, hacienda peons appear to have prioritized labor-related demands—
i.e., job security, pay raises, employee benefits, better working conditions, and
better living conditions—even before mobilizing with unions.[6] Indigenous
institutions' failure to adequately represent these claims led Indigenous communities to pursue closer ties to class-based institutions, including peasant
unions. These ties began in Peru in the mid to late 1920s and peaked in the
1960s. Several factors promoted these linkages. First, the poor working conditions on haciendas led many young people to migrate to work temporarily in
other areas. For instance, hacienda workers in the central Peruvian department
of Junín fled to work in the La Oroya copper refinery in the 1950s and 1960s;
as Handelman (1974) observes, "the few young men who returned to their
haciendas from the refineries brought the reformist ideology of the . . . labor
unions with them. Frequently they used their union experience in the creation
of Yanamarca's hacienda *sindicatos* [unions]" (95).[7] Children of peons often
moved to Lima before returning to form a union on the haciendas where their
families lived and worked. These individuals had the language and methods
to articulate peasant demands and understood labor organizations' potential
to obtain concessions from the government and landowners. For example,
Manuel Llamojha Mitma left his hacienda community at a young age to live
and work in Lima. Llamojha details the story of his return to his community,
Jhajhamarka, in Ayacucho:

---

6. The five union demands listed here are those identified by Mateos Mar (1964, 370).

7. The threat of exiting the hacienda to work in a mine also facilitated worker negotiations
with landlords. As Mallon (2014) observes, "the mining industry paid a higher wage and was
always looking for workers. On the haciendas . . . peasants would threaten to go to work in the
mines unless a particular demand was met" (219).

I organized a tenants' union and we began the struggle. I started to draw up documents. I went with my typewriter. I drew up documents and got peasants to sign them. I always walked around with my typewriter, I wrote petitions, and got all the people to sign. The documents said, "a series of abuses are committed on this hacienda, so the people want the hacenda-dos to retreat. If they don't, the pueblo will take charge." And then I took the documents to Lima myself, to deliver them to the ministry. I always did this, because the national government would readily order an investi-gation, whereas if you just presented your documents in Ayacucho, no one would investigate. So, I took documents directly to the ministry, to the gov-ernment itself. That's what I did, to the point that I made the hacendados tremble! (Llamojha Mitma and Heilman 2016, 49)

Perhaps the most well-documented case of this migrant mobilization occurred in the department of Cusco. La Convención, Paruro, and Paucar-tambo merit special attention. In 1876, Indigenous peoples in each province constituted a majority of the population.[8] These are also the only three provinces in southern Peru that had a hacienda population of over 50 percent in 1876, making them areas of "early hacienda expansion."[9]

Hacienda expansion in these areas generally reduced community mem-bers' willingness to invest in Indigenous institutions. Because the *hacendado* controlled and mediated Indigenous community members' access to land, anyone who challenged that authority could be expelled (Cotler 1976, 327). Organizing collective action to reclaim land and achieve concessions from landowners thus became increasingly difficult for Indigenous elites. A 1962

8. Indigenous peoples were 86 and 89 percent of the population in Paucartambo and Paruro, respectively, in the late eighteenth century (Mörner 1975, 17). La Convención's Indigenous pop-ulation share was likely greater than these two provinces. However, this data is not available as the region was not colonized at this time (see, e.g., Mörner 1975, 16). By 1876, the Indige-nous population was 76 percent, 59 percent, and 68 percent for Paucartambo, Paruro, and La Convención, respectively.

9. Almost all other provinces with large hacienda populations were on the north and central coasts. See Appendix Table OA1. Despite key similarities on variables of interest, the provinces differ in important ways. For example, Paucartambo and Paruro are located at a much higher altitude than La Convención. Paucartambo has historically produced potatoes for consumption in the capital city of Cusco and barley for a beer plant in the same city (Zimmerer 1997, 59). Haciendas in Paruro have engaged in similar forms of agricultural activity. La Convención, by contrast, has a subtropical climate that is more conducive to the production of coca, cocoa, and, perhaps most importantly, coffee (Hobsbawm 1969).

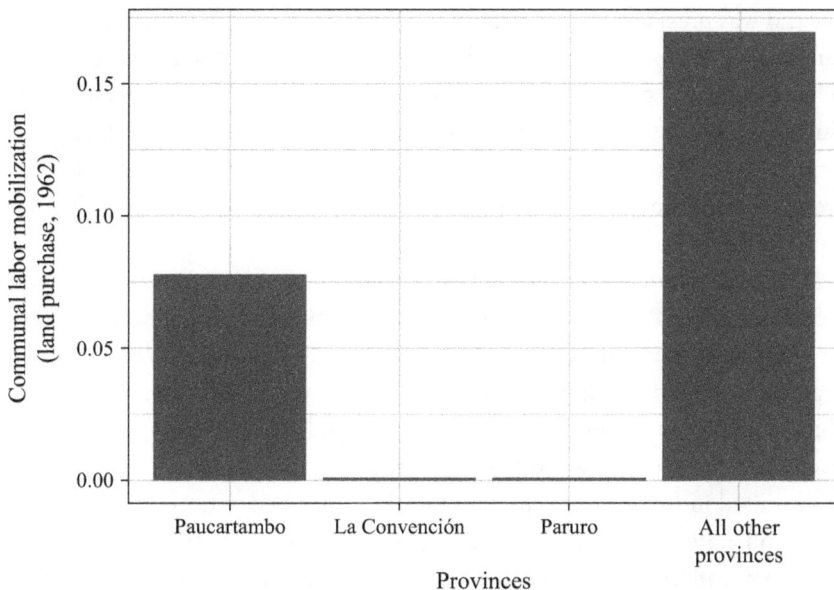

FIGURE 5.2. Early hacienda expansion and Indigenous institutions in 1960s Peru.
*Note*: The analysis includes only provinces in the department of Cusco. Paucartambo, La Convención, and Paruro were the provinces that experienced the earliest expansion of haciendas (rural elite extraction). Data taken from a 1962 survey of Indigenous leaders, which asked Indigenous leaders about their ability to mobilize communal labor to purchase land.
*Sources*: Dobyns (1964).

survey conducted by Dobyns (1964) found that Indigenous leaders were substantially less likely to mobilize unpaid communal labor to reclaim land in areas of early hacienda expansion, compared with other provinces in Cusco (Figure 5.2).

Lacking the capacity to mount an endogenous challenge to landowners, many Indigenous leaders turned to rural unions and agrarian leagues for assistance, leading to widespread unionization in La Convención, Paruro, and Paucartambo.[10] Silvestre Alvarez of the Maska Community of Paruro observed in

10. Mobilization in coastal areas is beyond the scope of this book, which concentrates on highland areas. The climate on the coast was conducive to growing profitable plantation crops, such as sugar and cotton, and was likely to have non-Indigenous workers (including Chinese and Japanese migrants). However, the predictions for highland areas also hold for the coast. Union mobilization efforts were especially prevalent in the provinces of Chancay and Cañete in Lima—both of which had large haciendas and appear in Appendix Table OA1 (Paige 1978, 159).

1984, "I was president of the community when I joined the Pachacutec Agrarian League. We were demanding that lands be transferred to the community. They helped us. For that reason, we regained our lands" (Seligmann 1995, 189). Such outside assistance was necessary; *hacendados* often controlled local politics, so those organizing to demand concessions could be not only expelled from their communities but also labeled "extremists" and arrested (Cotler 1976, 327).

La Convención is perhaps the best-documented case of peasant mobilization in southern Peru. The first union in the province was organized in 1947 at the Maranura hacienda and achieved a number of concessions, including an eight-hour workday and permission for peasants to sell their agricultural produce outside the hacienda (Eberhart 1977, 34).[11] These efforts expanded in 1952 when members of seven other haciendas organized independent unions; they united in 1958 to form the Provincial Peasant Federation of La Convención and Lares (Handelman 1974, 73). Craig notes that "the major part of the organization and development, particularly during the early phase from 1952 to 1960, was primarily an autonomous development within the valley and constituted an unusual Latin American phenomenon of a rural labor union organizing itself from the bottom up—rather than being organized and directed from outside" (Craig 1972, 287).[12]

La Convención's peasant movements benefited from ties to outside individuals and groups. They formed linkages with lawyers in Cusco, who helped articulate demands to landowners and the Ministry of Labor, and the Cuzco Labor Federation (FTC), "the department capital's leading worker's group" (Handelman 1974, 73). The Federation, spurred by the rapid unionization in La Convención, grew from 40 locals with 5,500 members in 1959 to 122 locals with 12,500 members in 1962 (Eberhart 1977, 37).

Two key factors helped boost mobilization during this period. First, demonstration effects of successful union mobilization in Lima and other urban areas provided a roadmap: rural residents who worked in urban areas and then returned home played an essential role in disseminating strategies and developing networks. Second, the end of an economic boom in the early

---

11. Hobsbawm (1969, 45) maintains that the Maranura union organized as early as 1934.

12. Like the unions discussed above, migrants played an important role in directing these efforts (Eberhart 1977, 35).

1960s resulted in the fall of a dictatorial regime and thereby provided a political opening for union expansion (Hobsbawm 1969, 46).

Union mobilization, however, may have provoked political opening as much as it benefited from it. The peasant movement in La Convención had notable successes in obtaining labor and land rights for otherwise disenfranchised peasants. Following a 1961 general strike to protest the mistreatment of workers, the Peruvian government filed a scathing report against landowners in the province, resulting in the abolition of unpaid labor in La Convención.[13] The unions in the province also obtained land rights for otherwise landless peons. In response to labor mobilization in La Convención, all presidential candidates in the 1962 elections committed to agrarian reform (Wright 2001, 113). Recognizing that they needed to respond to popular demands in the countryside to maintain stability and social control, the military government issued individual land titles that year to the peasants of Lares and La Convención (Watters 1994, 75).

Journalistic and academic accounts of the events at La Convención often attribute the peasant movement's success to Hugo Blanco, a Trotskyist and the son of a Cusco lawyer. While Blanco undoubtedly played a critical role as a leader, organizer, and messenger, the labor movement in La Convención was strong well before his arrival. When asked in a 2011 interview about the state of peasant unions when he arrived in Cusco in 1958, Blanco responded, "At this time, complaints respecting working conditions, health, matters of fairness and the like were being brought to the landowners themselves. . . . Then suddenly there would be a paro, which is a short general strike of one to three days—it was clear that the situation was radicalizing. . . . There were meetings happening all over, in Quechua" (Ward 2011, 653).

Paucartambo and Paruro followed a path similar to La Convención's. On some haciendas, workers led the way in forming unions. For instance, Saturnino Huillca was a monolingual Quechua speaker and son of hacienda workers, who "around 1948 . . . heard that a law had been passed that forbade unpaid labor on haciendas . . . [and] walked to Cusco to see if this was true and established contact with a labor union" (Mayer 2009, 45). Leveraging his growing connections with labor organizers, he formed new unions throughout Paucartambo. He met with members of other hacienda communities at religious festivities—including the important Fiesta de la Virgen del

13. See, e.g., Eberhart (1977, 37–38) and Paige (1978, 181).

Carmen—to convince them to join his union (Huillca and Samanez 1975, 76–78).

Yet, overall, outside actors played a more pivotal role in mobilization efforts in Paucartambo than in La Convención. Noted peasant organizer Emiliano Huamantica "visited Paucartambo frequently" to unionize hacienda workers (Fonseca Martel and Mayer 1991, 363, fn. 10, author translation). The Federation of Peasants of Cusco also played a key role in these efforts, unionizing "all Paucartambo valley haciendas between October and December 1963" (Cotler 1970, 544). Fonseca Martel and Mayer (1991) argue that outside assistance was necessary for labor union activity during this period because "hacienda peasants were almost all illiterate and although conscious of their situation of exploitation felt unable to assume leadership of a provincial-level movement" (363, author translation).

Unions in Paucartambo were able to secure several valuable concessions for hacienda peons. For example, they organized a strike that led to the signing of an "act of conciliation" between hacienda owners and peasants that outlawed some of the most notorious landowner practices of coercing unpaid labor (Cotler 1970, 544–545). In the late 1960s, Cotler (1970) surveyed hacienda workers and non-hacienda community members about their most important demand; 23 percent said that having more time to work their land was most important—second only to education (36 percent). Only 1 percent of respondents from non-hacienda communities named control over labor as their central demand (Cotler 1970, 556).

Paruro also experienced high levels of hacienda penetration and peasant mobilization. As Seligmann (1993) observes of the province's Huanoquite region, "At the time of the 1969 reform, the majority of the peasants, many of whom claimed membership in either ayllus or formal communities, continued to work as temporary or permanent laborers on large and medium-sized estates whose owners had been in the Huanoquite region for many generations" (31). As in La Convención, hacienda peons benefited greatly from external resources provided by provincial agrarian leagues, which "allowed them to recuperate their lands" (Seligmann 1995, 189). Peasants in the region were also inspired by the efforts of Hugo Blanco, a Paruro native who, as discussed above, achieved enormous success mobilizing the peasants of La Convención (Seligmann 1995, 120-121).

The mobilization of hacienda peons by unions endured through the two mechanisms hypothesized in Chapter 3: union ties to the government and the concessions that labor organizations obtained from private actors. First, unlike ethnic forms of mobilization, which generally struggled to gain traction after the repression of Indigenous movements in the 1920s, class-based organizations maintained close ties to the government. While the government repressed the Federation of Indigenous Workers of Peru (FIORP)—an anarcho-syndicalist federation that sought to unite Indigenous peasants with urban workers—major national actors, including the Peruvian Communist and APRA parties, continued to articulate FIORP's class-based demands in the 1930s and 1940s (Hirsch 2010). Ties to these influential national-level organizations reinforced the strength of unions and their demands for class-based rights; Peruvian Indigenous community members' only path to national political influence at this time was through their ties to labor organizations and the left parties that represented their interests *as peasants*.

Second, unions achieved concessions from landowners. Strikes often resulted in higher wages, better working conditions, and an end to unpaid labor; the demonstration effect of large-scale organizing in Cusco encouraged landowners in other departments to capitulate to peasant demands (Handelman 1974, 106). Even when landowners suppressed unions or responded to strikes with arrests and dismissals, the solidarity of peasant workers remained relatively high, and mobilization continued in the hope that the government would intervene or *hacendados* would ultimately capitulate.[14] While *local* unions could obtain concessions from individual landowners, they could also form alliances with national-level labor federations to coordinate more significant and effective acts of resistance. For example, the national-level Peasant Confederation of Peru became strongly associated with organizing large-scale invasions of peasants to claim hacienda land. Heilman (2015) observes, "An estimated 300,000 Peruvian campesinos participated in the efforts to recover hacienda land in this period [the 1960s], and their efforts pushed the successive Belaúnde and Velasco governments to enact agrarian reforms" (172).

To formally test the relationship between hacienda population, union strength, and workers' demands, I first compile a dataset of hacienda presence using the same measure as above: the percentage of the rural population residing on large estates in 1940. I then pair this data with information on Peruvian peasant movements between 1956 and 1964. I code each movement's demands and the organization responsible for mobilization. I aggregate the movement data to the provincial level, the second-level subnational administrative tier in Peru—the unit at which data can be coded confidently and consistently.

14. See, e.g., Handelman (1974, 94).

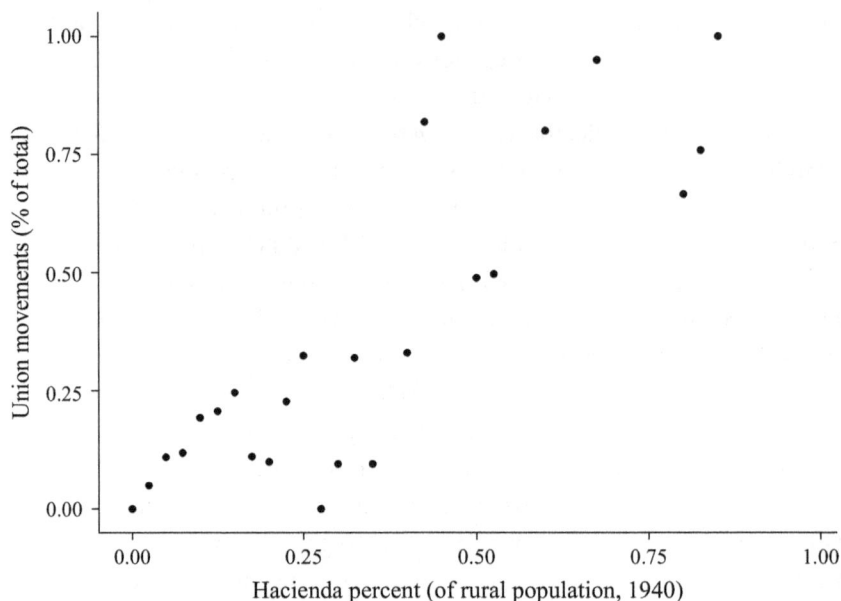

FIGURE 5.3. Rural elite extraction and union-led mobilization
*Note*: Author-coded data based on analysis of peasant movements. Data has been binned and aggregated to provincial level ($N = 109$).
*Sources*: Perez (1972) & Guzmán and Vargas (1981).

I begin by investigating the correlation between hacienda population (rural elite extraction) and union mobilization in the 1960s. I calculate the percentage of peasant movements organized partially or entirely by a union. The data yield a clear and robust positive correlation between the rural hacienda population—which was almost exclusively Indigenous—and union mobilization (Figure 5.3). The larger the hacienda population, the greater the number of union movements ($F > 28$, $p < 0.01$).

These union efforts to mobilize Indigenous communities on haciendas coincided with more labor-related claims and ultimately, assimilation. The Lauramarca hacienda in Cusco, for example, was mobilized by communist-led unions that advocated "no free labor, better salaries, and eight-hour workdays" (de la Cadena 2000, 188). The local union leader in Lauramarca emphasized that achieving these demands required abandoning ethnic identities and customs and acquiring literacy: "[N]ot knowing how to read makes us more Indian, easy victims of the gamonales [local strongmen] and their lackeys" (de la Cadena 2000, 129).

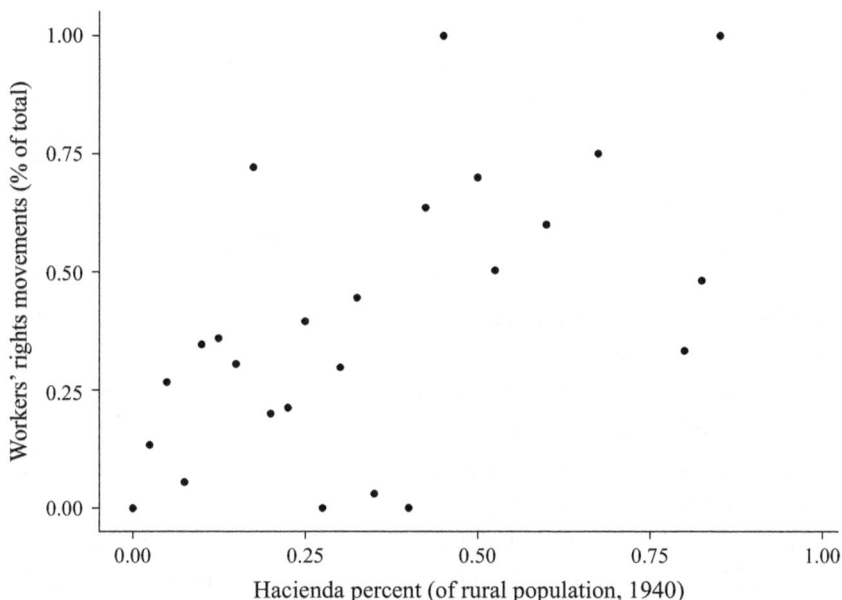

FIGURE 5.4. Rural elite extraction and the content of Indigenous demands
*Note*: Author-coded data based on analysis of peasant movements. Worker-related demands include those involving employer abuses, firings, mistreatment, imprisonment, and efforts to thwart unionization. Data has been binned and aggregated to the provincial level ($N = 109$).
*Sources*: Perez (1972) & Guzmán and Vargas (1981).

I further analyze whether rural elite extraction coincided with more class-based claims by coding the central demand of Indigenous movements between 1956 and 1964. Some demands focused on land, while others concentrated on labor. I code class-based demands as those that denounced an employer for abuses, wages, union suppression, dismissals, and imprisonment. Consistent with my theoretical predictions, I find a strong, positive correlation between the rural population residing on haciendas and the incidence of labor-related demand-making (Figure 5.4, $F > 20$, $p < 0.01$).

A final step of my argument suggests that rural elite extraction—and subsequent union-backed class demands—should have increased the likelihood of assimilation. In Peru, this could have occurred through multiple channels. First, corporatist policies under the leftist military government (1968–1975) targeted unionized areas. The head of the military regime, Juan Velasco, sought to "mobilize indigenous people into peasant federations and other corporatist organizations, such as the Sistema Nacional de Apoyo a la Movilización (SINAMOS, or National Support System for Mobilization). Accordingly, Velasco declared the social death of Indians" (Mainwaring 2006, 260). These efforts disproportionately focused on hacienda communities; through co-optation, Velasco sought to curb the autonomy of peasant unions, which had caused economic and political disruption. These unions also had long-standing ties to the APRA Party, a key opponent of Velasco's government.[15] Demands were to be channeled through government-recognized (and, frequently, government-run) unions; Velasco used these labor organizations to incentivize mobilization for peasant, rather than Indigenous, rights (Starn 1999, 59). Rice (2012) argues, "By structuring group representation and regulating official channels for demand making, the state corporatism of the Velasco era attempted to assimilate indigenous peoples into the dominant mestizo culture by reconstituting them as national peasants" (93).

Velasco further encouraged assimilation by separating hacienda communities and free ones, undermining future opportunities for cross-community ethnic solidarity. The agrarian reform, for example, expropriated hacienda land to give to hacienda peons.[16] Non-hacienda communities opposed these efforts as they argued that hacienda land had been stolen from them. Ultimately, these "free" communities were excluded from the reform (Yashar 2005, 243). As my theory predicts, the free communities adopted demands for ethnic rights, while the cooperatives (i.e., communities benefiting from the land reform) primarily made class-based claims.

Beyond the Velasco government, Peruvian peasant unions also encouraged assimilation. They and their overarching federations deemphasized ethnic identities to promote a broader cross-ethnic alliance of workers. Class consciousness and conflict thus became "an empowering banner . . . that replaced former notions of racial-cultural differences . . . [and] privilege[d] class over all other forms of identity" (de la Cadena 2000, 191). Hacienda communities reinforced these trends, calling for "education and better working conditions," which helped peasants "build alliances with student and labor movements" (Cant 2021, 23).

I now analyze whether hacienda communities, which were more likely to mobilize with unions and left parties, were more likely to experience

---

15. Evidence suggests, however, that unions remained strong and even became more robust—despite efforts by the government to co-opt and weaken them (McClintock 1981, 168).

16. The land was to be operated as a collective enterprise.

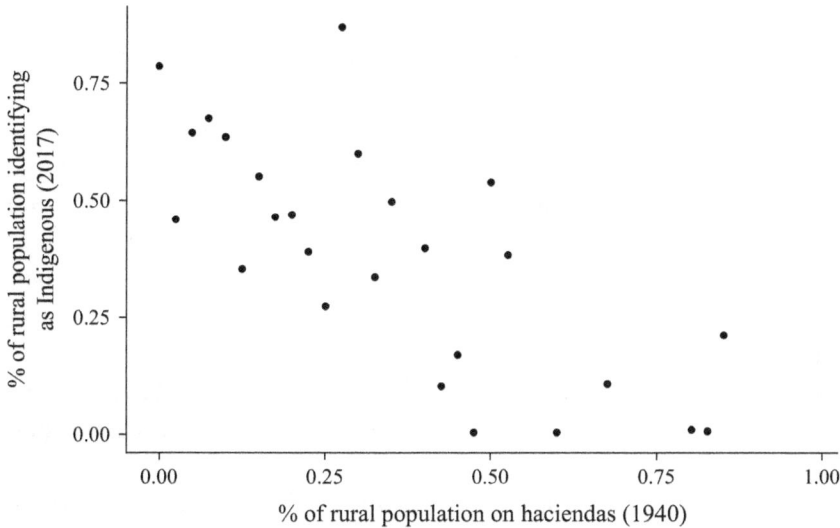

FIGURE 5.5. Relationship between hacienda prevalence and assimilation
*Note*: Binned means plotted. Self-identification measure taken from the
2017 Census: "According to your customs and traditions, do you consider
yourself . . . ?" Answers included Indigenous and non-Indigenous (white, *mes-tizo*, Afro-descendant) identities. I code answers indicating an Indigenous group
(e.g., Quechua, Aymara) as 1 and all others as 0. Hacienda population data taken
from Perez (1972).

assimilation. To measure assimilation, I calculate the percentage of the
population that identifies as Indigenous. My theory would predict that
hacienda prevalence is negatively correlated with contemporary Indigenous
self-identification. The data is consistent with this hypothesis. Examining
an ethnic self-identification measure from the 2017 Peruvian Census, I find
a strong and negative correlation between the rural hacienda population
in 1940—the same measure of rural elite extraction used above—and the
percent of the rural population that identifies as Indigenous (Figure 5.5).

Alternative explanations cannot easily account for the results in Figure 5.5.
Hacienda expansion, for example, may be more likely to occur near cities,
where agricultural products can be bought and sold and where economic elites
are more likely to reside; it may also be the case that certain aspects associated with urban life (e.g., education and intergroup contact) are more likely to
promote assimilation. Relatedly, we might be concerned that hacienda expansion is most likely to occur in areas that are better connected to infrastructure.
These places may be closer to markets, promoting hacienda growth. They

may also have been more legible to the state and thus more exposed to the assimilationist policies frequently adopted by national governments in Peru. To address these potential confounders, I include controls for urban population and completed roads in the early twentieth century. Incorporating these covariates does not reduce the strong association between hacienda population and assimilation ($p < 0.05$, Appendix Table OA5). My theory also finds qualitative support in Alberto Escobar's interviews with two community members and two hacienda workers in the early 1970s. The community members hoped their children would learn to read and write in Quechua, an Indigenous language. The hacienda workers he interviewed spoke Quechua at home; however, neither wanted their children to learn to read and write in the language, fearing it would lead to discrimination (Escobar 1972, 25).

In addition to a decline in Indigenous *identities*, hacienda communities are also associated with a long-term reduction in Indigenous institutions. In a 2017 survey I conducted with Indigenous leaders in Cusco, I asked how many communal labor projects they organized each year through traditional Indigenous institutions.[17] The number of projects in provinces that experienced early hacienda expansion (Paruro and Paucartambo) was about half that of other provinces (0.47 vs. 0.93). Most community leaders in Paruro and Paucartambo (57 percent) said they had not mobilized *any* traditional labor institutions in the past year. This was true of fewer than 40 percent of community presidents in other provinces in Cusco.[18]

## 5.2   Hacienda Expansion and Assimilation in Bolivia

As in Peru, Bolivian Indigenous communities experienced a sustained assault on their land in the late nineteenth and early twentieth centuries. Indigenous *ayllus* (communities) controlled two-thirds of Bolivia's cultivable land in the 1850s but only one-third by 1950 (Soliz 2021, 23). This decline corresponded to an increase in the number and size of large estates and, consequently, an expansion of debt peonage arrangements, or *pongueaje*. Despite these disruptive

---

17. Because these institutions require community members to contribute unpaid labor for several days at a time, they are costly, particularly in places with greater market integration—i.e., where opportunity costs are high.

18. See Appendix Figure OA7.

changes, many Indigenous communities remained intact within the bounds of haciendas as "ex-communities" (Soliz 2014, 598, fn. 4).

One of the primary ways that Bolivian hacienda owners ensured a steady supply of peasant labor was by buying off the leaders of traditional Indigenous political institutions. Soliz (2021) observes, "In some petitions, ex-comunarios [ex-community members] complained that caciques apoderados [traditional Indigenous leaders] sold communal property when bribed, or they demanded money from comunarios to recover their property" (125). Klein similarly notes, "In some cases the owners were known to interfere with the appointment of the jilakatas [Indigenous community leaders] on their estates, and sometimes there were accusations of overly intimate relations between the jilakatas and the mayordomos or owners, which resulted in complaints or exploitation of the regular peasant families" (Klein 1993, 148). Mayer finds evidence of collusion between landowners and Indigenous authorities: "To compound the lack of community solidarity, by 1951 many community leaders had worked out an economic partnership with some of the most exploitative landowners in the province" (Mayer 1995, 184).

Landowners' often successful efforts to undermine Indigenous institutions allowed outside organizations to form ties with hacienda peons, who sought an ally that would faithfully articulate their grievances. Dandler and Torrico A. (1987), for example, notes of the pro-peasant National Indigenous Committee: "In the case of the haciendas the alcaldes de campo and kurakas [traditional Indigenous authorities] were men not necessarily loyal to their communities, and the committee, therefore, sought to identify those local leaders with the organizational capacity, tact, or courage to elude control by the patrones [hacienda owners]" (Dandler and Torrico A. 1987, 344). Unions, as the most powerful national and regional non-Indigenous societal organizations in mid-twentieth-century Bolivia, were the most significant potential beneficiaries of these opportunities. On the haciendas, they found a willing base of potential members with few alternative, locally legitimate leadership structures.

Hacienda peasants formed the first peasant union in Ucureña, Cochabamba in 1936 with the goal of "freeing themselves from the feudal obligations of service to the latifundium owners" (Patch 1960, 120). Allying with teachers and lawyers, the union members quickly achieved concessions, including a rural school on the hacienda. The movement soon spread throughout the Cochabamba valley, forming "a network of twenty four unions in the upper

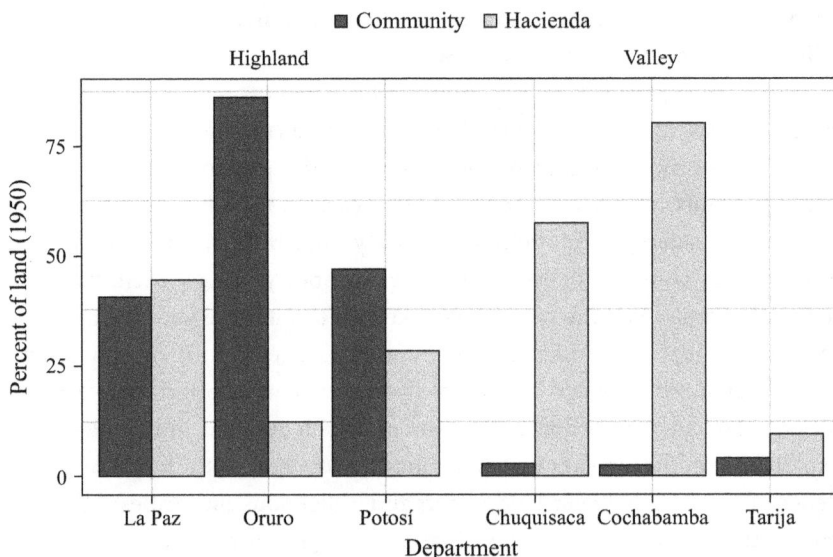

FIGURE 5.6. Haciendas and communities (% of total land) in 1950 Bolivia
*Note*: Other non-plotted land tenure systems include smallholding, renters, or other (non-specified) arrangements.
*Source*: Fundación TIERRA (2009).

valley" (Albó 1999, 796–797), which had the largest hacienda population share in the country in 1950 (Figure 5.6).

The labor movement quickly spread to "the hacienda regions of La Paz, Oruro, Potosí, Chuquisaca, [which] witnessed a new form of struggle: the sit-down strike" (Albó 1999, 797). Peasant unions were especially powerful in Oruro, where an urban-based anarcho-syndicalist federation was central in organizing rural hacienda workers (Gotkowitz 2008, 154). Unions made two key demands at the time. The first was an end to unpaid labor, which was especially common on highland estates. The second was for land rights; a familiar refrain was "The land is for those who work it" (Albó 1987, 381).

Not coincidentally, perhaps, this first phase of union mobilization coincided with the 1936 creation of the Bolivian Ministry of Labor, which provided "novel forms of redress," such as investigative committees that could "circumvent biased local officials" (Gotkowitz 2008, 147). Other events bolstered the growing peasant union mobilization, including the relatively pro-labor regimes of Presidents David Toro (1936–1937) and Germán Busch (1937–1939). Toro, for example, made union membership compulsory, which "helped speed up the organization of workers throughout the country" (Rivera Cusicanqui 1987, 44). News of this changing government approach to labor spread quickly through Bolivia. As one peasant noted:

> We noticed things were changing during the Busch administration, when periodicals and various individuals published articles and pamphlets speaking in favor of the campesinos. . . . [Despite] what we heard about these decrees and promises, no one helped us, and by order of the patrón [hacienda owner] we were treated more cruelly than ever. . . . But by this time we were beginning to defend ourselves as men. (Dandler and Torrico A. 1987, 339)

The Chaco War (1932–1935), South America's first modern military confrontation, also helped mobilize Indigenous peasants. This territorial conflict between Bolivia and Paraguay over the Chaco region resulted in an embarrassing military defeat for Bolivia.[19] As such, it redefined the political system by discrediting the traditional governing elite, which the public held responsible for both the conflict and the deaths of the overwhelmingly Indigenous military conscripts. New left parties emerged to capitalize on these grievances and formed an "intimate bond" with dissatisfied hacienda workers (Albó 1987, 381). At first, the most important of these parties was the Stalinist *Partido de la Izquierda Revolucionaria* (PIR, Revolutionary Leftist Party), which had formed close—and perhaps co-optive—relationships with many of the country's trade unions. In 1942, the PIR organized the First Congress of Quechua-speaking Indians, which, despite its name, made class-based demands, including an end to *pongueaje*, the return of stolen land, and reform of taxes that were viewed as harming the peasantry (Rivera Cusicanqui 1987, 48).

In 1943, Gualberto Villarroel assumed the presidency of Bolivia, having undertaken a successful coup with the assistance of the *Movimiento Nacionalista Revolucionario* (MNR, Revolutionary Nationalist Movement). The MNR had long been an ally of Bolivia's labor movement, and its substantial presence in the new government—including in crucial cabinet positions—emboldened peasant groups, which initiated a series of strikes throughout the country (Rivera Cusicanqui 1987, 49). While the MNR historically had maintained strong ties to the mining unions, it had weaker links to peasants, who had traditionally supported the PIR. To solidify its support among

---

19. See Chesterton (2016); Niebuhr (2021); de Quesada (2011); Sapienza et al. (2020) for a detailed description of this conflict.

rural workers, in 1945, the MNR conceded to hacienda peasants' demands to hold an Indigenous conference in the capital of La Paz. Indigenous peoples from throughout the country attended the conference; many expressed their support for Villarroel, whom they called *tata*, or "father" in Quechua and Aymara (Rivera Cusicanqui 1987, 50). Villarroel encouraged this paternalistic relationship in his speech at the conference: "Today begins the work of the government that will watch over you like a father caring for his sons. The abuses will end" (Dandler and Torrico A. 1987, 353). To control future peasant mobilization and uprisings, the government sought to limit the demands of conference attendees to those it could feasibly address, privileging labor concerns over land.[20] On the last day of the conference, Villarroel decreed an end to *pongueaje*.

Peasant unions quickly spread the word that forced labor was now illegal. Labor organizations then shifted their focus to land, most notably, launching invasions of large estates. Villarroel had little control over peasant leaders, who felt they had the government's unwavering support. Furthermore, a lack of state capacity prevented Villarroel from controlling the rural elite, who violently suppressed peasant movements and their leaders (Dandler and Torrico A. 1987, 361). Dissatisfaction was so great that in July 1946, a coalition that included both conservative interests and the leftist PIR overthrew the Villarroel government. The ex-president was assassinated and "hung from a lamppost outside the Government Palace alongside the corpses of several other high-ranking officials" (Gotkowitz 2008, 233).

Indigenous peasants rebelled across Bolivia immediately after Villarroel's overthrow, and the unrest continued until 1947. Consistent with my theory, the data suggest that these peasant uprisings were more likely to occur in areas where haciendas were dominant. Mobilization was particularly strong in Larecaja, Omasuyos, and Yungas in La Paz; Charcas in Potosí; and Tomina in Chuquisaca, all of which had experienced a strong decline in Indigenous communal land (approximately 80 percent) between 1850 and 1900. I conduct a quantitative analysis to probe further whether movements were more likely to occur in areas where haciendas were dominant (Figure 5.7). I use a binary coding to indicate whether provinces were sites of rebellions in the aftermath of Villarroel's overthrow (Rivera Cusicanqui 1987, 55). I code the

---

20. The Villarroel government had the authority to approve (or reject) any decrees issued by the conference.

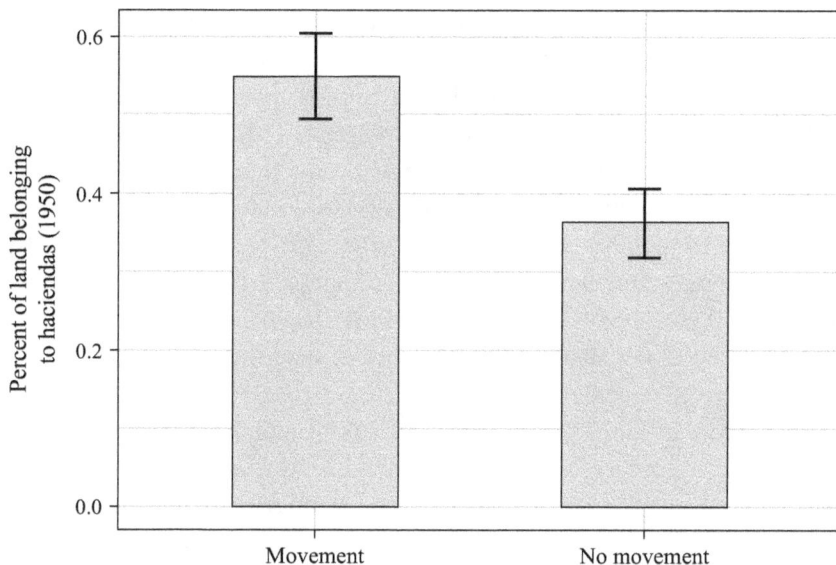

FIGURE 5.7. Hacienda prevalence and peasant movements, Bolivia, 1950
*Note*: Hacienda land plotted as percentage of total land. Movements coded based on whether there was a peasant movement in 1946 or 1947. 95% confidence intervals plotted.
*Sources*: Bolivia Dirección General de Estadística y Censos (1956), Rivera Cusicanqui (1987, 55).

1950 prevalence of large estates using the percent of a province's land occupied by haciendas Bolivia Dirección General de Estadística y Censos (1956).[21] On average, haciendas accounted for about 55 percent of the total land in provinces with a peasant movement, compared to 35 percent in those without such a movement.

At least two alternative explanations could account for the findings in Figure 5.7. First, as described above in the Peruvian analysis, communities with better connections to infrastructure may have been more likely to experience rural elite extraction; this same infrastructural access may have also facilitated collective mobilization. As such, connections to infrastructure—rather than rural elite extraction—may account for the observed effects.

21. This is technically post-treatment (measured after the independent variable), but I do not expect—nor does the historical record suggest—that 1950 land distribution fundamentally changed in response to the 1946–1947 unrest.

Yet, controlling for the presence of roads and railways does not change the strong relationship between hacienda prevalence and peasant mobilization (Appendix Table OA6). A second possibility is that hacienda expansion and peasant mobilization arose where Indigenous identities were initially weaker. Hacienda owners may have targeted communities with weak preexisting Indigenous identities and institutions; these same places may have been more likely to mobilize with peasant unions, as they lacked the option to organize along ethnic lines. This does not appear to be the case: accounting for whether a province is considered a historically Indigenous "core area," as defined by Grieshaber (1980), does not change the strong relationship observed in Figure 5.7.[22]

An analysis of individual instances of peasant mobilization likewise suggests that peasant uprisings arose on large estates. In February 1947, "10,000 Indian peasants took arms" in the highland region of Ayopaya in Cochabamba, "forcing several landlords to flee and killing at least two of them" (Rivera Cusicanqui 1987, 57). Unlike in the valleys of Cochabamba, in Ayopaya "the hacienda exerted its nearly hegemonic domination over property in land, production, and peasant labor" (Dandler and Torrico A. 1987, 336). Peasants in these areas, known as *laris* or "Indians of the estate," often mobilized for class-based rights, the most important of which was compensation for their (otherwise unpaid) labor. These workers did not demand Indigenous rights and autonomy; such claims were more likely to emerge in traditional Indigenous communities "where peasants held some sort of territorial space of their own from whence to unite" (Dandler and Torrico A. 1987, 371).

The movements in Ayopaya and elsewhere influenced Indigenous communities' demand-making, which endured through the two mechanisms of persistence I theorize. First, hacienda communities forged linkages with the MNR and other left parties, mediated by union officials. Local leaders of the Ayopaya rebellion, for example, claimed to have ties to the MNR, the Communist Party, or the PIR, and almost all had participated in the 1945 Indigenous Congress (Gotkowitz 2008, 238, 241). Villarroel was a major inspiration for the rebellion, and some peasants claimed they had participated to avenge his death. One rebel actor said, "as we swore before at the [1945 Indigenous] Congress at La Paz, Villarroel said he was prepared to die for us, and now we are ready to die for him" (Dandler and Torrico A. 1987, 366). Ultimately, the government violently repressed the movement and imprisoned its leadership.

22. See Appendix Table OA6.

After the rebellions of 1947, the MNR sought to harness, co-opt, and, most importantly, control peasant dissatisfaction. Even the MNR's failed attempt to take power through a civil war in 1949 did not incorporate peasant fighters; as one militant stated, "some of the leaders of the MNR had scruples about letting loose a peasant movement, the results of which were unforeseeable" (Kohl 2020, 166). Yet, the MNR did seek alliances—especially in the run-up to the 1951 elections—with peasant leaders, such as Antonio Mamani Álvarez, the self-proclaimed "Chief executive of the Bolivian Peasantry" (Kohl 2020, 136, 166). The military's annulment of the 1951 elections led the MNR to organize another revolution, once again with little peasant participation. However, this time their attempt to take the Bolivian state was successful.

While peasants played a limited role in the revolution, the MNR's tenure in office depended on their continued support. Albó observes:

The MNR's populist model took root most in those areas long dominated by the hacienda, as in Cochabamba or Achacachi. It was there more than elsewhere that the MNR, first as a party and later as the government, seemed to the *colonos* (serfs) a superior and powerful ally, a new and to a certain extent unexpected one, with which to fight and eventually defeat their most visible enemy: the landowners (Albó 1987, 384).

The MNR's mobilization efforts primarily targeted Cochabamba, which had a demonstrated capacity for disruption that the government sought to co-opt and control. In 1952, peasant unions organized a series of land invasions to reclaim hacienda property (Clark 1968, 162). As peasants took land for themselves, the government feared the potential disruptive capacity of the movement and the rural destabilization it might provoke. Meanwhile, unions grew stronger, empowered by the MNR's rhetoric around the need for land reform. These labor organizations "owed nothing to the government and could act independently of it" (Patch 1961, 129). Controlling the growing rural, class-based movement became "critical for the consolidation of the new Government . . . [as] direct appropriation of land threatened to be beyond the government's control" (Rivera Cusicanqui 1987, 80).

To exert greater control over organized labor in rural areas (especially Cochabamba), the MNR established its own peasant unions. As Albó explains, "it wanted a new peasant participation, but it wanted the MNR to remain in the driver's seat" (Albó 1987, 383). The party expected and demanded loyalty from the members of its unions, and "any attempt to show ideological independence was systematically marginalized, and potentially dangerous sectors were subordinated" (Rivera Cusicanqui 1987, 77).

The government, therefore, sought to co-opt Cochabamba's peasant union structure for its own purposes. The MNR's network of patronage ties with union leaders effectively curbed the autonomy of peasant organizations and gave the party control over peasants (Rivera Cusicanqui 1987, 79). Unlike other regions of Bolivia, which featured alternative forms of mobilization under Indigenous leaders and institutions, the union in Cochabamba was able "to establish itself as the only body that could unify and align the demands of the peasant smallholders" (Rivera Cusicanqui 1987, 97). The MNR's land reform also encouraged membership in government unions; in fact, the government mandated that any beneficiary of the land reform be affiliated with the MNR-created National Confederation of Bolivian Peasant Workers (Confederación Nacional de Trabajadores Campesinos de Bolivia, CNTCB).[23]

The ties between Indigenous communities and rural unions were reinforced not only by these government concessions but also by benefits that unions obtained from landowners. Take, for example, the case of wage employment on haciendas in the Cochabamba valley versus estates in the La Paz altiplano (high plateau). In the former, hacienda workers achieved wage employment by the 1940s, while in the latter, peasants rarely received compensation for their labor (Smith 1977, 235). Creating and strengthening an employment relationship in Cochabamba placed hacienda laborers more firmly within the working class and further tightened peasants' connections with a growing labor movement, which endured over time.

This class-based mobilization had significant consequences for the maintenance of Indigenous identities; as in Peru, the corporatist policies of the MNR government generally encouraged assimilation. Postero notes, "For Indians, the corporatist political system took the form of state-sponsored peasant unions, which integrated Indians into the state as producers and not as Indians per se. . . . Indians were called campesinos, their organizations were converted to *sindicatos* (peasant unions or leagues), and the government indigenous office was submerged into the peasant ministry" (Postero 2007, 38).

The MNR's ideology explicitly emphasized such assimilation. Silvia Rivera Cusicanqui describes the party's beliefs about ethnicity and class:

23. See, e.g., Albó (2002a, 75).

The Indians' demands did not fit into the MNR's plan to create a culturally unified nation by means of inter-marriage, Hispanicization, and the domestic market. . . . The Indian programme, in so far as it implied a strengthening of the Andeans' ethnic sense of identity, therefore stood in the way of the idea of a "decent" mestizo-Creole nation. . . . The MNR tried to turn the Indian movement into a "peasant movement"; they set up structures for co-optation and union control to convert the rural masses. They were to be passive receivers of the new civilizing proposals. Hundreds of Indian agitators were incorporated into this enveloping movement, which gradually caused them to change even their perception of themselves. They slowly abandoned their ethnic attachment and assimilated the illusion of equality among citizens. (Rivera Cusicanqui 1987, 60)

The MNR's ability to mobilize Indigenous peasants—and thus achieve its assimilationist goals—can be attributed to a combination of electoral success and path dependence. Villarroel's ability to form connections with peasants through the 1945 Indigenous conference and subsequent decrees created an enduring support base for the MNR among hacienda peasants. Had the PIR become Bolivia's main left party instead, hacienda communities may have felt less pressure to abandon their ethnic identities.[24] The PIR was more tolerant of ethnic difference; it sought to *accommodate* rather than eliminate Indigenous identities. For instance, it advocated education in the Quechua and Aymara Indigenous languages (Dandler and Torrico A. 1987, 34).

The labor unions themselves also played an essential role in encouraging assimilation. Trotskyist leaders of major labor organizations, such as José Rojas in Cochabamba, frequently argued that class-based identities should supersede ethnicity. "The only solution to the *indigenous problem*," Rojas said, "is to nationalize the land without compensation and to hand it over to the *peasants* immediately" (Rivera Cusicanqui 1987, 80, emphasis mine). Ironically, the interests of socialists and nineteenth-century liberals now seemed aligned: to create a nation of smallholding peasants. The central difference was that while the socialists sought to break up haciendas to provide the land for this reform, liberal politicians looked to eliminate Indigenous communal land altogether.

Given my theory and the discussion above, we would expect demands for assimilation to arise among hacienda communities due to their closer linkages

---

24. This may have led to demands for integration, as outlined in Chapter 7.

with peasant unions (and, thus, the MNR). The results of a survey I conducted in Bolivia support these theoretical expectations. I asked 1,000 self-identified Indigenous respondents to indicate their preferences for Indigenous institutions. I first asked them to indicate how important communally held land was to them on a 1-to-4 scale; I coded responses of "very important" as 1 and all others as 0. I also asked respondents to use a seven-point scale to indicate the degree to which they would agree with their municipality converting to an autonomous, Indigenous municipality (AIOC). I coded responses of "Agree" or "Strongly agree" as 1, and all others as 0. Finally, I asked respondents whether they belonged to an Indigenous community or Indigenous organization and coded them as 1 if they belonged to at least one of these.

As expected, residents of Cochabamba, which had the most substantial hacienda penetration (Figure 5.6), consistently scored lowest or second lowest on each measure (Figure 5.8); 54 percent of respondents in Cochabamba said that government recognition of Indigenous communal land was very important to them, compared with 65 percent in other departments. Only about 25 percent of the self-identified Indigenous respondents from Cochabamba said they belonged to an Indigenous community or organization, compared with an average of 35 percent for other departments. Perhaps most striking is the finding on political autonomy, which exhibited an especially large gap between Cochabamba respondents and those from other regions of Bolivia. Just over half (55 percent) of Cochabambans said they would support their municipalities seeking Indigenous autonomy, compared with an average of 73 percent in other departments. Finding these discrepancies even among those who identify as Indigenous—most of whom continue to speak an Indigenous language—is telling. On average, Cochabamba residents appear to be less likely to prefer autonomy and are more likely to pursue or otherwise experience assimilation.[25] Patch seems to confirm this in his observation, "In all probability, the aspirations of the Quechua speakers in Cochabamba to the status of mestizo [a person of mixed Indigenous and European ancestry] . . . was more keenly developed than in other parts of the Andes" (Patch 1961, 128).

---

25. Examining only those who consider themselves Indigenous likely provides a conservative estimate of assimilation; if one could consider the full population of interest—those who no longer consider themselves Indigenous but are descendants of former members of Indigenous communities—differences between Cochabamba and other departments might be even greater. See also Postero (2007, 39–40).

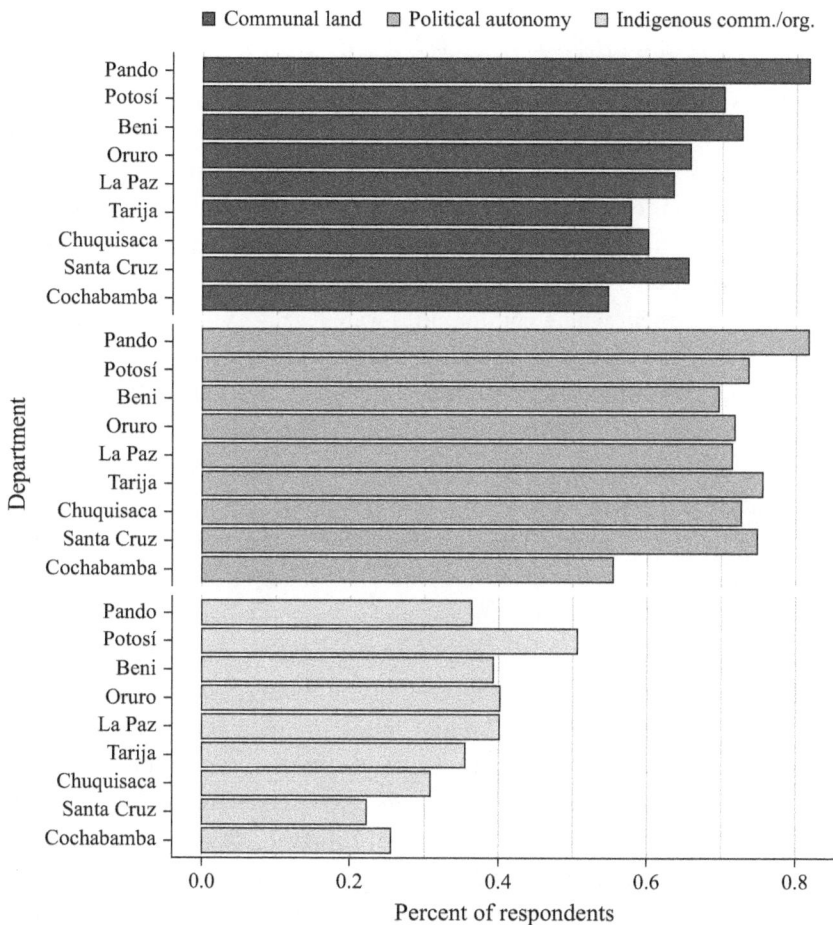

FIGURE 5.8. Support for Indigenous rights by department, Bolivia

*Note*: Responses taken from a survey of Indigenous Bolivians conducted by the author in 2020. Political autonomy was coded using responses to the question: "How much would you agree with your municipality pursuing autonomous status?" The full question also gave respondents information about autonomy. I coded answers of "strongly agree" or "agree" as 1. Communal land was coded using responses to the question: "How important is government recognition of Indigenous communal land to you?" Respondents chose answers on a four-point scale, and I coded answers of "very important" as 1. Finally, respondents were asked whether they belonged to an Indigenous organization or an Indigenous community: I coded "yes" responses as 1. $N = 1006$.

At this point, it is helpful to ask: why did Cochabamba differ from other highland areas of Bolivia? As I establish in Chapter 7, Indigenous communities in many parts of the country resisted land privatization. In Cochabamba, however, they often "accepted" it, initially purchasing titles to the individual parcels of land where they resided (Gotkowitz 2008, 33). They then sold their plots to large landowners; Indigenous farmers were allowed to stay on their land in exchange for working for the landlord—as such, "they became colonos on their own property" (Gotkowitz 2008, 72). Likewise, Cochabamba was the only department where communities were legally exempt from state-led labor conscription.[26] As I discuss in more detail in Chapters 6 and 7, in other departments, resisting road conscription reinforced the authority of Indigenous institutions and—even when resistance to hacienda expansion failed— helped leaders of these institutions mobilize and advocate ethnic rights within unions and left parties.

Cochabamba's relatively unique response to land privatization increased linkages between Indigenous communities and labor unions. It also divided communities in two ways that complicated future mobilization around communal, ethnic identities. First, by purchasing titles to their land and then selling them, smallholders further eroded the bonds that held Indigenous communities together. Second, some community members became *colonos* while others did not, which increased inequality within communities, eroded long-standing institutions, and complicated future collective mobilization.

Thus, in Bolivia, the expansion of haciendas in the late nineteenth century gave rise to the unionization of Indigenous peasants; these peasant unions formed linkages with left parties—most notably, the MNR. After taking power in the 1950s, the MNR sought to control peasant groups through large-scale land reform, party-sponsored unions, and an assimilationist ideology. As Rivera Cusicanqui (1987) observes, "With the 1952 revolution, the role played by the Indian authorities was largely undermined and union mediation gradually began to exert greater influence in community-state relations." This was nowhere truer than in Cochabamba.[27]

Given these differences between Cochabamba and other departments, alternative explanations—outside of rural elite extraction—may account for Cochabamba's higher rates of assimilation. First, Indigenous identities may

26. For the exemption of the Cochabamba department from road conscription, see the Ley de 23 de Octubre de 1915.

27. See also Appendix Figure OA8.

have been weaker at baseline in Cochabamba, leading to a greater willing-ness of Indigenous community members to divide communal land and sell it to hacienda owners. The population of Indigenous peoples was indeed smaller in Cochabamba even before colonialism, and haciendas had captured many Indigenous communities well before the turn of the twentieth century (Grieshaber 1980; Lagos 1991; Larson 1998, 10). Nevertheless, the number of Indigenous peoples—as measured by the population subject to the Indian tribute—remained substantial in the region; as late as 1877, more Indigenous people lived in Indigenous communities than on haciendas in three of the Cochabamba's six provinces: Tapacarí, Misque, and Arque (Grieshaber 1980, 32–35).[28] And while it was weaker and fragmented during the colonial period, Cochabamba's Indigenous population experienced a period of "ethnic revital-ization" at the turn of the twentieth century, which featured efforts to recoup both communal land and traditional forms of authority (Gotkowitz 2008, 11). Thus, weaker baseline ethnic identities do not appear to easily explain the differences between Cochabamba and other departments.

A second alternative explanation for the cross-regional differences I observe involves the much earlier and more severe experience of colonial-ism in Cochabamba, particularly in the fertile valley areas (Grieshaber 1980, 243). The Spanish quickly outnumbered the Indigenous population in the region, which may have encouraged Indigenous residents to seek assimila-tion to avoid discrimination, exploitation, and even genocide (Lagos 1991). Yet, Cochabamba's Indigenous communities were not alone in experienc-ing substantial marginalization and discrimination. Most of Bolivia's leaders in the colonial and post-independence period were of European descent, and the dominant rhetoric and policy in most of the country's regions was strongly anti-Indigenous. As such, demographic differences and the incen-tives to assimilate that they generate seem unlikely to explain cross-regional variation in preferences for Indigenous identities and institutions.

Notwithstanding the significant cross-regional differences analyzed in this section, substantial within-region variation exists. Many Cochabambans still value and invest in Indigenous identities (Figure 5.8). Many Cochabam-bans have preserved Indigenous languages and cultural practices even as they primarily identify as peasants (Lagos 1991, 146). These values are often

28. In Tapacarí and Arque, the number of communities also exceeded the number of haciendas: 157 to 94 in Tapacarí and 266 to 1 in Arque (Grieshaber 1980, 245).

articulated through the class-based organizations (unions and left parties) discussed in this chapter. The resulting demands often call for *integration*, which emphasizes Indigenous identities alongside a broader set of class-related claims. I return to these points in Chapter 7.

## 5.3 Conclusion

The growth of haciendas at the turn of the twentieth century in Latin America had lasting effects on Indigenous communities. The debt peonage arrangements typical of large estates often co-opted or eroded Indigenous institutions. Rural sector unions stepped into this void. Inspired by Marx and Trotsky, leaders of these labor organizations sought to emphasize class identities over ethnic ones in the hopes of generating a workers' alliance that included both urban and rural laborers. In mid-twentieth-century Peru and Bolivia, left governments targeted these unionized areas for mobilization, seeking to cooperate with or co-opt labor unions. These left parties also sought to deemphasize Indigenous identities and to emphasize class-based ones for ideological and strategic reasons. Ultimately, these processes encouraged demands for assimilation.

Elsewhere in Latin America, hacienda expansion had a similar impact. In the Mexican state of Yucatán, debt peonage was especially common among Indigenous peoples (Knight 1986). Many of Yucatán's Indigenous peasants were affiliated with the Mexican Communist Party in the 1930s, which linked them to the corporatist regime of Lázaro Cárdenas (1934–1940). Cárdenas advocated a massive agrarian reform, which he tested in Yucatán because of its large hacienda population (Fallaw 2001, 2).[29] As in Bolivia, integration into the corporatist regime had lasting consequences for Indigenous peoples' demands and identities in Yucatán. Mattiace (2009) argues, "Maya peasants had so little relative autonomy under the corporatist regime (1940s–1980s) and official peasant leagues that they were constrained in using the experience garnered in these leagues for subsequent ethnic-based organization" (138). As in Peru and Bolivia, hacienda expansion and subsequent class-based mobilization in Yucatán appears to have increased pressures for assimilation and frustrated movements for autonomy.

---

29. The other region where he tested the reform was La Laguna, a cotton-growing region in the northern states of Durango and Coahuila (Fallaw 2001, 2).

The next chapter evaluates the conditions under which communities demand autonomy. I highlight the importance of another form of labor extraction—by the state—that paradoxically strengthened Indigenous institutions and identities. Unlike rural elite extraction, which at times generated closer relationships between Indigenous communities and (especially left) governments, state-led extraction generated profound community mistrust of the government. These communities doubled down on their existing institutions and identities; those that made these investments were better able to withstand pressures to assimilate and were more likely to demand autonomy.

# 6

# Explaining Autonomy Demands

"The resistance to road conscription leaves no room for doubt about public sentiment regarding this service. The indigenous race, when invited to speak, has spoken in terms that are quite categorical. The Indigenous Congress, among other demands, advocated two years ago the repeal of this law. The Indians in the sierra have declared themselves against road conscription. The coast, which does not and will never suffer it with the same severity as the mountains, is also voting against it.

—JOSÉ MARIÁTEGUI, "LEY DE CONSCRIPCIÓN
VIAL," MUNDIAL, 1926

RURAL ELITE extraction encouraged mobilization for *assimilation*, but state-led extraction at the turn of the twentieth century often led to demands for *autonomy*. During this period, government extraction most commonly involved conscripting Indigenous labor to work on large-scale infrastructure projects without pay (Chapter 4). The effects of this conscription were far-reaching and distinctive from both rural elite extraction *and* previous instances of state-led extraction. It often circumvented, rather than co-opted, Indigenous elites, who subsequently organized their communities to reinvest in Indigenous institutions to resist extraction. These institutional investments and patterns of ethnic mobilization endured and promoted long-term autonomy demands.

Drawing on the cases of Bolivia and Peru, this chapter examines how state-led labor conscription shaped communities' investments in Indigenous institutions and organizations, as well as their later likelihood of demanding autonomy. I test the argument using a natural experiment and archival data on labor conscription, collective mobilization, and demands for autonomy.

Early rural elite
extraction

Hacienda          *No*     State-led           Later rural elite
*expansion in*        extraction       extraction          *No*   **N. Potosí, Bolivia**
*Bolivia (pre-1888)*               *Yes*                       **Quispicanchi, Canas,**
*& Peru (pre-1920)*     *Labor*             *Hacienda*              **& Canchis, Peru**
                            *conscription*        *expansion*               **(b)**
                            *in Bolivia*         *in Bolivia*
                            *(1888–c.1950)*   *(c. 1900–c.1950)*
                            *& Peru*          *& Peru*
                            *(1920–1930)*     *(1930–c.1967)*

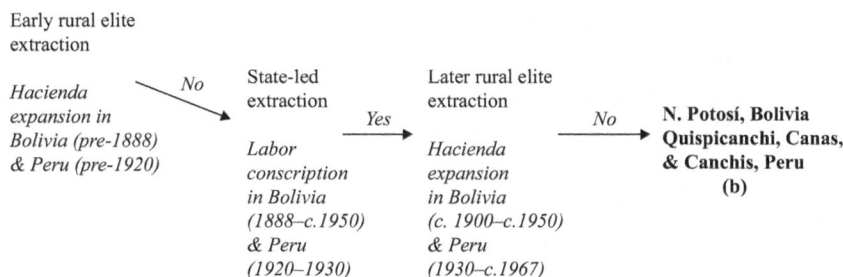

FIGURE 6.1. Extractive sequences in Peru and Bolivia: State-led extraction

I further interrogate these claims through case studies of three Peruvian provinces (Quispicanchi, Canas, and Canchis) in Cusco and the northern region of the Bolivian Department of Potosí (Figure 6.1).

## 6.1   Labor Conscription and Autonomy Demands in Peru

Chapter 4 discussed Peruvian President Augusto Leguía's (1919–1930) road-building program, which entailed a highway connecting the northern and southern parts of Peru for the first time since the fall of the Inca empire. To build this road, Leguía conscripted unpaid Indigenous community labor using provincial-level road-building committees ( *juntas viales*)—rather than Indigenous leaders and institutions.

Indigenous leaders responded to this conscription program by mobilizing and reinventing traditional, ethnic institutions. In Ayacucho, they developed quasi-military organizations to resist conscription violently (Heilman 2010b). Throughout central and southern Peru, Indigenous leaders organized uprisings to oppose road conscription (Hirsch 2010, 265; Mayer 1995, 280). When Leguía was ousted in 1930, "hatred of the [road conscription] law erupted into violence" as Indigenous communities throughout the country "sacked government offices and burned conscription files" (Davies 1974, 85). Indigenous elites also organized non-violent forms of collective action to resist conscription, including petitions and protests (Calisto 1993, 111; Heilman 2010b). Between 1922 and 1930, there were 837 documented Indigenous movements, 213 of which can be directly linked to abuses by local authorities and the road conscription program (Kapsoli 1982, 61); there were only 137 documented movements during the first two decades of the twentieth century (Marín and Castilla 1973, 38–39).

The quantitative evidence similarly suggests that Leguía's road conscription program provoked a backlash among affected Indigenous communities. As discussed in Chapter 4, communities located in a province containing the Qhapaq Ñan (pre-colonial Inca Road) were more likely to be drafted to work on Leguía's road for two reasons. First, Leguía designed his road to follow the route of the Qhapaq Ñan. Second, by law, community members could only be drafted to work if they resided in a province containing Leguía's road. Communities in Qhapaq Ñan provinces should, therefore, have been more likely to be conscripted and—if my theory holds—to mobilize against the state to resist conscription. To measure labor conscription, I code provinces based on whether they contained a portion of the Qhapaq Ñan.[1] I examine Indigenous mobilization using data from Kapsoli (1982), Kapsoli and Reátegui (1987), and Kammann (1982). I supplement these secondary sources with primary data from bulletins issued by the Section on Indigenous Affairs (1922–1930). This dataset thus includes all documented Indigenous movements that occurred between 1920 and 1930—the time frame for which data is available.[2] I link community names with their municipalities—as of 1920—and use as an outcome whether an Indigenous mobilization occurred in a given municipality.[3] I include any mobilizational event by Indigenous communities that explicitly targeted abuses by state officials during the period of conscription.

I analyze this data to determine whether anti-state Indigenous movements were more likely to occur in conscription-eligible provinces during this period. The results provide robust evidence that such movements were concentrated in provinces eligible for road conscription. Of the 111 documented Indigenous movements that occurred during the period of conscription (1920–1930), 104 (94 percent) took place in Qhapaq Ñan provinces.[4] Other measures of exposure to road conscription yield similar results. Table 6.1 provides an ordinary least squares (OLS) regression of a binary, municipal-level indicator of Indigenous mobilization on three measures of exposure to labor conscription: a dichotomous measure of whether a municipality was located in a province containing a portion of the Leguía road, a continuous

1. For more information, see Appendix A.

2. The data fully covers the departments of Apurímac, Cusco, Puno, Ayacucho, and Huancavelíca. Other departments are—at least—partially covered. Appendix A discusses how I address potential missing data issues.

3. This is the only outcome coded at the municipal level as community-level data was not available.

4. See Online Appendix Figure OA9.

TABLE 6.1. Road conscription and Indigenous movements in 1920s Peru

| | Dependent variable: | | |
|---|---|---|---|
| | Probability of movement against the state (1920–1930) | | |
| | (1) | (2) | (3) |
| Leguía road (thousands of km built) | 0.0005*** (0.0001) | | |
| Leguía road (dummy) | | 0.205*** (0.037) | |
| Qhapaq Ñan province (Y/N) | | | 0.264*** (0.026) |
| Constant | 0.104*** (0.019) | 0.128*** (0.015) | 0.022 (0.019) |
| Observations | 686 | 675 | 687 |
| $R^2$ | 0.030 | 0.045 | 0.128 |
| Adjusted $R^2$ | 0.029 | 0.043 | 0.127 |

Note: $*p < 0.1$; $**p < 0.05$; $***p < 0.01$. Results are from an OLS regression of dependent variables on independent variables.
Sources: Kapsoli (1982), Kapsoli and Reátegui (1987), Kammann (1982), Regal (1936); Ministerio de Fomento (1930); Díez Canseco and Aguilar Revoredo (1929); Peru (1929); Portaro (1930); and Boletínes de Asuntos Indígenas between 1922 and 1930.

indicator of the kilometers of Leguía road built in the municipality's province, and a dummy indicator for whether the municipality is in a province that contained a portion of the Qhapaq Ñan. All three measures of exposure to road conscription have a strong, positive, and significant relationship with the number of Indigenous movements between 1920 and 1930.

This bivariate analysis of labor conscription and Indigenous mobilization may generate at least two concerns. First, national governments may target labor conscription to communities with higher levels of preexisting collective action capacity and stronger institutions—either to weaken them or to use their institutions to facilitate conscription. Second, if communities were drafted based on their proximity to a road, the treatment may be bundled in a way that makes it difficult to isolate the effect of labor conscription. As such, subnational comparisons across communities may be confounded.

One way to address these concerns is to limit the analysis to communities just on either side of a provincial border dividing a Qhapaq Ñan province from a non-Qhapaq Ñan province. My research design draws on this logic by using a geographic regression-discontinuity design (RDD).[5] "Treatment" is defined as eligibility for the road conscription program, which is determined by a community's location vis-à-vis provincial borders. Because labor was conscripted from only the provinces where the road passed through, clusters of municipalities within a given province were assigned to either treatment (i.e., subject to the Leguía draft) or control.

I use the Qhapaq Ñan route—rather than the number of conscripts or Leguía's road—to code treated provinces for two reasons. First, all communities in provinces with a portion of the Qhapaq Ñan (which Leguía used as his guide for the road) were eligible for conscription.[6] Because most communities that were eligible for conscription ultimately worked, eligibility should have a similar effect as (and perhaps be a conservative estimate of) experiencing conscription. Second, data on road conscription in Peru is only partially available. I thus conduct an intent-to-treat (ITT) analysis, which estimates the effect of eligibility for labor conscription.

I define the study group as provinces located in the mountainous Andean region that neighbor or are themselves a Qhapaq Ñan province.[7] The running variable is a municipality's distance to a *border* dividing a Qhapaq Ñan province from a non-Qhapaq Ñan province—not the distance to the road itself. As a result, while the effects capture conscription, they do not necessarily indicate broader effects of exposure to the Qhapaq Ñan or later roads.[8]

A further benefit of analyzing communities on either side of provincial borders is that we should expect no differences in pre-conscription community characteristics. For any pair of neighboring provinces, there may have been pre-treatment differences resulting from how the specific border was drawn

---

5. The RDD approach yields local average treatment effects (LATEs) and does not provide identification of causal effects for communities far away from the cut point (i.e., a treat-control border). Nevertheless, plausibly exogenous assignment to treatment among a narrower subgroup of cases is generally preferable to possibly confounded comparisons among the full universe of cases. An analysis of provincial-level outcomes (average community scores on autonomy) using a standard OLS—where comparisons are likely confounded—does not yield significant effects.

6. Appendix Table OA2 shows a strong relationship between where Leguía's road was built and the location of the Qhapaq Ñan, suggesting the two roads followed one another.

7. See Figure 4.5 and FN9.

8. It is true that for the full sample, proximity to the road increased the likelihood of conscription. However, proximity is not necessarily predictive of conscription among the set of communities for which an effect is identified—i.e., those closer to a treat-control border.

or from historical differences in provincial-level administration. However, this threatens inference only if these pre-treatment differences are systematically correlated with the presence of the Qhapaq Ñan. There is no reason to expect this to be the case because the location of the Qhapaq Ñan was not well known at the time that provincial borders were drawn.[9] Provincial boundaries were fluid until 1850, nearly three centuries after much of the Qhapaq Ñan was destroyed in wars between the Spanish and Indigenous groups; the road was never rebuilt, and the parts that had not been destroyed quickly fell into disuse (Esquivel 2013, 34–35).[10] Furthermore, the administrative boundaries drawn during Spanish colonial rule, some of which became the borders of modern provinces, were "imprecise" and "vague," with borders running "along the peaks of mountains, in stream beds, or in relatively unpopulated stretches of the high puna" (Cook 2003, 415–416).[11] Thus, I do not expect communities on either side of a treat-control border to—in expectation—exhibit discontinuous changes in key baseline covariates.[12] I provide support for this and other key assumptions of the RDD in Appendix A. The RDD estimates plotted in Figure 6.2 are largely consistent with the bivariate analyses. Labor conscription increased the likelihood of a municipality having an Indigenous movement by about 30 percentage points ($\approx$ 0.8 standard deviations, or $SDs$).[13]

Ethnic institutions and identities persisted and, perhaps, strengthened through three mechanisms of reproduction. First, the act of resisting conscription triggered a reinvestment in, and strengthening of, long-standing Indigenous institutions. Traditionally, community leaders occupied a position of relative equality with other community members. Resistance to road

9. One potential concern is that the Qhapaq Ñan primarily traversed highland provinces where Indigenous identity may have historically been stronger. For this reason, I limit my study group to highland provinces (Figure 4.5). Furthermore, analyses presented in the Appendix suggest no significant difference in altitude between treated and control provinces.

10. See FN21 in Chapter 4.

11. Gonzáles (2011) argues that the pre-colonial Inca empire generally lacked fixed territorial borders (97–98).

12. When communities were located near more than one treat-control border, I used the distance from the closest border.

13. Movements occurred in 16 percent of sample municipalities. Thirty-one Indigenous movements during this period occurred directly in response to the Road Conscription Program (Kapsoli 1982, 61). The actual number of mobilizations targeting the conscription program was likely much larger; often, however, demands were more generally stated in the historical record as protesting "abuses by local authorities."

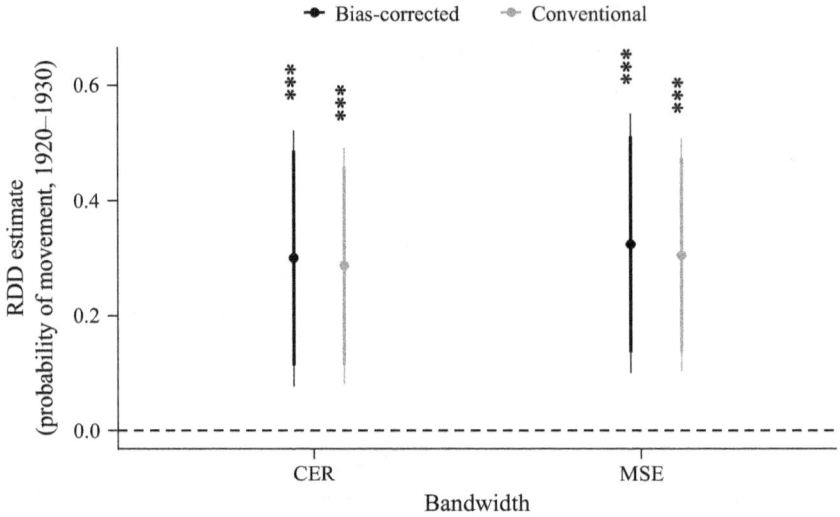

FIGURE 6.2. Labor conscription and community mobilization in Peru
*Note:* $*p < 0.1$; $**p < 0.05$; $***p < 0.01$. Point estimates taken from a local-linear regression-discontinuity analysis with border-pair fixed effects. The dependent variable is whether a municipality experienced Indigenous mobilization against local officials between 1920 and 1930. The running variable is the municipality's distance from a border dividing a treated (i.e., Qhapaq Ñan) province from a control one. SEs clustered at the province level. P-values adjusted for multiple comparisons using a Benjamini Hochberg procedure. Bias-corrected estimates include robust confidence intervals ($N = 687$).
*Sources*: Kapsoli (1982), Kapsoli and Reátegui (1987), Kammann (1982), and Boletínes de Asuntos Indígenas between 1922 and 1930.

conscription, however, allowed these leaders to take on new and more pow-erful roles. In 1920s Peru, some Indigenous community leaders reclaimed pre-colonial titles of Inca, the Quechua word for "nobleman" or "king," while others adopted the military title of colonel (Heilman 2010b; Kapsoli and Reátegui 1987). Indigenous peasants eagerly mobilized behind these tradi-tional leaders "because of their profound anger at official government author-ities and their agents" (Heilman 2010b, 501). Salcedo (1921) describes how Indigenous communities in Arequipa during the period of labor conscrip-tion were "willing to fight ... against enemies of the community at the orders of leaders" (50). Indigenous leaders capitalized on this willingness to act collectively. They formed military branches to defend their communities against road conscription and established "brigades and local cell groups to foment public disorder" (Mayer 1995, 305). Leaders deployed this collective mobilization to burn villages, assassinate officials of the *juntas viales*, and seize local government offices.[14]

Second, investments in ethnic identities and institutions persisted through communities joining Indigenous organizations. In the 1920s, the most prominent national-level Indigenous organization was the Tahuantinsuyo Pro-Indigenous Rights Committee (*Comité Central Pro-Derecho Indígena Tahuantinsuyo*, CPIT).[15] A primary goal of the CPIT was to end Leguía's road conscription program. The first item on the agenda of its Second Indigenous Congress, held in 1922, was "Elimination of the Road Conscription Law" (Kapsoli 1984, 230).[16] The CPIT encouraged Indigenous communities not to comply with the road conscription program (Hirsch 2010, 265). In Huanta, in the department of Ayacucho, the local branch of CPIT was accused of "stirring up the area's Indians" to resist conscription (Heilman 2010a, 65). The subprefect of Canta, a province in Lima, noted that two of the members of an uprising against conscription in the community of Lachaqui belonged to CPIT (Meza Bazán 1999, 155–156). *La Prensa*, a major newspaper in Lima, said the CPIT would protect Lachaqui, and, thus, community members "did not have to fear" reprisals for their resistance (Meza Bazán 1999, 133, fn.149, author translation).

Subcommittees of the CPIT emerged throughout Peru to facilitate Indigenous mobilization—particularly against conscription.[17] Of the 50 CPIT subcommittees established in Peru between 1922 and 1927, over 80 percent were formed in conscription-eligible provinces.[18] These subcommittees emerged from neither a purely top-down nor a completely bottom-up process. Instead,

14. See, e.g., Heilman (2010b); Kapsoli (1982); Kapsoli and Reátegui (1987); Kammann (1982).

15. Some of Peru's most celebrated intellectuals formed the committee, which began as a peasant organization in 1909. Starting in 1920, however, the Committee evolved into "a powerful force for indigenous mobilization" (Lienhard 1992, 292).

16. Juan Pevez, a noted peasant activist, spoke forcefully against the road conscription program at the close of the Third Indigenous Congress in 1923, asserting, "the Road Conscription Law, which no matter how fair some may believe its implementation to be, will never cease to be in practice for our race anything other than slavery and an attack on all individual rights" (Kapsoli 1984, 229).

17. De la Cadena (2000) documents a contemporaneous account of the spread of these and other Indigenous organizations, noting that not all the founders were literate or from urban areas: "The best men among the Indians are organizing and leading Indigenous societies (Sociedades Indígenas) in spite of their relative lack of literacy" (94).

18. See Appendix Figure OA10.

they arose in response to both supply- and demand-side forces. The national-level committee indeed sought to organize Indigenous communities at the subnational level. However, without the buy-in of local Indigenous authorities, their organizing efforts were unlikely to be successful in either the short or the long term. Thus, the CPIT targeted areas affected by conscription, where Indigenous leaders were also most eager to mobilize against conscription. The committee's resources and networks promised to facilitate these efforts.

While the subcommittees of the CPIT were almost fully disbanded and repressed by Leguía in 1927, they provided important socialization experiences for Indigenous leaders. For example, Tarma was one of the centers of CPIT mobilization; its leaders' experiences defending their communities during the period of conscription (and their coordination with CPIT) had enduring effects:

> One finds certain parallels in the position of the two protagonists in Carhuamayo and Huasahuasi who led the defense of their communities in the 1920s and 1930s. . . . The protagonists were crucial figures who drew on and synthesized many different influences and experiences as they became community leaders. Through this, they could improve connections and build bridges between the political and the cultural. They had become leaders in parallel spheres, however at the heart of both trajectories was the struggle for the recognition and defense of their community. (Wilson 2018, 164, author translation).

The CPIT also promoted the formation of an enduring Indigenous identity. Wilson (2018) argues that between 1920 and 1930, "a new political subjectivity was emerging among those who could identify with being 'indigenous' in new ways . . . fostering cultural renewal by drawing on and adapting a national imaginary from the pre-colonial past to comment on the shortcomings and abuses of the present" (164, author translation). The organization's name, Tahuantinsuyo, was the Quechua name for the pre-colonial Inca empire, and its logo drew on traditional Andean symbology (de la Cadena 2000, 92). Subcommittees organized events designed explicitly to promote an Indigenous identity within and beyond Indigenous communities. One of the most important events they organized was a festival commemorating the death of the last Inca emperor, Atahualpa. Leibner (2003) observes:

> The Committee's commemorations differed from traditional local ceremonies in at least two main aspects. First, the ceremonies took place near

or inside the provincial towns, transcending the realm of the local and intimate village or community and congregating thousands of peasants from
a vast region. Secondly, some creole or mestizo prominent guests, mostly
pro-Indigenous rights activists, indigenista allies, and sympathetic authorities and intellectuals were invited. Since the ceremonies invaded the urban
public space, many other mistis (non-Indigenous) in the Andean towns
were converted into spectators, even if reluctant ones. . . . From the point of
view of the peasant communities, they were being asked to unite and put
aside local and regional rivalries and specific local traditions, and to consider the identification with Atahualpa and the Incan traditions as a public
and political question, not only an internal local tradition. In this way, the
Committee was pushing toward the consolidation of an alternative, Incan
and Indigenous nationalism. The deliberate invitation and noticeable presence of non-Indian supporters signified that not all the mistis should be
excluded or considered enemies. (Leibner 2003, 11)

The increased salience—and assertion—of an Indigenous identity further reinforced Indigenous institutions and their leaders, who community
members increasingly relied on as legitimate intermediaries with the state.
Traditional Indigenous leaders became prominent officials within the influential Peruvian Communist Party and the populist Alianza Popular Revolucionaria Americana (APRA) party (Arroyo 2004, 206). The founding and
promoting of the CPIT subcommittees, often at the municipal level, proved
to other organizations that Indigenous leaders could serve as valuable allies
in forming the grassroots base of national organizations. As I demonstrate
in Chapter 7, this capacity gave leaders some leverage to dictate the terms of
their cooperation: if unions and left parties wanted to partner with community
leaders, they would have to concede to Indigenous elites' demands for ethnic
rights.

A final mechanism of persistence arises from the enduring memory of
exploitation that conscription created. Peruvian communities have long com-
memorated experiences of exploitation and, especially, resistance to it. For
example, the memory of the Tupac Amaru rebellion in Peru in the late eighteenth century persisted through oft-mythologized community histories that
emphasized an Indigenous identity. According to Galindo (2010), "While his-
torians converted Tupac Amaru into a precursor of Peruvian independence
and ignited a dreadful debate about his reformist or revolutionary character, oral traditions conserved the identification of the movement with the

Andean world" (105). Similar oral histories preserved the collective memory of conscription. Because the *juntas viales* used child labor in road conscription, first-hand accounts of working on Leguía's road persisted even into the late 1990s (del Busto Duthurburu et al. 2004, 524). Ancestors passed down stories of conscription to their descendants—often in a somewhat mythologized way—through song, dance, and pilgrimages to work sites. Written accounts also document the conscription period. One of the CPIT's main goals was to increase local education (Heilman 2010a, 52–53). As a result of these efforts, many Indigenous leaders became literate and wrote down their experiences, including those with conscription, resistance to it, and the Tahuantinsuyo subcommittees. Wilson analyzes three such written testimonies from the 1920s and observes:

> The extension of literacy through rural school education had inaugurated a new type of historical record, memories that offered social and political commentary from an indigenous perspective. . . . For the historian, this makes the Oncenio [eleven-year term of Augusto Leguía] a special period in the sense that by the 1920s the "invisibility" of the indigenous Andean populations, as Guerrero refers to it, is no longer completely maintained. The historical record is not obscured to the extent that it was previously. . . . Documentary evidence can reveal very different scenarios from the "ventriloquist" representations given to indigenous people by the writing of the powerful about indigenous perspectives. (Wilson 2018, 164, author translation).

Many of these memories indicate that Indigenous communities experienced a growing sense of empowerment during this time; they used ethnic identities and institutions to stand up to powerful non-Indigenous elites—with varying degrees of success. This sense of pride perhaps arose from rhetoric promulgated by the CPIT and its local affiliates around the exploitation of (often illiterate) Indigenous communities by literate, non-Indigenous actors. Such coordination and consistent messaging were generally absent from previous acts of rebellion against state actors and rural elites. It also meant that, regardless of their success, rebellions could serve an expressive purpose to demonstrate opposition to existing racial hierarchies.

Government repression of these movements did not discourage future mobilization, as had been the case with past uprisings. The 1896 rebellion in Huanta, for example, led the military to "[raze] several Huanta communities, destroying houses, burning fields, and killing thousands of peasants"

(Heilman 2010a, 64). This harsh state reaction led Indigenous peasants to avoid mobilizing against the state: "campesinos whose relatives, friends, and neighbors died as a direct result of the 1896 repression probably wanted to do all they could to assuage provincial authorities' concerns about a looming uprising. Shying away from participation in the Tawantinsuyo Committee served that purpose" (Heilman 2010a, 64).[19] Repression of conscription-era rebellions, however, generated enduring "anger at—and opposition to— abusive authorities [that] continued across subsequent decades" and facilitated later mobilization (Heilman 2010b, 525).

The sustained memory of conscription—and especially of a community's resistance to it—became markers of local identity for some communities.[20] Wilson (2018) observes, "[The CPIT] was put down by presidential decree. However, in the Andean provinces, popular opposition to the traditional political order did not disappear but rather increased its reach and brought about a surge of . . . Indigeneity" (156–157, author translation). The way these communities mobilized similarly highlighted the continuing importance of Indigenous identities. De la Cadena (2000), for example, documents peasant uprisings organized by unions in Cusco in the 1960s, writing, "Peasants wielding Quechua, and filling the Plaza de Armas [central square] in their wool ponchos and chullos (caps) made it clear that the uprising had a cultural identity, even if the leadership subordinated it to class rhetoric" (190). These expressions of a broader ethnic consciousness extended beyond the borders of individual Indigenous communities and even reached intellectuals in the capital of Lima. Flores Galindo (1993) posits, "Without these [1920s] rebellions . . . would [the Indian] consciousness [among writers, artists, and men of science and politics] have been possible?" (340). The memory of these rebellions shaped Peruvian Indigenous communities' future efforts to make demands on the state.

Ethnic institutions and identities, which began with collective resistance to conscription, persisted throughout the twentieth century. Using data from Dobyns (1964), I construct an index of public goods, including bridges,

19. Ultimately, however, these communities did resist conscription with the help of local hacienda owners, who opposed state-led extraction for the reasons discussed in Chapters 4 and 5 (Heilman 2010a, 68).

20. In many cases, an *ethnic* identity persisted. In others, ethnic identities gave way to mobilization around a class identity (Heilman 2018). As I demonstrate in Chapter 7, even in these cases, a community's ethnic character was often not fully lost.

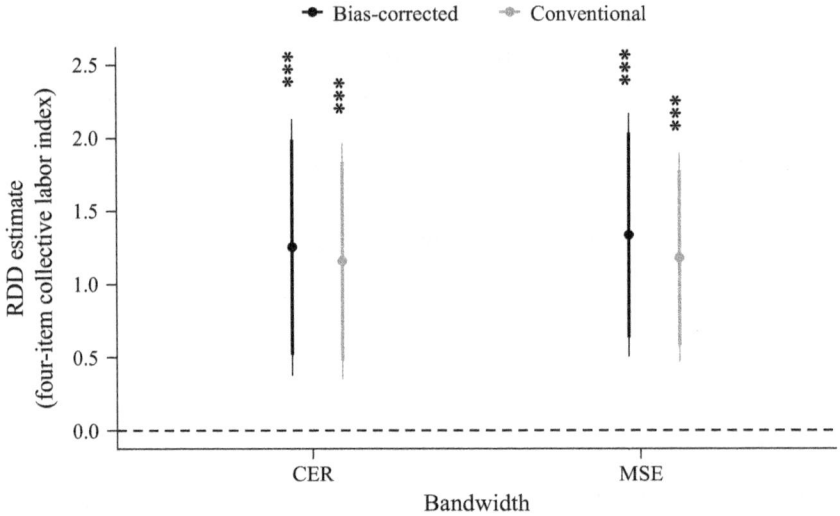

FIGURE 6.3. Labor conscription and Indigenous institutions in 1960s Peru
*Note*: *$p < 0.1$; **$p < 0.05$; ***$p < 0.01$. Point estimates are taken from a local linear regression-discontinuity analysis where the dependent variable is the number of infrastructure projects (out of a total of four) for which communities use unpaid collective labor. The running variable is the municipality's distance from a border dividing a treated (i.e., Qhapaq Ñan) province from a control one. The analysis includes border-pair fixed effects. SEs are clustered at the province level. P-values are adjusted for multiple comparisons using a Benjamini Hochberg procedure. Bias-corrected estimates include robust confidence intervals. $N = 230$.
*Source*: Dobyns (1964).

roads, schools, and irrigation canals produced through traditional labor institutions.[21] I again compare communities on either side of a provincial border dividing a conscription-eligible province from a non-conscription-eligible province. Figure 6.3 indicates that conscription eligibility had a strong, positive, and significant effect on the persistence of traditional Indigenous institutions.

The reinvestment in Indigenous institutions that occurred in the wake of conscription appears to have persisted even to the present. To demonstrate this, I analyze the 2012 Indigenous community Census, which asked community presidents about three key traditional, Indigenous institutions (*ayni*, *minka*, and *mita*). It also asked whether communities still have traditional Indigenous leaders; whether leadership positions are undertaken

21. See Appendix Figures OA11 and OA12.

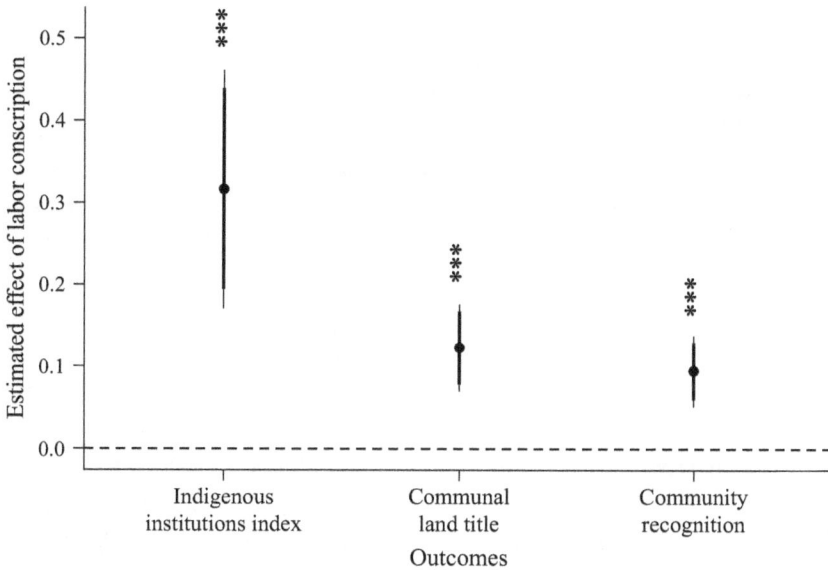

FIGURE 6.4. Labor conscription, Indigenous institutions, and autonomy in 2012 Peru

Note: $^*p < 0.1$; $^{**}p < 0.05$; $^{***}p < 0.01$. Point estimates taken from a local-linear regression discontinuity analysis. The "Indigenous Institutions Index" outcome consists of seven items: *ayni*, *minka*, *mita*, traditional leaders, collective labor, communal farming, and the cargo system. The "Communal land title" and "Community recognition" outcomes are binary. The running variable is the municipality's distance from a border dividing a treated (i.e., Qhapaq Ñan) province from a control one. SEs are clustered at the province level. Bias-corrected estimates include robust confidence intervals. $N = 2{,}333$.
Source: Instituto Nacional de Estadística e Informática (2014).

on a rotating, unpaid basis (i.e., a *cargo* system); whether community members participate in communal labor; and whether collective farming is still used. I employ these measures to construct a seven-item index of Indigenous institutions.[22] Using the RDD design, which compares communities on either side of a treat-control border, I find that conscription has a strong, significant, and positive effect on the persistence of Indigenous institutions (Figure 6.4). Eligibility for conscription increases the value of the seven-item index by about 0.3 units ($\approx$ 0.2 standard deviations). Thus, the experience of conscription—and resistance to it—appears to have bolstered Indigenous institutions, which served as the basis of later autonomy claims.

22. Each item enters the index as a binary variable with equal weight.

A core part of my argument is that these investments in Indigenous institutions promoted future demands for autonomy. The case of communal land illustrates how this occurred in Peru. Titles to collectively held land were available to all Indigenous communities beginning in 1920, but there were several barriers to achieving these rights. Community leaders first had to convince their members to engage in the long and often costly process of obtaining a title. Next, leaders needed to secure bureaucratic, legal, and financial resources. Lawyers and researchers were needed to prove a community had resided on its land from time immemorial, surveyors had to be contracted to define the community's borders, fees had to be paid to the government, and in some cases translators were needed to help community leaders navigate Spanish-language legal documents. Finally, even after submitting all documents to the government, communities often pressured state agencies and officials for years or decades before receiving their titles. Handelman (1974) describes the difficulties communities faced in obtaining collective land titles in the mid-twentieth century:

> [Communities] often lacked the necessary funds and knowledge to secure government recognition. Yet those very communities were most in need of protection. Moreover, villages that applied for ministry recognition often lacked sufficient titles to prove which land was theirs. A village's sixteenth-century titles might be too vague to be legally acceptable.... When a community presented its claims to a court, it might find that the *hacendado* whom they were challenging had real or forged titles to the same land. (Handelman 1974, 33)

Communities that experienced labor conscription have been more willing and able to bear the costs of autonomy. Returning to the regression-discontinuity design, communities that experienced road conscription have been 12 percentage points more likely to obtain a completed communal land title (Figure 6.4). These results are strong ($\approx 0.3$ SDs) and significant ($p < 0.01$). Communities that experienced conscription have also been 10 percentage points ($\approx 0.3$ SDs) more likely to seek and achieve recognition from the government ($p < 0.01$).

Most communities did not pursue autonomy immediately after experiencing conscription. Figure 6.5 presents a series of OLS regressions where the dependent variable in each model is a dummy indicator for whether a community received recognition in that decade, and the independent variable is a dummy indicator for whether the community is in a province that Leguía's

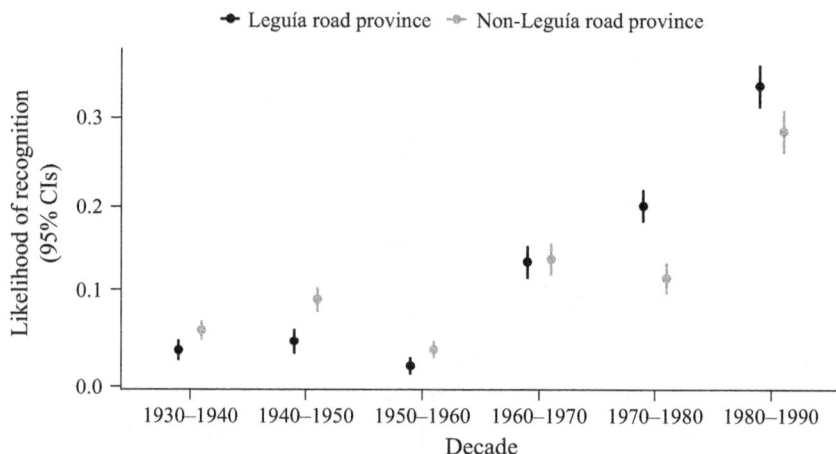

FIGURE 6.5. Labor conscription and the timing of autonomy demands in Peru
*Note*: Point estimates taken from a series of OLS regression where the dependent variable for each model is a dummy indicator for whether communities received recognition in a given decade. The independent variable is a dummy indicator measuring whether a community is located in a province that contained a portion of Leguía's road. $N = 1,880$.
*Sources*: Data taken from Ministerio de Vivienda, Construccion, y Saneamiento (2009); Regal (1936); Ministerio de Fomento (1930); Díez Canseco and Aguilar Revoredo (1929); Peru (1929); Portaro (1930).

road passed through.[23] The analysis suggests that before 1960, communities that did *not* experience conscription were more likely to seek recognition. This delay was perhaps due to initial skepticism and distrust of the government in the aftermath of conscription. However, by the 1970s, those that experienced conscription had become significantly more likely to seek recognition.[24] Thus, an initial mistrust of the state appears to have waned with time, but preferences for alternative institutions to those provided by the state (autonomy) persist.[25]

Autonomy demands have been much less likely to arise in areas that were not subject to conscription. For example, the municipality of Carhuanca in

23. Standard errors are clustered at the province level, the smallest administrative unit for which road construction data is available.

24. In the 1960s, communities that did and did not experience conscription were statistically indistinguishable in their likelihood of seeking recognition.

25. I return to these points in the conclusion, discussing similar delays in autonomy demands among the Navajo in the United States.

Cangallo province had no documented roads built under Leguía, and, thus, there is no evidence of labor conscription. The Indigenous communities there subsequently abandoned traditional Indigenous institutions, and community members' memories of these institutions are mostly negative (Heilman 2010a, 103). While communities in the province were affiliated with the CPIT, few now remember the movement or its strong ethnic component (Heilman 2010a, 57–59). Carhuaquinos are now more likely to make demands "in class rather than ethnic terms," which, according to my theory, suggests a low likelihood of autonomy demands (Heilman 2010a, 70).

In tracing the effects of state-led labor conscription, I specified and evaluated several alternative mechanisms that could account for the observed positive relationship between conscription and autonomy demands. I first explored whether Indigenous leaders collaborated with the government to mobilize workers for conscription and then leveraged these ties to demand (and later achieve) autonomy. I found no evidence that they did. In fact, Leguía abolished the position of the community leader in 1921 in an effort to delegitimize certain traditional authorities (Davies 1974, 72). Second, I investigated whether the Tahuantinsuyo Committee, which Leguía supported early in his administration, was used to establish a paternalistic relationship between the Peruvian government and Indigenous communities. If it was, co-optation—rather than collective mobilization—might explain why communities later demanded and achieved autonomy. However, the Committee appears to have functioned autonomously: it openly opposed the government after 1924, and Leguía ultimately banned and repressed it (Arroyo 2004).

I also analyzed three further explanations that might account for the positive relationship between labor conscription and autonomy demands. First, governments could have offered Indigenous communities autonomy in exchange for participating in road conscription—or to atone for past wrongs, absent community pressure. If this were the case, affected communities should have been the first to be recognized. However, the data discussed above suggests that road conscription led to much later community recognition (Figure 6.5). A second alternative explanation posits that eligibility to work on Leguía's road may have been tied to exposure to the road network itself, which could have increased community ties to external markets. There is no evidence of this.[26] In fact, a key criticism of the conscription law during debates over its

---

26. See Appendix Figure OA15.

adoption was that Indigenous groups would be responsible for building the road but—because of their isolation—would not generally benefit from it (de la Cadena 2000, 96). A third potential concern is that communities located in a Qhapaq Ñan province were also closer to the Inca Road and thus had stronger Indigenous institutions and identities prior to conscription.[27] I find that the communities for which an effect is identified—i.e., those close to a treat-control provincial border—are, on average, quite distant from the Qhapaq Ñan. The average straight-line distance between a treat-control provincial border—using the point on the border closest to the Qhapaq Ñan—and the Qhapaq Ñan is 28 km, a significant distance in the mountainous terrain of the Andes.[28] Figure 4.5 further suggests that most treat-control borders are not especially close to the Qhapaq Ñan.

Thus, the experience of resisting labor conscription in Peru reinforced autonomy demands through three key mechanisms. First, the act of organizing resistance strengthened Indigenous institutions. Traditional leaders assumed greater power within their communities, which they could use to encourage or force community members to invest in Indigenous institutions. Second, conscription generated linkages between communities and Indigenous organizations; these partnerships demonstrated that ethnic identities and institutions could be enduring tools of mobilization vis-à-vis the state. Third, the memory of conscription created a sustained grievance against the state, which made traditional forms of governance more attractive. Together, these factors promoted the persistence of Indigenous institutions and identities in the face of deep structural changes and growing threats from states and markets. In turn, demands for autonomy have also endured.

The effects of conscription can be further illuminated through case studies of three Cusco provinces that experienced relatively limited hacienda expansion: Quispicanchi, Canas, and Canchis. By 1940, hacienda residents accounted for only 24 percent, 11 percent, and 5 percent of these provinces' rural population, respectively. In addition to limited rural elite extraction, all

27. These communities may have also been economically stronger, giving them more power to make demands (Franco et al. 2021).

28. I make two conservative choices in this analysis: using the straight-line measure and using the closest point on a provincial border to the Qhapaq Ñan. This understates the true travel distance between borders and the road. Furthermore, the 28-km distance is outside the 20-km bandwidth used by Franco et al. (2021) in their RDD analyzing the long-term effects of the Qhapaq Ñan.

three provinces experienced high levels of labor conscription. Leguía built over 150,000 km of road in Canchis, over 130,000 km of road in Canas, and nearly 200,000 km of road in Quispicanchi—by far the most road construction in Cusco outside the capital (see Appendix E).

As my theory predicts, all three provinces experienced Indigenous mobilization in the 1920s, led by traditional ethnic leaders. Communities formed local chapters of the CPIT: one in Canas, one in Quispicanchi, and *eight* in Canchis (Melgar Bao 1988). A 1921 newspaper headline noted the organizational strength of Indigenous leaders in Canas: "Indigenous uprising in the Province of Canas. Five hundred Indians under the command of the aboriginal supreme chief, Valentín Choqueneyra. He orders the Indians to obtain the newspaper *Tawantinsuyo* [since it] contains information about indigenous rights" (quoted in de la Cadena 2000, 99).

Community leaders' strength persisted in these provinces. A 1962 survey by Dobyns (1964) found that community leaders in all three reported organizing communal labor for a wider range of projects than community leaders in other provinces of Cusco.[29] My 2017 survey of community leaders in Cusco revealed that Indigenous institutions remained strong in these areas. Community presidents in Canas were 15 percentage points more likely to report using communal labor than those in other provinces in Cusco (74 percent versus 59 percent).[30] As my theory predicts, communities in these three provinces have also been more likely to demand autonomy than those in other provinces— as measured by their likelihood of obtaining a completed communal title (90 percent versus 79 percent) and achieving government recognition (96 percent versus 92 percent).[31]

Ultimately, the case studies and quantitative evidence suggest that in Peru, Indigenous communities that experienced state-led extraction (but not rural elite extraction) now have more robust ethnic institutions and stronger ties

---

29. The 13 types of communal labor events included using unpaid communal labor to build schools, bridges, irrigation canals, community offices, sports fields, churches, or roads; to engage in communal farming, water development, land purchases, joint harvests; to contribute tools to projects; or to perform other miscellaneous forms of collective labor. Canchis, Quispicanchi, and Canas community leaders reported using communal labor for about 3.6, 3.25, and 3.3 different types of projects, respectively; this figure was 3.1 for all other provinces in Cusco.

30. See Appendix Figure OA13. I did not survey community leaders in Canchis or Quispicanchi.

31. See Appendix Figure OA14.

to Indigenous organizations.[32] Over the long term, these communities have also been more likely to demand—and achieve—autonomy. This suggests a necessary addendum to prior work on Peruvian Indigenous politics. Opportunities for coordination around ethnic identities at the regional and national levels have been limited, as Yashar (2005) describes.[33] However, Indigenous communities have organized at a more local level to claim essential autonomy rights. They have mobilized to demand the government comply with the community recognition and collective land rights it promised under the 1920 Constitution.[34] Increasingly, individual Indigenous groups are also claiming self-governance rights. The Wampis nation in northern Peru, for example, has organized to demand political autonomy, which Peruvian courts have subsequently recognized.

How can we reconcile the successful ethnic mobilization for Indigenous autonomy with the relatively low salience of ethnic identities in Peru? Once again, the level at which organization occurs may be informative. While linguistic, tribal, and overarching Indigenous identities may be of relatively low salience in Peru, communal identities remain important. As a Cusco community leader told me in 2017, "First, I am a *comunero* (community member), then a peasant, then a Peruvian."[35] In a survey of 300 current and former community presidents, I included a trust game that varied the information participants received about their partner. Those who were told their partner was a *comunero* shared more money than those who were told that their partner was from Cusco (Carter 2021).

32. The provincial case studies, however, mask important within-province variation. In areas of these three provinces with haciendas, Indigenous leaders often embraced demands for class-based rights and assimilation (Chapter 5). On the Lauramarca hacienda in Quispicanchi, for example, "Indigenous leaders adopted class vocabulary and activities in their political work: they self-identified as *campesinos* (peasants) . . . and organized *sindicatos rurales* (rural unions) as part of their struggle" (de la Cadena 2000, 129, emphasis in original).

33. Scholars have often noted the important role of the civil conflict of the 1980s in destroying the "political associational space" for rural organizing in Peru (Yashar 2005, 246). One can also highlight the Velasco regime's repression of unions as an important reason why labor organizations failed to mobilize Indigenous communities in the country. However, as I demonstrate in the analysis in Figure 7.4, union mobilization of Indigenous communities was comparatively limited even before the military government.

34. By the time Velasco and the military assumed control of the Peruvian government in 1968, a third of Peru's Indigenous communities had achieved recognition; today, nearly 80 percent have.

35. Author interview, Pisac, July 2017.

Communal identities are complex. They are technically class-based (i.e., peasant), but they often represent a commitment to long-standing Indigenous practices, such as reciprocity, communal landholding, and social insurance. Many communities maintain Indigenous languages and institutions (i.e., *ayni, minka, mita*). Peru's Indigenous communities have reinterpreted ethnic identity to fit the nature of their mobilization. Rather than making demands as "Indigenous" groups, they often call for "community" rights—entitlements granted under the colonial government that they expect the post-independence Peruvian state to maintain. In this way, ethnic identities are not primordial. Instead, they were constructed and redefined through the colonial experience and the institutions imposed by the Spanish Crown. As a result, the claims of Peruvian Indigenous communities often look quite different from those of their Bolivian neighbors.[36] The following section further elaborates on these ideas by examining the effects of labor conscription in Bolivia.

## 6.2   Labor Conscription and Autonomy Demands in Bolivia

Bolivian labor conscription covered more domains, started earlier, and was more enduring than Peru's road conscription program. In addition to highway construction, conscripts in Bolivia were drafted to build railways.[37] The systematic conscription of Indigenous labor to build infrastructure occurred through the *prestación vial*, a program introduced during the 1880s that endured well into the mid-twentieth century.

The *prestación vial* became especially important for the Bolivian government in the wake of the Zárate Willka Indigenous rebellion in the 1890s. This was true for three reasons. First, the revolt was part of a broader civil war that ultimately brought the Liberal Party, which Willka had briefly supported, to power. The party sought to provide modernity, civilization, and progress—all defined by the country's non-Indigenous governing class—to

---

36. The *ayllu*, which is more prevalent in Bolivia, resembles pre-colonial territorial arrangements much more closely than the community, which is dominant in Peru. The persistence of the *ayllu* may be attributed to the greater distance of most Bolivian Indigenous communities from the viceregal capital in Lima and key economic ports.

37. Railroads generally provided even fewer benefits to Indigenous communities than roads. Transporting goods to market via rail was more expensive, and few Indigenous communities were located near railheads.

Bolivia's rural, majority Indigenous population. Roads and railways were a key part of this plan, and the *prestación vial* offered a way to produce this infrastructure. Second, Willka's rebellion reinforced the government's notion that establishing order in the hinterland should be a priority, and large infrastructure projects were crucial to this goal. Finally, the uprising led the Bolivian state to engage in a new campaign to repress "rebellious" Indigenous communities; part of this strategy included an increase in forced labor. Thus, for reasons related to ideology, state capacity, and revenge, the Bolivian state expanded its use of the *prestación vial*, a program that allowed the state to reach previously isolated areas by exploiting Indigenous labor (Gotkowitz 2008, 43).

As in Peru, Indigenous leaders in Bolivia organized resistance to the *prestación vial*. Mayer observes:

> By August [1938] the Indians of Copacabana had organized into opposition groups against the prestación vial, counterfeiting work tickets and distributing them throughout not only [the province of] Omasuyos but the entire department of La Paz. The organized resistance was an effort to disrupt the labor draft which was being used to construct the railroad between La Paz and the lowlands. (Mayer 1995, 168)

In the Bolivian province of Cinti, the president deployed the national police to "enforce the conscription levies" and quell the "strident resistance by Indians to ... forced road construction" (Kohl 2020, 16). In Pucarani in the department of La Paz, Indigenous community members resisted conscription, refusing to provide unpaid labor for road-building projects (Preston 1978, 174).

These acts of resistance had a lasting impact through the three hypothesized mechanisms of persistence. First, the process of organizing collective resistance to conscription strengthened Indigenous political institutions; Indigenous leaders assumed more powerful positions within their communities. These leaders reestablished pre-colonial institutions—such as the *cacique apoderado* (legal chief), an enduring, community-level political office with substantial authority. Gotkowitz (2008) elaborates how Bolivian *caciques* "created their own institutions, and sought official recognition of their titles" (87). Irurozqui (2000) observes that *caciques* institutionalized this authority by forming organizations that they sought "to strengthen ... in the face of an adverse climate" (105). And in the wake of particularly severe labor extraction in Chayanta, Bolivia, for example, an Indigenous leader "took the title of heir of the Incas, stirring up the Indians with promises to ... reestablish the rules of his race in all branches of public administration" (Platt 1987, 309). *Caciques* in the La Paz municipality of Jesús de Machaca organized a rebellion in 1921 to protest abuses by local government officials, which included using violent tactics to collect the *prestación vial* tax (Choque Canqui and Ticona Alejo 1996, 52).[38]

Second, Indigenous leaders institutionalized this collective resistance by creating ethnic organizations that articulated demands for "specific ethnic programs" (Platt 1987, 304). For example, the Oldest Autonomous Mayors (AMP), an ethnic movement and network of Indigenous community leaders that opposed the *prestación vial*, argued that "Indians could no longer be subjected to 'forced' labor" (Ari 2014, 102). A key priority of the AMP was protecting communal land, and *caciques* throughout Bolivia organized networks to pursue "a coordinated legal defense of community lands" (Soliz 2014, 296, fn. 3). Another powerful Indigenous organization also emerged during this time, forming a national-level network that made it perhaps the most potent ethnic movement of early twentieth-century Latin America (Gotkowitz 2008, 46). The movement—which consisted of the aforementioned *caciques apoderados*—made a heterogeneous set of demands, including rights to their traditional lands, an end to property taxes, an expansion of schools, elimination of road conscription, and an abolition of debt peonage (*pongueaje*).[39] Its most vocal demands, however, were for autonomy. Like Peru's CPIT, the *caciques apoderados* network was based in its country's capital city; as Soliz (2014) observes, "Indigenous leaders worked out of the city of La Paz so that different communities could develop a common strategy" (296, fn. 3). The network was especially powerful in areas affected by labor conscription, including "nearly all provinces of La Paz, highland areas of Cochabamba, western Oruro, northern Potosí, and some valleys of Chuquisaca" (Rivera Cusicanqui 1991, 608). Opposition to conscription played a central role in structuring its activities. In 1919, the organization led a successful boycott of road conscription in Jesús de Machaca, where it sought to establish an autonomous Indigenous government (Ticona Alejo 2003). The *caciques apoderados* network endured in subsequent decades and continued to articulate demands for ethnic rights. Gotkowitz (2008) observes that "a 1940 petition from Andrés Marka T'ula

38. The communities of Jesús de Machaca were among those drafted to build a railroad from La Paz to Arica under the *prestación vial* (Bolivia Congreso Nacional Cámara de Senadores 1909, 529–535).

39. See, e.g., Ramos Flores (2016).

(son of Santos Marka T'ula) and other caciques from all nine departments of Bolivia . . . requested the election, recognition, and protection of alcaldes mayores, regidores, alguaciles, escribanos, and other indigenous authorities" (151). She goes on to say that this petition "underscores the importance that indigenous leaders continued to place on the election of their own authorities, and it shows how they creatively merged scattered utterances from ambiguous rulings to advance those pleas" (152).

Third, the memory of conscription and resistance to it reinforced the near-term mobilization effects of labor conscription. Writing on the experiences of resisting conscription, Cussi et al. (1999) observe,

> Our grandparents and our history record that the *corregidor* [mayor] Lucio Estrada was one of the *gamonales* [political bosses] that committed unbearable abuses against the community members of the ayllus of San Andrés and Jesús de Machaqa, charged each person for road conscription (even though they had already done the physical labor) and also imposed, for whatever reason, fines. All of these inhumane abuses and outrages motivated the rebellion of the Indigenous people of Jesús de Machaqa. The legal documents did not work [to stop overcharging of road conscription]. The abuses continued and our [caciques] *apoderados* were labeled "Indian rebels." (Cussi et al. 1999, 53, author translation)

My 2020 survey of Indigenous citizens in Bolivia revealed evidence of the persistence of such memories. I asked respondents to indicate whether their community had previously experienced state-led extraction of their land or their labor. To analyze variation in *actual* exposure to conscription, I leverage the fact that all Indigenous citizens initially had to contribute labor to fulfill their obligations under the *prestación vial*. Beginning in 1915, however, the government of the Cochabamba department required all Indigenous and non-Indigenous residents to pay the tax *in cash*. As a result, Indigenous communities in Cochabamba were not subject to road conscription after this time.[40]

---

40. The origins of this exemption are unclear. It may be because there were relatively few Indigenous people in Cochabamba, which—when compared to other departments—lowered the returns to mobilizing unpaid, Indigenous labor. According to the 1900 Census, Indigenous Bolivians accounted for only 23 percent of the department's population; the department with the next lowest Indigenous population was Chuquisaca, at nearly 40 percent. Furthermore, landowners could benefit from charging the tax in cash—rather than labor; fewer workers would be taken off haciendas to work, and those residing in "free" Indigenous communities (i.e., those whose land had not been seized by large estates) might be forced to labor on large

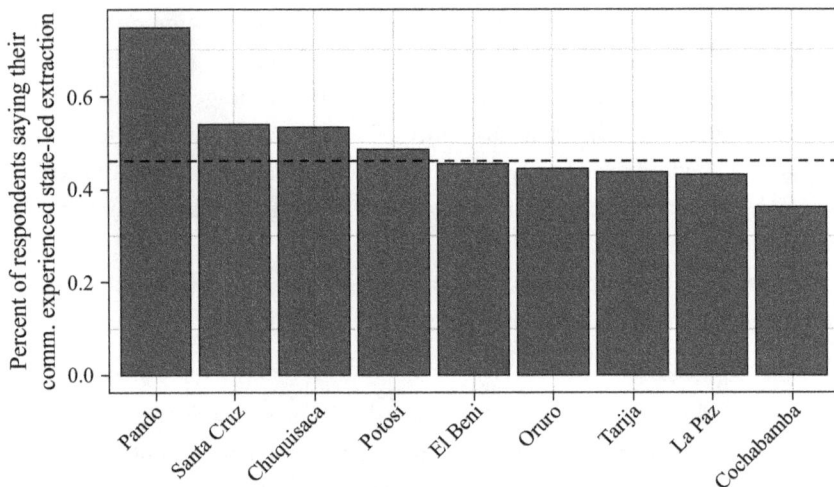

FIGURE 6.6. Memory of state-led extraction in Bolivia, 2020
*Note*: Data taken from the author's survey of Indigenous residents of Bolivia. I subset the data to the 329 respondents who report being members of an Indigenous community. The dependent variable codes responses to the question: "To your knowledge, has your community experienced pressure by the state to take land, labor, or natural resources?" The options were "Yes," "No," or "Don't know." "Yes" answers are coded as 1, and all other options are coded as 0. The dashed line indicates average support for autonomy across all respondents.

Therefore, we might expect communities in Cochabamba to be less likely to report experiencing state-led extraction than those in other departments. This is precisely what the data suggests: fewer respondents in Cochabamba reported that their community experienced state-led extraction compared to respondents in other departments (Figure 6.6).

Communities maintained the memory of conscription by forming a collective consciousness of shared racial identity. These efforts were triggered and facilitated by the often traumatic experience of conscription. Conscripts observed that "only *comunarios* [community members] were to be drafted . . . [which] stimulated a consciousness of exploitation" (Mayer 1995, 58). As such, conscription generated a shared grievance among the members of otherwise diverse communities; it also forced community members into contact with one another and created spaces where they could commiserate and

---

estates to obtain money to pay the tax. This was particularly important in Cochabamba, where landowners faced a severe labor shortage (Grieshaber 1980, 244–246).

form enduring networks. Subsequently, communities affected by conscription collaborated to organize uprisings—such as the ones in Omasuyos and Chayanta described above. Irurozqui (2000) observes the enduring "impact the rebellions had on Indian national and political consciousness" (87). At the local level, the common participation in rebellion became a marker of an ethnic identity that spanned multiple communities.

Ultimately, I expect these experiences of state-led labor conscription to have promoted demands for autonomy. To test this prediction, I embedded an experiment in my survey of 1,000 Indigenous Bolivians. All respondents were first asked about their support for adopting Indigenous autonomy in their municipality and their support for autonomous Indigenous governments more generally. Respondents were then provided information about Charagua, Bolivia's first autonomous Indigenous municipality. Half were then given a prime to suggest that autonomy has helped Charagua resist state-led extraction: respondents were told Charagua's deliberative assembly has the right to reject any government extractive or development project in the municipality.[41] The other half (the control group) was not provided with this additional information. After this intervention, all respondents were again asked about their support for adopting Indigenous autonomy in their municipality and their support for Indigenous autonomy more generally.

My theory suggests that the effects of the experimental prime should be strongest among respondents with a memory of state-led extraction. As such, I analyze heterogeneous treatment effects based on whether respondents report that their community has experienced state-led extraction in the past. Figure 6.7 demonstrates that respondents are more likely to support autonomy after learning it can help their communities resist government-led extractive projects. While the difference between the extraction subgroups is not statistically significant, the evidence is generally consistent with my theory. The effect of the prime is significant (albeit at $p < 0.1$) only for respondents who report that their community has experienced state-led extraction. For those communities, the experimental prime—that autonomy can help communities avoid state-led extraction—increases support for autonomy by about 0.2 units on a 0–3 scale. Thus, as was true in Peru, state-led

---

41. The treatment did not focus specifically on labor coercion, as this is no longer the primary extractive threat communities face. Instead, communities often fear the loss of land or natural resources to state extraction and development.

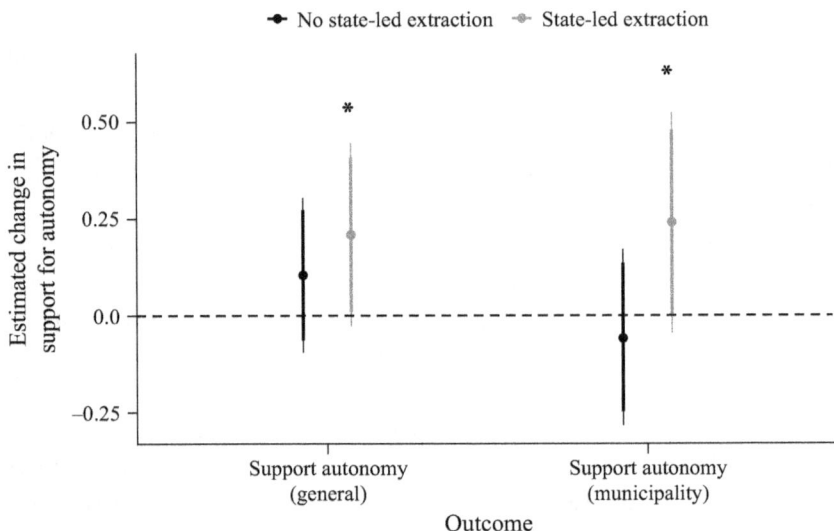

FIGURE 6.7. Memory of state-led extraction and autonomy in Bolivia
*Note*: Data taken from the author's 2020 survey of Indigenous residents of Bolivia. Half of the 1,006 respondents were randomly selected to receive information about how autonomy requires prior consultation with an Indigenous municipal government prior to state officials undertaking extractive or developmental projects. The outcomes are differences in pre- and post-treatment responses to questions asking respondents (1) whether they believe Indigenous autonomy is positive for the country and (2) whether they would support their municipality's adopting Indigenous autonomy. Respondents could choose "Strongly agree," "Agree," "Somewhat disagree," and "Strongly disagree." The results are disaggregated based on whether respondents claim their community had experienced state-led extraction in the past.

extraction appears to have increased communities' likelihood of supporting ethnic autonomy, especially when they believe it will curb future government extraction.

Analyzing community applications for autonomous status—as an indication of revealed preferences for autonomy—likewise yields evidence consistent with my theory. Of the 21 municipalities that have begun the process of becoming autonomous municipalities (AIOCs, Indigenous First Peoples' Peasant Autonomies), eight are in Oruro, five are in Santa Cruz, four are in La Paz, and three are in Chuquisaca. Not a single municipality in Cochabamba, which was exempt from state-led labor conscription, has started the process to obtain autonomy, even though over 90 percent of municipalities in the department are eligible for AIOC status (i.e., they have a majority-Indigenous population).

An analysis of the northern region of the Potosí department offers further support for my argument. In the valley areas (i.e., the *puna*), there was relatively little hacienda penetration (Cusicanqui 1990, 105). However, unpaid labor for road conscription was common. The department government reported in 1916 that nearly 40 percent of men in northern Potosí (Bustillo, Charcas, Chayanta) were required to contribute labor for infrastructure construction compared with just under 32 percent in the rest of the department (Prefecto de Potosí 1916, 83–84).[42] Subsequently, this region experienced notably high levels of *ethnic* mobilization. It was here that "ayllus finally coalesced into regional confederations that claimed a 'national' identity . . . probably the closest remnants to the older nations of the preconquest period" (Klein 1993, 59). Silvia Rivera Cusicanqui similarly observes that communities in northern Potosí proved especially effective at resisting union mobilization. She notes that "the union apparatus and the *ayllus'* system of representation and authority was . . . radical and irreconcilable" (Cusicanqui 1990, 105). Instead, the communities "continued to be governed by the ethnic authorities rather than by the artificial union structures created under state auspices" (Cusicanqui 1990, 105). It is, therefore, unsurprising that communities in Potosí now support ethnic rights and autonomy at high rates (greater than 75 percent).[43]

A comparison across Bolivian regions raises important empirical concerns; departments may differ beyond their exposure to road conscription. These differences may correlate with the likelihood of experiencing road conscription and long-term autonomy demands. Relatively high levels of bilingualism and a large mestizo (individuals of mixed Indigenous and European descent) population, for example, led scholars in the early twentieth century to claim "Cochabamba long ago ceased to be an Indian country [*sic*]" (McBride 1921, 20). A small Indigenous population could account for why the department had limited exposure to conscription and why it has fewer documented instances of autonomy demands today. Yet, this does not explain why—when subsetting

---

42. I calculate this statistic using the data in Prefecto de Potosí (1916) and the male population from the 1900 Census (Oficina Nacional de Inmigración, Estadistica y Progpaganda Geográfica 1904). Many roads were built in 1916–1917 using forced labor in this area (Prefecto de Potosí 1916, 83).

43. See Figure OA8.

to the Indigenous populations in my survey—I find results largely consistent with my theory. Furthermore, highland areas in western Cochabamba share many similarities with neighboring departments in the *altiplano*.[44] Yet, municipalities just across the border from Cochabamba in La Paz (Inquisivi) and northern Potosí (Chayanta) have pursued autonomous status; no municipality has yet done so in highland Cochabamba.

## 6.3   Summary and Discussion

The findings in this chapter demonstrate that exposure to labor conscription led Indigenous communities to invest in long-standing ethnic institutions, which has increased demands for autonomy. I have tested these claims using evidence from Peru and Bolivia, but similar effects can be observed across Latin America. Indigenous leaders often mobilized their communities to resist labor conscription for roads and railways. In late nineteenth-century Ecuador, for example, "Indigenous communities rebelled against . . . intolerable state demands" the most common of which was labor conscription (O'Connor 2007, 79). The largest such uprising occurred in Chimborazo, where "thousands of Indian men and their wives rose up against White-Mestizo society," killing local officials and burning down villages (O'Connor 2007, 79). Indigenous rebellion in these cases generally did not achieve its immediate goal of stopping conscription. Those convicted of participating in the Chimborazo rebellion, for example, were sentenced to labor on public roads, which "promoted [President] García Moreno's agenda for building up national infrastructure while punishing [rebels] with one of the burdens against which they had rebelled" (O'Connor 2007, 81). Yet, these acts of resistance set a precedent and established the capacity for future mobilization. Baud (2007), for instance, links communities' resistance to conscription to the emergence of a "new Indigenous self-consciousness" in Ecuador (86). Similar trends can be observed in Mexico. Smith (2020), for example, draws on evidence from Oaxaca, Morelos, Veracruz, Puebla, Estado de Mexico, and Tabasco to argue, "Opposition to the use of communal labor for road building was extremely widespread" (289). In some cases, Indigenous leaders used this resistance to achieve government recognition of deliberative

44. As McBride (1921) observes, "But in the Provinces of Arque and Tapacarí [both in Cochabamba] that lie in the hill country adjoining the Departments of Oruro and Potosí there are localities where Indians retain their land in common as upon the altiplano" (20).

assemblies, which mirrored long-standing Indigenous institutions (*usos y costumbres*).[45]

In addition to conscripting Indigenous labor to build infrastructure, Latin American states also compelled Indigenous men to serve in the military—with similar effects. In Peru, members of native communities constituted the overwhelming majority of service members at the turn of the twentieth century (Forment 2013, 174–175). Traditional Indigenous leaders mobilized their communities to resist military conscription (Hunefeldt 2018, 377–384). Even though the government violently repressed this mobilization, it generated enduring collective action (Thurner 1997, 92). The communities that resisted military conscription became future "centers of rebel activity" (Mallon 1995). In Bolivia, Indigenous veterans used their status to make complaints and demands on the state, "claim[ing] credibility and authority based on their personal participation in the war and the collective contribution of the many indigenous men who had fought on the front lines" (Shesko 2020, 128). These leaders received attention from national politicians and the press. Shesko (2020) observes, "Unlike in the prewar period, the mainstream press in 1945 was willing to present Chipana Ramos [an Indigenous veteran] as speaking with authority and making claims for Indians' place in the nation as 'sons of the same soil'" (126). Like road conscription, military service—albeit through a different mechanism—appears to have reinforced Indigenous community leaders' ability to demand rights for their communities.

These results do not suggest that labor conscription had a uniformly positive long-term impact on affected communities. Autonomy, even when communities achieve it, is unlikely to offset the costs Indigenous workers and their families incurred from conscription, which included a decline in material wealth, loss of human life, and enduring trauma. Instead, my findings highlight how groups can respond to government exploitation and abuse by investing in their collective action capacity—what Finkel (2015) calls the "phoenix effect of state repression."

The effects of labor conscription provide a cautionary tale for the state. In their efforts to bypass and weaken Indigenous authorities, governments unintentionally sowed the seeds of future ethnic mobilization. Far from solidifying the state's monopoly of control over peripheral areas, labor conscription encouraged communities to reinvest in Indigenous authority and strengthen

45. See, e.g., Smith (2020, 291–292).

their long-standing—and resilient—political, economic, and cultural institutions as substitutes for those of the state.

## 6.4   Looking Ahead

This chapter's treatment of the effects of labor conscription as separate from those of rural elite extraction (discussed in Chapter 5) is empirically justified. Facing labor scarcity, state officials and rural elites competed over a limited supply of Indigenous workers. Elite opposition amounted to a free-rider problem: most elites wanted to benefit from the public goods created by state-led labor conscription without contributing their own laborers to produce them. Heilman (2010b) observes of the Peruvian case, "Across Ayacucho, in turn, many departmental hacendados who were not otherwise active opponents of the Leguía regime opposed the conscripción vial, most likely because they wanted their hacienda workers laboring on their land, not on distant road projects" (517). In Bolivia, landowners similarly opposed the conscription of their workers (Langer 1989, 54). In some cases, Indigenous community members even fled to large estates to avoid their labor obligations to the state. While legal, this strategy was harmful to the government and its efforts to conscript Indigenous workers. Williams (2007) explains that in Ecuador "suspicious state officials . . . increasingly blamed the hacienda system as the principal impediment to labor recruitment. Combating these alliances of convenience and other resistance by landlords to national road projects quickly became the focus of state recruiting strategies" (51).

In addition to damaging rural elites' economic interests, conscription also projected central state power into peripheral areas through roads and railways. These changes threatened to disrupt the centuries-long stronghold that local notables held over politics. The state's wresting Indigenous workers away from economic elites symbolized the broader power struggle between the core and periphery at the turn of the century. Clark (2007) argues that "controlling labor recruitment practices for local public works . . . became an important way in which the [Ecuadorian] state undermined local landowners' power" (94).

Despite the apparent conflict between state-led and rural elite extraction, many communities experienced both labor conscription and rural elite extraction. The following chapter examines this more complex extractive experience. It sheds light on why Indigenous identities, languages, and organizations remain stronger in Bolivia than in Peru despite similarly high levels of hacienda expansion in both countries. I discuss how Indigenous leaders in various parts of Bolivia—mostly outside of Cochabamba—mobilized their longstanding institutions to resist this expansion. Even when this resistance failed, Indigenous identities remained relatively strong in "captive" communities (those trapped on large estates). Eventually, these ethnic identities would prove foundational to developing *integration* demands.

# 7

# Explaining Integration Demands

The current leaders are resolved that they do not accept and will not accept any
class reductionism, only becoming "peasants." Neither do we accept nor will
we accept any ethnic reductionism that turns our struggle into a confrontation
of "Indians" against "whites."

—UNIFIED SYNDICAL CONFEDERATION OF RURAL
WORKERS OF BOLIVIA (CSUTCB), 1983

"The *ayllus* have not been passive in the face of these new attacks from the
dominant creole-mestizo society. They have developed several forms of
resistance and self-defence [*sic*], ranging from selective and conditional
acceptance of the unions . . . to open hostility manifested in multiple
testimonies and defiant attitudes."

—SILVIA RIVERA CUSICANQUI, 1990

THE PREVIOUS two chapters demonstrated that state-led and rural elite
extraction have distinct and opposing effects. This chapter explores outcomes
in communities exposed to both forms of extraction. Most of these communities experienced state-led extraction (i.e., labor conscription) first, followed
by hacienda expansion.[1] In fact, state-led extraction often *provoked* future rural
elite extraction; the end goal of labor conscription—to expand transportation

1. Landlords exercised tighter control over their labor force than the state did and were
thus better able to prevent competing forms of extraction. This is due to landowners' in-depth
local knowledge, the greater importance of a given subset of Indigenous workers to rural elites
(compared to the state), and the temporary nature of state-led conscription compared to more
permanent debt peonage relationships.

infrastructure—helped landowners move wool and agricultural products to markets more quickly and efficiently. Owners of large estates sought to expand the labor supply under their control to take advantage of this new market access. The expansion of railways in Peru, for example, allowed cattle ranchers to supply dairy and meat products to the capital of Lima (Smith 1991, 91) and wool producers to transport their products to key regional markets in Arequipa and Cusco (Orlove 2014, 46).[2]

This extractive sequence—labor conscription followed by hacienda expansion—increased Indigenous communities' demands for *integration*. State-led extraction encouraged increased community investments in Indigenous institutions to resist conscription (Chapter 6). In these cases, hacienda owners subsequently captured Indigenous land without the same collaboration from traditional Indigenous authorities that I described in Chapter 5. Indigenous leaders, who remained strong, then became important intermediaries between their communities and the unions that sought to mobilize hacienda peasants. They leveraged their gatekeeping power, exchanging access to their communities for union leadership positions and recognition of certain ethnic rights. However, these leaders generally achieved only the concessions that unions found least costly: recognition of Indigenous identities but not Indigenous institutions.

This chapter focuses first on the case of Bolivia, where many communities experienced labor conscription before hacienda expansion. I demonstrate that this extractive sequence generated demands for integration in the regions where it occurred, notably highland La Paz, Oruro, and southern Potosí. I use archival data, secondary historical sources, and a survey of Bolivian Indigenous peoples to test my argument.

I then turn to the Peruvian case, where integration demands have been much less common. Systematic, post-independence labor conscription started later in Peru than in Bolivia; many communities had already experienced hacienda expansion when the road conscription program started in 1920. I combine historical data on extraction with an analysis of the content of demands from over 600 peasant movements (1956–1964). A notable exception to Peru's limited incidence of integration demands is the province of

---

2. The construction of highways created even greater incentives for hacienda owners to seize Indigenous land and labor, as native communities were often located much closer to a road than to a railhead.

Early rural elite
extraction

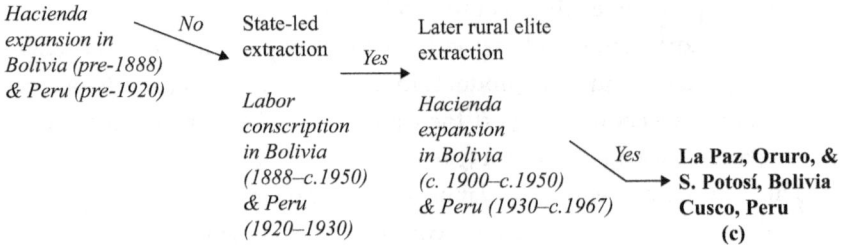

*Hacienda*
*expansion in*        *No*       State-led                Later rural elite
*Bolivia (pre-1888)*            extraction     *Yes*    extraction
*& Peru (pre-1920)*

                                *Labor*                  *Hacienda*
                                *conscription*           *expansion*
                                *in Bolivia*             *in Bolivia*        *Yes*    **La Paz, Oruro, &**
                                *(1888–c.1950)*          *(c. 1900–c.1950)*           **S. Potosí, Bolivia**
                                *& Peru*                 *& Peru (1930–c.1967)*       **Cusco, Peru**
                                *(1920–1930)*                                         **(c)**

FIGURE 7.1. Extractive sequences in Peru and Bolivia: Both forms of extraction

Cusco—located in the department of the same name—where conscription preceded hacienda expansion (Figure 7.1).

## 7.1  Extractive Sequences and Integration Demands in Bolivia

As discussed in previous chapters, Indigenous leaders in Bolivia sometimes organized their communities around coherent and consistent Indigenous identities. The Oldest Autonomous Mayors (*Alcaldes Mayores Particulares*, AMP) and networks of Indigenous *caciques* (chiefs) I discussed in Chapter 6 were led by traditional leaders who primarily demanded ethnic rights, including autonomy. In contrast, the Indigenous leaders analyzed in Chapter 5 mostly disappeared or otherwise promoted class-based mobilization. For example, the hacienda communities of Cochabamba tended to mobilize through assimilation-promoting unions and left parties.

The more complex—and arguably more common—path in Bolivia arose through the alliances that emerged among Indigenous leaders, labor unions, and, in some cases, political parties. These partnerships created a more heterogeneous set of demands that included ethnic rights *and* class-based claims. Power imbalances between Indigenous authorities and non-Indigenous organizations often limited the expression of ethnic rights, constraining the degree to which ethnic leaders could achieve meaningful policy change. Nevertheless, these efforts laid the foundations for future Indigenous and peasant mobilization in Bolivia. They demonstrated that individuals could hold both class and ethnic identities and that achieving labor rights did not necessarily preclude the recognition of Indigenous ones.

One of the first examples of this hybrid (i.e., class and ethnic) mobilization occurred in the late nineteenth century. Members of the Liberal Party sought to displace the long-governing Conservative oligarchy. The Liberals sought the support of the country's Aymara population, who resisted the state's assault on their lands that had begun in the 1870s. Liberals allied with Zarate Willka, an Indigenous *cacique* (chief), who had gained influence by mobilizing and defending Indigenous communities that were under attack from large estates (Larson 2004, 231–233).

Willka derived power and legitimacy from his position as *apoderado*, the legally recognized representative of his community; *apoderados* defended Indigenous communities against land seizures and fraudulent purchases by large estates.[3] They were often regarded as "descendants of the ancient *mallkus* (authorities), for which community members regarded them as faithful representatives" (Teijeiro 2007, 153, author translation). Willka's four main demands reflected the needs of both hacienda peons—who constituted the core of his army—and Indigenous *comuneros* (community members): the government should (1) restore communal land, (2) install an autonomous Indigenous government, (3) end hacienda expansion by white landlords, and (4) recognize that the Bolivian government did not have legitimate command over Indigenous troops (Rivera Cusicanqui 1986, 85–86).[4] These demands reflected a fusion of Indigenous and peasant claims, emphasizing both work-related claims and a return of communal land—the fundamental Indigenous right.

Willka's partnership with the Liberal Party achieved short-term gains but ultimately backfired. Hacienda expansion slowed after the 1898–1899 civil war but resumed with renewed vigor soon thereafter under the newly installed Liberal government that came to power in 1899 (Gotkowitz 2008, 38–39). In 1904, for example, only 141 Indigenous land plots were sold in the department of La Paz, followed by 319 in 1905, 350 in 1906, and 1,245 in 1907 (Grieshaber 1990, 76). The Liberal government viewed Willka as a threat and eventually executed him in 1905 (Condarco Morales 1983, 414).

Over the next 30 years, Indigenous leaders, inspired by Willka, built networks and organizations of *caciques* and *alcaldes mayores*, described in

3. See, e.g., Gotkowitz (2008, 37) and Teijeiro (2007, 153).

4. The demands of Indigenous groups who mobilized under Willka's banner diverged from those of the Liberals, who "emphasized the need to modernize and liberalize the Bolivian state to favor better the export sector" (Rivera Cusicanqui 1986, 84).

Chapter 6. While these organizations prioritized demands for Indigenous rights, they strategically sought alliances with non-Indigenous actors, including political parties, labor unions, and urban intellectuals (Irurozqui 2000, 105). As such, they eventually adopted demands for both peasant and Indigenous rights. The *caciques apoderados* both "hoped to stop the [land] usurpation, which in many regions used the absence of [colonial] titles to declare communal lands vacant and proceed with their sale," and sought "to unify the isolated struggles of the community members against the landowners in a single movement" (Rivera Cusicanqui 1991, 609, author translation).

One of the clearest examples of this hybrid mobilization was led by Martín Vásquez, an Indigenous *cacique* from an area that experienced both state-led labor conscription and hacienda expansion. In the early 1900s, the Bolivian government had forced members of his community—located in the Pacajes region of La Paz—to build a portion of the railroad from the capital of La Paz to the Chilean port city of Arica (Bolivia Congreso Nacional Cámara de Senadores 1909, 529–535). This new railway had a doubly negative effect on nearby communities. It was built using their unpaid labor, and it connected their communities to ports, increasing the value of their land to expansionist landowners (Kohl 2020, 122). These dynamics triggered widespread rebellions in affected areas; communities made a variety of ethnic and nonethnic demands, including Indigenous representation in Congress, an end to forced labor, a return of communal land, and a government chosen by peasants (Rivera Cusicanqui 1987, 32). To articulate these demands, Vásquez sought alliances with non-Indigenous individuals, including members of the purportedly pro-Indigenous Republican Party (Gotkowitz 2008, 47).

In the mid-1910s, Vásquez relinquished his position and named Santos Marka T'ula to be his successor. Like Vásquez, T'ula sought to form alliances with external actors, particularly with emergent labor organizations, such as the Local Workers Federation (FOL, Federación Obrera Local). These were attractive opportunities for Indigenous leaders and union officials. The latter sought to work with established social leaders who had demonstrated an ability to organize local collective action. Such partnerships promised to expand unions' fledgling membership base. A chapter of the FOL, the Oruro Workers Federation, named T'ula its Secretary of Peasant Affairs in 1926, "which meant that some Aymara networks subsequently appeared as peasant sindicatos (syndicates) in FOL paperwork even though they remained autonomous and had their own ayllu [traditional community] structure" (Ari 2014, 42). In the 1930s, T'ula leveraged his networks and experience in the union to form his own organization, the Indigenous Society, which adopted a layered set of demands: land for Indigenous communities and freedom from labor abuses for hacienda workers (Ari 2014, 43).

Other Indigenous leaders pursued similar strategies. Eduardo Leandro Nina Quispe was born in a native community in the province of Ingavi, just north of Pacajes. As was the case with T'ula and Vásquez, Quispe's community was located near the La Paz-Arica railway line. As a result, the community experienced labor conscription between 1905 and 1911, and after the railroad was complete, it faced a new threat from non-Indigenous landowners (Mamani Condori 1991, 61–62, author translation). The combined effects of these two forms of extraction "in areas traditionally dominated by ayllus . . . stimulated a resurgence of organized, Indigenous resistance" (Mamani Condori 1991, 62, author translation). Nina Quispe emerged as the leader of these movements, organizing a 1920 rebellion, after which he was forced to flee to the capital city of La Paz (Mamani Condori 1991, 128).

In La Paz, Nina Quispe sought to link the *ayllus* he represented in exile with urban unions. He collaborated with the butchers' union—among the most powerful labor organizations in the city. In exchange for their support, he taught union members' children to read and write (Mamani Condori 1991, 128,130).[5] Nina Quispe advocated Indigenous education as a tool of liberation and advancement. Key government officials and intellectuals were receptive to his promotion of literacy. Ticona Alejo (2010) describes him as "a spokesperson and leader of the ayllus and communities in different areas of the country, with broad power to represent Aymaras, Quechuas and Tupi-Guaraníes before the governments of the day" (18, author translation). His work even gained him an audience with Bolivian President Hernando Siles (1926–1930), which Nina Quispe described as follows:

I timidly entered the palace, but after I talked with the gentleman Siles my fear disappeared. I explained my proposals to him and he congratulated me on my work, promising to help me in everything. When I said goodbye he hugged me affectionately. His words encouraged me so much that I happily told my students about my interview, making them see how the primary authority [of the country] was a great advocate for us. (Ticona Alejo 2010, 19, author translation)

5. He continued to form relationships with other unions, mostly comprised of Indigenous migrants, that represented milkmen, stone cutters, and bricklayers.

Nina Quispe was not without his detractors. Leaders of the Indigenous organization, the AMP, criticized him and Santos Markos T'ula for being too eager to compromise on demands for Indigenous rights. Another La Paz *cacique*, Titiriku, denounced Nina Quispe's literacy program as being too focused on teaching Spanish rather than Indigenous languages (Ari 2014, 52). Ari (2014) further observes, "Compared to the AMP's project, however, both [Santos Marka T'ula and Nina Quispe] were too receptive to Westernization and assimilation" (52).

Yet, such a critique oversimplifies Nina Quispe's goals. He founded the Sociedad Centro Educativo de Qullasuyo in 1930, which sought to educate Indigenous children in Spanish and spread the doctrine of resistance to oppression. Ticona Alejo (2010) notes, "In these schools, the connection between instruction and the fight for territorial and cultural recognition of the Indigenous peoples was always present" (29, author translation). Nina Quispe believed "the recognition of indigenous territory and autonomy could be the basis for the nation's advance" (Gotkowitz 2008, 50). Far from advocating assimilation, he sought to give Indigenous communities the tools they needed to protect and reinforce their cultures.

Santos Marka T'ula and Nina Quispe headed extensive (and often overlapping) networks that covered Indigenous communities and ex-communities— as those subsumed by haciendas were known—throughout the country (Ticona Alejo 2010, 50). Their demands, which they disseminated to their followers, reflected their experiences with state-led conscription and hacienda expansion; they called for both ethnic and class-based rights, including increased representation of Indigenous groups in government, access to markets, an end to forced labor and tribute, and a return of communal land lost to haciendas (Rivera Cusicanqui 1987, 37). These claims were subsequently adopted by hundreds of other *caciques* in Bolivia during the 1910s and 1920s (Gotkowitz 2008, 50). The Chaco War (1932–1935) fundamentally transformed patterns of Indigenous mobilization in Bolivia by creating new incentives to mobilize and new techniques of doing so (Rivera Cusicanqui 1987, 47). As I described in Chapter 5, the conflict amplified Indigenous groups' grievances against the state because native men had comprised the bulk of the military and were forced to fight for a cause few understood. The war also resulted in a military defeat that delegitimized the Bolivian government. Left parties channeled this popular dissatisfaction to challenge the traditional political establishment.

In the early 1940s, a national-level peasant organization attempted to create "an ample network of contacts with local leaders in the committees and haciendas . . . [and] sought to identify those local leaders with the organizational capacity, tact, or courage necessary to elude control by the patrones [patrons]" (Dandler and Torrico A. 1987, 344). Teams of Indigenous *caciques* and labor organizers sponsored regional and national conferences, where participants demanded ethnic *and* class-based rights (Gotkowitz 2008, 161). Unions named Indigenous *caciques* to key union positions, including "Secretaries for Indian Affairs" (Rivera Cusicanqui 1987, 49). The rise of unions and left parties increased the salience of class-based demands, but Indigenous leaders remained influential even in these contexts. As Gotkowitz (2008) recounts,

> the burgeoning labor organizations gave new impetus to the longstanding struggles of the cacique apoderado networks. Those earlier movements had changed significantly during the Chaco War years, but they were not fully suppressed. Although the national network no longer maintained the same level of coordination, the "caciques indígenas" continued to submit petitions to national politicians. And while the demands that hacienda colonos expressed during the late 1930s and early 1940s figured centrally in Bolivia's first indigenous congresses, community-based leaders also influenced those events (162).

In addition to assuming leadership roles in unions, Indigenous leaders continued mobilizing their communities to resist various forms of extraction. In Omasuyos, a province in La Paz, Indigenous leaders mobilized their communities against the government's labor draft. Community leaders printed counterfeit certificates stating that their members had completed their labor service for the year and distributed copies for other communities throughout the department to use; these efforts complicated the government's efforts to build a railway line from La Paz to Bolivia's lowland areas (Mayer 1995, 168). The rapid expansion of large estates also generated a sometimes violent peasant movement, which was based in Achacachi, a municipality in the Omasuyos province. These forms of resistance created "a class of community leaders which could potentially be an alternative network of rural contacts for the government" (Rivera Cusicanqui 1987, 83).

For this reason, after the 1952 revolution, some, though by no means all Indigenous leaders became key allies of the Leftist Revolutionary Nationalist Movement (MNR) government, which endeavored to mobilize Indigenous communities through state-sponsored unions. These unions were anathema to many community leaders, as they were often run by non-Indigenous towns-people, "the traditional exploiters of community members" (Alejo et al. 1994, 51, author translation). Furthermore, as Rivera Cusicanqui (1987) argues, "The union was to be yet another link in the chain of proposals to assimilate and civilize the Indians put forward by the dominant Creole class to solve what was known as the 'Indian problem'" (93). Indigenous leaders could either resist these efforts—if they had the capacity to do so—or collaborate with them.

I now analyze where Indigenous elites were most likely to resist these state and union efforts to assimilate their communities. Following the logic outlined in Figure 3.6, I hypothesize that communities that experienced early hacienda expansion were more likely to demand assimilation, while those that experienced only state-led labor conscription were more likely to demand autonomy. Communities that endured state-led conscription followed by hacienda expansion were more likely to demand integration.

I draw on several sources to test these predictions. To measure "early" land loss to haciendas, I examine provincial-level changes in the Indigenous community population between 1833 and 1877 (Grieshaber 1980). To measure the later presence of haciendas, I use a measure from the first Agrarian Census (*Censo Agropecuario*), administered in 1950, which documents the percentage of land in each Bolivian province occupied by haciendas.[6] To construct a measure of state-led extraction (labor conscription), I analyze documents on Bolivian highway and railroad construction in the first decades of the twentieth century.[7] I code the province in which the highway or railroad was located to measure exposure to labor conscription (the *prestación vial* program). I adopt this measure for two reasons. First, governments used unpaid Indigenous labor to build most roads and railways during this period. Second, Indigenous workers were supposed to be taken from no more than three leagues ($\approx$ 15 km) from the construction site (Bolivia 1902). Thus, proximity to roads and railways should indicate communities' exposure to conscription. Using present-day provinces, which are much smaller than those in the early twentieth century, increases the likelihood that communities in each province were close enough to an infrastructure project to have been drafted to work. Table 7.1 summarizes these variables for highland, Indigenous departments of Bolivia. I include only departments with highland provinces that

6. Importantly, this measure was taken prior to the 1953 land reform.
7. These include Marsh (1928) and Walle (1914).

TABLE 7.1. Rural elite and state-led extraction in Bolivia

| Department | Comm.pop. change (1833–1877) | Hacienda prevalence (% land, 1950) | Labor conscription (% of provinces) | Predicted demands |
|---|---|---|---|---|
| Chuquisaca | +223 | 60% | 25% | Assimilation |
| Cochabamba | −757 | 60% | 0% | Assimilation |
| La Paz | +1103 | 51% | 55% | Integration |
| Oruro | +1814 | 43% | 63% | Integration |
| Southern Potosí | +580 | 40% | 57% | Integration |
| North Potosí | +4065 | 12% | 20% | Autonomy |

Note: Community population change is the average of the provincial-level change in number of community members who paid the tribute between 1833 and 1877. The prevalence of the hacienda is the percentage of all land occupied by large properties that have *colonos* (serfs). The labor conscription variable is the percentage of provinces in a department that contained a highway or a railroad built under the *prestación vial* program before 1915.

Sources: Grieshaber (1980); Marsh (1928); Walle (1914); Fundación TIERRA (2009).

Grieshaber (1980) considers part of the traditional "Indian core." Following existing work, I also separate northern Potosí from the rest of the department (Rivera Cusicanqui 1987; Platt 1982).

The table indicates that the population size of most communities in the sample grew between 1833 and 1877—the first year after the Law of Expropriation was passed (column 2 of Table 7.1). The lone exception is Cochabamba, where each province lost, on average, 757 community members during this period. This observation is consistent with prior work, which suggests that hacienda expansion began much earlier in Cochabamba (McBride 1921, 20). Chuquisaca and La Paz had caught up to Cochabamba by 1950 in their levels of hacienda expansion (Table 7.1); both had 50 percent of their land occupied by haciendas in the middle of the twentieth century. As noted above, La Paz experienced a substantial expansion in large estates at the beginning of the twentieth century following the construction of government roads and railways. The same was true around Sucre in Chuquisaca, where haciendas and debt peonage arrangements grew at unprecedented rates, mirroring what had occurred much earlier in Cochabamba (Langer 1989, 76). Hacienda expansion remained more limited in Oruro and northern Potosí; in the former, it was generally concentrated on a few large estates (Jackson 1989, 276–277).

The northern provinces of Potosí represent a unique example within Bolivia (see Chapter 6). Indigenous communities staved off hacienda expansion throughout the nineteenth century, even in fertile valley areas conducive to wheat production (Grieshaber 1977, 250–251). Faced with growing threats in the early twentieth century, Indigenous leaders reestablished "tributary pacts" with the state (Platt 1982).[8] By reentering these agreements, which had begun during the colonial era but partially eroded following independence, Indigenous leaders gained protection for their communal land in exchange for paying head taxes, which provided much-needed revenue to the departmental government. As an economic elite observed in a report to the Potosí prefect in 1906, the provinces of Charcas and Chayanta in northern Potosí were "the only [provinces] that support the Treasury" (Platt 1982, 138, author translation). In 1918, a prefect noted Indigenous elites' authority to collect revenue in these provinces: "the *padrones* [tax rolls] are in the hands of the curacas [Indigenous leaders], who don't trust anyone, and the Departmental Treasury does not have the authentic lists of taxpayers because no state authority can provide it" (Platt 1982, 139–140, author translation).

Examining the final column of Table 7.1, state-led labor conscription appears in highland areas of every department except for Cochabamba.[9] Cochabamba experienced no labor conscription, which supports a core assumption of my theory: that the early expansion of haciendas made future state-led labor conscription less likely. The limited incidence of labor conscription could be observed even before the 1915 law that required Cochabamba's *prestación vial* to be collected in cash. In a 1902 discussion of Cochabamba's department budget in Bolivia's Chamber of Deputies, one deputy observed, "the prestación vial has not had the effectiveness [in Cochabamba] that it has achieved in other departments" (Bolivia Congreso Nacional Cámara de Diputados 1902, 615, author translation).

Conscription was much more common in La Paz, as the central government attempted to extend its reach beyond the capital. Conscription rates were also high in Oruro and many regions of Potosí. The high altitude of many *altiplano* (high plain) regions was no deterrent to constructing roads and railways. Travelers recounted the impressive achievement of Bolivia's building

---

8. See Chapter 3 for a discussion.

9. Importantly, railroads and roads were built in valley and non-Indigenous core areas of Cochabamba. The evidence from the departmental government's *memorias* (annual reports) and congressional debates is inconclusive about how successful authorities were in mobilizing Indigenous labor for these projects.

"the highest railroads of the world, the marvel of railway engineering . . . to connect mining centers" (Pan American Union 1918, 780).

Figure 7.1 outlines the predictions that arise from the extractive sequences. Cochabamba's highland provinces experienced early hacienda expansion and no documented state-led labor conscription. My theory predicts that in these areas, unions would have replaced Indigenous leaders as the primary organizers of community mobilization. As I discussed in Chapter 5, that is precisely what occurred. Alejo et al. (1994) argue that in Cochabamba, "the unions quickly came to be the only, widespread form of communal organization" (55, author translation).

In northern Potosí, most Indigenous leaders successfully resisted the expansion of large estates.[10] They did, however, experience state-led extraction, both through the *prestación vial* and, especially, through head taxes.[11] The strength of Indigenous leaders created an "internal cohesion and capacity to renew social relations regulated by traditional law" in the *ayllus* of northern Potosí, and, consequently, these leaders resisted the efforts of the post-1952 MNR government to (1) break up their communal lands and (2) impose government-run unions (Cusicanqui 1990, 104). Ultimately, the *ayllu* leaders in this region retained substantially more power as organizers of Indigenous peasant mobilization (Alejo et al. 1994, 52). As my theory predicts, these leaders lobbied for collectively held titles and a degree of local autonomy (Cusicanqui 1990, 104).

In the *altiplano* departments of La Paz, Oruro, and southern Potosí, Indigenous communities experienced hacienda expansion (and were targeted by large landowners) *after* state-led labor conscription. My theory argues that this extractive sequence should have generated demands for integration, which is what the data suggests. Indigenous leaders in these *altiplano* regions did not fight the unions but pursued power within them. The *ayllu* structure coexisted with the union, which was often "subordinated to the traditional organization" (Alejo et al. 1994, 53, author translation). Ultimately, many Indigenous

10. When the threat became serious in 1927, Indigenous leaders organized one of the largest revolts in Bolivia's history in Chayanta.

11. Only one province in northern Potosí, Chayanta, experienced road and railway construction. This might be due either to the reestablishment of land-for-tax pacts that could have prevented conscription or to geography. However, the Bolivian government frequently constructed highways and rail lines between major cities during this period, but a route from the city of Potosí to the city of Cochabamba, which would have run through northern Potosí, was not constructed—or to my knowledge planned—in the first decades of the twentieth century.

Aymara groups agreed to unionize, but doing so "did not imply self-rejection or self-negation"; the unions thus became an opportunity for "reproducing the ancient organizational roles" (Rivera Cusicanqui 1987, 98). These cases exhibited more demands for integration. Indigenous leaders obtained power within unions—and the MNR, to which they were tied in the 1950s—which allowed them to lobby for Indigenous rights. These labor organizations used ethnic and class language, and, as such, "indigenous communities found a way to include their own political demands within revolutionary nationalism's broader agenda" (Soliz 2021, 140).

Indigenous leaders in these regions also sought to articulate their claims directly to left parties without involving unions. Soliz (2021) analyzes the petitions that Indigenous community leaders filed with the MNR government's Ministry of Peasant Affairs between 1952 and 1953. All but three of the 25 petitions came from La Paz, a department that experienced high levels of labor conscription—due to the construction of roads and railroads to and from the capital—and substantial hacienda expansion. All of the documented petitions came from La Paz, Oruro, or southern Potosí, as Table 7.1 predicted (Soliz 2021, 123).

Almost all Indigenous leaders demanded Indigenous rights—specifically, the restitution of communal lands. This pressure campaign was immediately successful. A May 1954 decree had amplified the prior land reform law to recognize Indigenous communal land.[12] Almost 30 percent of the 5,095 petitions filed in local agrarian courts between August 1954 and February 1955 involved Indigenous communal land. These "restitution" cases—calling for the return of communally held land—were especially likely to occur in La Paz, Oruro, and Potosí (Figure 7.2). In La Paz, such cases were four times more common than expropriation cases (involving private property). In Oruro, restitution cases were twice as common as expropriation cases. As expected, the cases filed in Cochabamba—which had the same level of hacienda penetration as La Paz in 1950 (Table 7.1)—overwhelmingly sought expropriation, suggesting a declining demand for Indigenous institutions and a rise in assimilation. Thus, while past work has characterized the MNR period as one of rampant assimilation, we see that Indigenous leaders initially demanded autonomy.

Indigenous leaders were ultimately forced to moderate their ethnic claims and articulate their demands using the MNR's preferred language of revolution and class. The MNR believed Indigenous forms of organization were

---

12. See Decreto Ley No. 3732, 19 de mayo de 1954.

■ Expropriation    □ Restitution

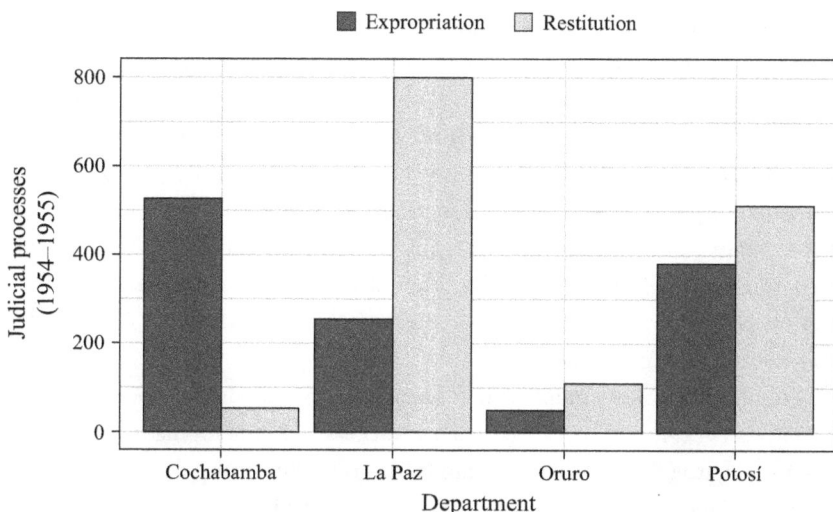

FIGURE 7.2. Divergent attitudes toward land reform in 1950s Bolivia
*Note*: Restitution cases involve recognizing Indigenous communal land. Expropriation cases involve issuing titles to land as private parcels. The data is taken from local judicial processes for land reform between August 1954 and February 1955.
*Source*: Soliz (2021, 133) based on Ayala Mercado (1955).

outmoded and "should be swept away on the road to 'progress' " (Rivera Cusicanqui 1987, 93). A hybrid form of mobilization eventually emerged that combined peasant and Indigenous identities. Albó observes that "at the root of every local union was the community with all its historical strength and depth, and behind that, the ayllu" (Albó 1987, 412). He goes on to explain that "with the deterioration of the model of dependence based on the MNR-PMC [military-peasant pact] . . . the Aymara communities had greater organizational reserves with which to reemerge as a force to be reckoned with" (Albó 1987, 412).[13]

New forms of hybrid organization emerged in the 1970s; the Kataristas were a group of current and former Indigenous community members who were inspired by Túpac Katari, the famed leader of a 1780 Aymara uprising against

13. A 1964 coup displaced the MNR and gave rise to a military regime, which implemented a military-peasant pact that substantially curbed the autonomy of Indigenous communities (Yashar 2005, 163). The formation of this military-peasant pact triggered a new phase of Indigenous organizing.

Spanish extraction.[14] The group opposed the government-run unions that had arisen under the MNR, viewing them as tools for controlling and assimilating Bolivia's Indigenous populations (Rivera Cusicanqui 1987, 117–118). However, the Kataristas were certainly not anti-union; they sought to reform, rather than eliminate, labor organizations. As Casen (2012) describes, "By joining cultural demands to political opposition, Katarism participated in this movement to emancipate peasant trade unions from government tutelage" (30). A common refrain was "*como indios nos explotaron, como indios nos liberamos* [they exploited us as Indians, we will liberate ourselves as Indians]" (Albó 2002b, 79–80, author translation).

The Katarista movement, which fused demands for Indigenous and peasant rights (*integration*), was particularly successful in the highland areas of La Paz and Oruro (Rivera Cusicanqui 1987, 117–119). The group developed strong ties to Indigenous leaders and sought to empower them as crucial intermediaries between communities and the government. In their first Manifesto of Tiahuanaco, issued in July 1973, the Kataristas contrasted traditional authorities with those of the government-run unions that had been imposed on many communities:

> Our past experience, and current one, tells us that when the altiplano peasantry is free to elect their *hilacatas, hilancos,* and other community authorities, they do so through the most democratic spirit and the highest decorum and respect for the opinion of others. The current internal fights among peasants have always been a reflection of the ambitions of external actors. (Hurtado Mercado 1986, 306, author translation)

The traditional Indigenous community, its institutions, and its authorities held both symbolic and practical importance. As Albó (1987) observes, "In the katarismo of the 1980s the [Indigenous] community is again the key engine" (413). This was particularly true among the "Indianist" branch of katarismo, which believed that the movement should be structured using the organizational form of the *ayllu*, rather than that of a union (Rivera Cusicanqui 1987, 153).

Eventually, the Kataristas merged with the Unified Syndical Confederation of Rural Workers of Bolivia (CSUTCB), and the Katarista demands were partially incorporated into the union's agenda, as noted in the epigraph to this chapter. However, the individual Katarista Labor Federations

14. See, e.g., Albó (1987, 379).

of Potosí, Oruro, and La Paz "chose to keep the name of Túpac Katari in [their] official acronym and the picture of the Aymara chief and other Indian cultural symbols on the CSUTCB logotype" (Rivera Cusicanqui 1987, 139). These emphases on ethnic symbols nurtured Indigenous identities but stopped well short of advocating the recognition of Indigenous institutions.

The Kataristas and CSUTCB sought a set of *integration* demands that would allow Indigenous groups to achieve equal status to non-Indigenous Bolivians without sacrificing their long-standing cultures. These goals were reflected in the 1978 Thesis of the Bolivian Peasantry (*Tesis del Campesinado Boliviano*),[15] the chief architects of which were the Kataristas and the future leaders of the CSUTCB (which was formed the following year). The thesis articulated demands for anti-discrimination, respect for Indigenous cultures, and intercultural education.[16] It also demanded "recognition of our right to be elected" and that "our [Indigenous] languages be incorporated into curricula [at all levels]."[17] These demands were likewise embraced by Bolivian Vice-President Víctor Hugo Cárdenas (1993–1997), an Aymara Katarista who sought greater Indigenous engagement with the state, "concrete inclusion," and "difference . . . at the very centre of national government" (Canessa 2000, 130).

My theory would predict that the Kataristas and the CSUTCB should have been most successful at mobilizing communities in Oruro, La Paz, and Potosí since these departments experienced the highest levels of (early) state-led and (later) rural elite extraction (Table 7.1). To test this prediction, I measure support for the Katarista political parties in the 1985 presidential elections—the first election for which provincial-level vote returns are available. Two Katarista parties ran for office that year: the Túpac Katari Revolutionary Movement (MRTK) and the Revolutionary Liberation Movement Túpac Katari (MRTKL). The Katarista movement struggled to form a viable electoral coalition, winning a tiny share of the total vote. As Albó (1987) explains, "the peasant, and the majority of the [Bolivian] populace, votes pragmatically for someone who has a real possibility of getting into power. . . . Up to this point, it has to be recognized, these parties, offshoots in one or

---

15. A copy of the thesis can be found in Hurtado Mercado (1986, 321-332).

16. Section "Asuntos Sociales, Culturales Y Educativos," items 3, 7, and 12.

17. These provisions are contained in sections "Asuntos Politicos y Sindicales," item 7, and "Asuntos Sociales, Culturales Y Educativos," item 9, respectively. Translation by author.

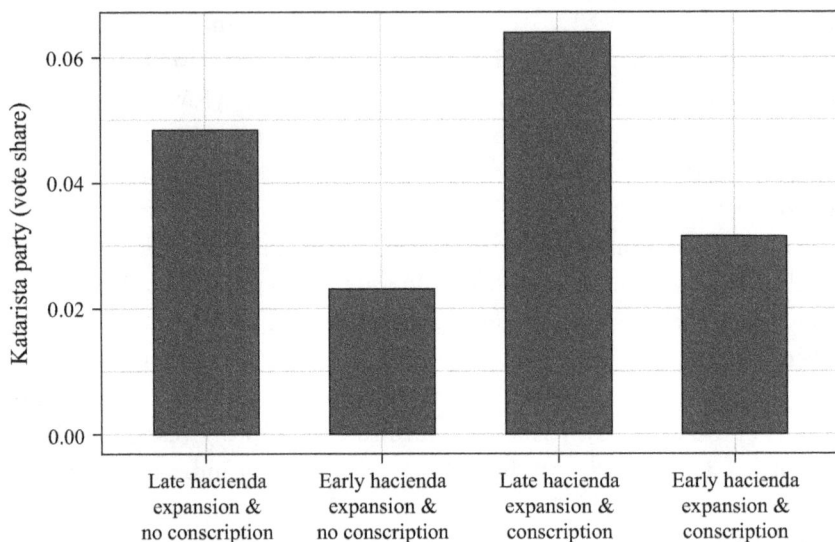

FIGURE 7.3. Extractive sequences and Katarista vote share
*Note*: Data coded at the provincial level. Includes highland and lowland provinces in Cochabamba, Chuquisaca, La Paz, Oruro, and Potosí. See Table 7.1 for information on extraction coding.
*Sources*: Atlas Electoral de Bolivia; Grieshaber (1980); Marsh (1928); Walle (1914); Fundación TIERRA (2009).

another form of katarismo, were simply 'symbolic' " (402). This strategic voting can be considered a feature of this measure of my outcome; individuals who voted for *katarismo* should most strongly support its integration ideas. Only in these areas would voters either believe it was strategically sound to vote for the Kataristas—because of the local strength of the movement—or sacrifice a strategic vote in favor of a sincere one. Consistent with this observation, the Katarista parties received much more support in La Paz (5.3 percent), Oruro (3.3 percent), and Potosí (4.1 percent) than in Cochabamba (1.2 percent).

I now combine the variables in Table 7.1 with information on provincial-level vote share in 1985. I would expect a combination of state-led conscription and later hacienda expansion to lead to greater support for the Kataristas; that is exactly what I find (Figure 7.3). The Katarista vote share is highest in provinces where (1) initial hacienda penetration was low (i.e., the community population increased between 1833 and 1877) and (2) state-led labor conscription occurred. The vote share for the Katarista Party in these provinces was substantially higher than in areas of late hacienda expansion that experienced no labor conscription and, especially, in areas of early hacienda expansion.

Those who supported the Kataristas embraced a set of demands for integration, which included bilingual education and guaranteed political representation. This strategy rested on the belief that ethnic identities should neither be denied through assimilation nor segregated into traditional institutions through autonomy.[18] These beliefs were transmitted from party leaders to members through unique decision-making structures within the Kataristas and, especially, the CSUTCB. When the Katarista leader, Jenaro Flores, was chosen to lead the CSUTCB, he permitted Indigenous communities to elect their own representatives—a key point of distinction with other labor organizations that often appointed local union officials (Yashar 2005, 178). The Kataristas drew on the legitimacy of these locally chosen leaders to "extend their influence and transmit their ideas through the union" (Ticona Alejo 1996, 14). Furthermore, radio transmissions in Aymara allowed the Kataristas to disseminate their message from La Paz to rural communities (Rivera Cusicanqui 1986, 180). These broadcasts, along with "research groups, . . . constituted an alternative public sphere that provided young rural leaders with a different vision of Aymara political identity" (Lucero 2008, 83).

Areas that experienced both rural elite and state-led extraction—and thus had a strong Katarista presence—should have also been more likely to embrace integration demands. To demonstrate this, I use evidence from my 2020 survey of Indigenous Bolivians. I created an index of integration demands, which includes two components: guaranteed representation of Indigenous peoples in state institutions and the provision of bilingual education (Chapter 2). Respondents were asked to score each issue on a four-point scale from not at all important to very important. Responses to each question are coded as a binary variable ($1 =$ very important; $0 =$ all other responses).[19] I sum the indicators to create a two-item index of integration demands.

18. In the 1990s, however, the CSUTCB began to shift its focus toward self-determination and autonomy under the leadership of Felix Quispe, but this was met by opposition from integration-minded members and leadership (Gutiérrez Aguilar 2014, 37–42).

19. I use "very important" because around 60 percent of respondents said the two items were "very important." Including responses of "important" in the outcome measure would have resulted in minimal variation in the dependent variable.

I regress the integration demands index on indicators of self-reported exposure to extraction. Respondents were asked whether (1) the state or (2) private
actors had extracted land, labor, or resources from their community.[20] I use as
independent variables whether respondents' communities faced only state-led
extraction, only rural elite extraction, or both forms of extraction. Consistent with my expectations, respondents who reported having experienced
both types of extraction were more likely to prefer integration rights ($p <$
0.05). This relationship is not observed for respondents from communities
that experienced only one type of extraction.[21] The results remain mostly
unchanged when I include a battery of individual-level controls (e.g., age,
education, gender, income) that might otherwise confound the relationships
I observe.[22]

In many ways, the country's Indigenous communities face the same struggle they did in the 1950s. Indigenous identities remain politically salient in
many parts of Bolivia, often occupying key spaces in left parties and labor
unions. Native groups have received symbolic concessions, such as the 2009
plurinational Constitution, which recognizes the diverse composition of the
Bolivian nation-state. Yet, more costly policy achievements, including political autonomy and collective land rights, remain heavily circumscribed. Few
municipalities have obtained political self-governance rights, and communally
held land, which accounts for a large portion of Bolivia's territory, covers only a
meager portion of Bolivia's Indigenous communities. Even under Indigenous
President Evo Morales, Indigenous groups were denied the right to resources
on their own territory. As Morales said in a 2009 speech: "In some regions,
some brothers say that because they have indigenous autonomy the natural
resources belong to them. . . . Hydrocarbons and [mineral] resources belong
to the national Government" (Tockman et al. 2015, 52).

20. These questions were asked after the outcome measures in the survey.

21. Crucially, however, the differences across the groups are not significant, perhaps due
to the few respondents who indicated experiencing only private (12 percent) or only state (15
percent) extraction, compared with those who experienced both (25 percent).

22. Age, for example, could shape the likelihood that a respondent remembers extraction
and could also affect attitudes toward integration. I also address potential satisficing behavior
by respondents who answer all questions with the highest possible positive response. To address
this concern, I examine a battery of 14 questions in the survey, which measures how important
a variety of concerns are for respondents. I exclude respondents who answer every question in
this set with the maximum value (i.e., "very important").

TABLE 7.2. Extraction and integration demands in Bolivia

| | Dependent variable: | | | |
| --- | --- | --- | --- | --- |
| | Integration demands index (0-2) | | | |
| | (1) | (2) | (3) | (4) |
| Both forms of extraction | 0.198*** | 0.177*** | 0.196*** | 0.189*** |
| | (0.058) | (0.058) | (0.063) | (0.062) |
| Private extraction only | 0.139* | 0.122 | 0.166** | 0.158** |
| | (0.076) | (0.076) | (0.080) | (0.080) |
| State extraction only | 0.030 | −0.007 | 0.020 | 0.001 |
| | (0.070) | (0.069) | (0.074) | (0.074) |
| Secondary education | | 0.014 | | −0.040 |
| | | (0.053) | | (0.055) |
| Age | | 0.008*** | | 0.007*** |
| | | (0.002) | | (0.002) |
| Income | | −0.073 | | −0.091* |
| | | (0.049) | | (0.052) |
| Intercept | 1.290*** | 0.975*** | 1.218*** | 1.055*** |
| | (0.034) | (0.103) | (0.036) | (0.103) |
| Satisficers included | Yes | Yes | No | No |
| Num. obs. | 934 | 934 | 841 | 841 |
| R2 | 0.014 | 0.049 | 0.014 | 0.035 |
| R2 adj. | 0.010 | 0.039 | 0.011 | 0.027 |
| F | 4.294 | 5.237 | 4.074 | 4.350 |
| RMSE | 0.72 | 0.71 | 0.73 | 0.72 |

Note: $^*p < 0.1$; $^{**}p < 0.05$; $^{***}p < 0.01$. Data is taken from an original survey administered by the author in 2020 to self-identified Indigenous Bolivian respondents. The independent variable is self-reported responses to a question about whether respondents' communities had experienced extraction of land, labor, and resources by (1) the state and (2) private actors. The outcome variable is responses on a 0 to 2 index of the degree to which respondents find (1) guaranteed representation for Indigenous peoples in existing state institutions and (2) bilingual education "very important." Columns 3 and 4 exclude satisficers—those who answer 14 straight questions with their highest possible value: "very important."

The hybrid forms of mobilization that characterized the *altiplano* throughout the twentieth century continue to shape politics today—sustaining the legacy of the early MNR, the Kataristas, and the CSUTCB. Contemporary ethnic parties have adopted "inclusionary" messages that promise leftist social policies alongside weaker demands for Indigenous rights; these parties, whose founders and leaders are often Indigenous, have advocated a wide-ranging set of demands that will appeal to both Indigenous and non-Indigenous voters

(Madrid 2008). Yet, Indigenous autonomy, for the most part, continues to be subordinated to class-based concerns.

## 7.2   Extractive Sequences and Integration Demands in Peru

In contrast to Bolivia, where the *prestación vial* (road conscription program) started in 1888 and remained in place for around 80 years, labor conscription in post-independence Peru was mainly confined to the 1920s. Many areas had, therefore, already experienced hacienda expansion when the Peruvian government adopted its *conscripción vial* (road conscription program). Hacienda owners were generally reluctant to allow the government to force their laborers to work on state infrastructure projects. Heilman (2010b) details two such examples from Ayacucho: "The owner of the Airabamba hacienda, in Vischongo, Cangallo, blocked 50 of her hacienda workers from carrying out their vial service in 1928, asserting that the law had been suspended. Similarly, Nicanor Carrasco, owner of the Viran hacienda in Carhuanca, Cangallo, urged campesinos from the adjacent community of Ocopa to abstain from their vial duties" (Heilman 2010b, 517). The burden of road conscription was, therefore, concentrated among the Indigenous communities that had resisted or otherwise avoided hacienda expansion.

In some cases, the need to resist conscription caused Indigenous demands to be layered onto or fused with peasant ones. Indigenous leaders formed alliances with various rural-sector unions to resist road conscription; as Hirsch (2010) explains, "The *Conscripción Vial* was a burning issue for the . . . indigenous peasantry in the 1920s. Anarchists and anarcho-syndicalists in the southern highlands and in Lima were responsive to this popular concern" (267). The Peruvian Regional Indigenous-Worker Federation (Federación Indígena Obrera Regional Peruana, FIORP) and Local Workers Federation of Lima (FOL-Peru),[23] for example, lobbied in the 1920s not only for greater protections for peasant workers but also for Indigenous communal land rights.[24]

The most substantial increase in organizations combining Indigenous and peasant concerns started in the 1940s. Ethnic authorities who had mobilized

---

23. I use FOL-Peru (rather than FOL) to distinguish the Bolivian FOL from the Peruvian one.

24. See, e.g., Bao and Indacochea (2002, 102); Hirsch (2020, 64).

their communities to resist conscription obtained leadership positions in powerful unions, including the Peasant Confederation of Peru (CCP).[25] Similarly, Handelman (1974) argues that community members became the "leadership nucleus" for unions in Cusco (100). The incorporation of Indigenous leaders into traditional labor organizations transformed unions into hybrid entities that articulated both class-based and ethnic demands.

My theory predicts that these hybrid organizations should have been most likely to emerge in areas that experienced labor conscription *and* hacienda expansion. I evaluate this prediction using provincial-level data from the early twentieth century. I code hybrid organizations from the dataset of 1920s organizations listed in Melgar Bao (1988). Examples include the Pro Indigenous Peasant Federation of Acomayo, the Indigenous Federation of the Valley of Chincha (also called the Peasant Federation of the Valley of Chincha), and the Workers Central Federation of Indigenous Peoples of the Region of Huancavelíca. Many of these organizations were affiliated with the FIORP. I measure hacienda expansion using the 1940 Census, which documents the percentage of the rural population that lived on haciendas (see Chapter 4). I code exposure to labor conscription based on the criteria used by Leguía to build roads under the *conscripción vial* program: whether a community was located in a province containing a portion of the Qhapaq Ñan (see Chapters 4 and 6).

Table 7.3 presents the results of a regression of the number of hybrid organizations in a province on the percentage of the rural population that lived on haciendas.[26] I conduct the analysis with and without department-level fixed effects and find that the size of a province's hacienda population predicts the formation of hybrid organizations. This effect is driven by provinces that experienced labor conscription. Among communities that experienced labor conscription, moving from no hacienda population to a 100 percent

25. See, e.g., Albó (1999, 779).

26. The outcome, measured in the 1920s, is earlier in time than the independent variable (measured in 1940) due to data availability. However, as I discuss in Chapter 5, the hacienda population in 1940 should be more highly correlated with the hacienda population in 1920 than the 1876 measure of hacienda expansion. Furthermore, we might expect unionization and the formation of hybrid organizations to discourage the formation of haciendas, perhaps even breaking up existing ones; it seems unlikely that hybrid organizations would directly or indirectly *encourage* the formation of haciendas. As such, measuring the hacienda population in 1940 should—if anything—offer more conservative estimates of the relationship between hacienda expansion and hybrid organizations.

TABLE 7.3. Hacienda expansion, labor conscription, and hybrid organizations in Peru

| | Dependent variable | | | |
|---|---|---|---|---|
| | Hybrid Organizations | | | |
| | (1) | (2) | (3) | (4) |
| Hacienda Population (1940) | 0.504* | 0.616** | 1.091** | −0.257 |
| | (0.259) | (0.282) | (0.478) | (0.226) |
| Constant | 0.070 | | | |
| | (0.081) | | | |
| Experienced labor conscription | | | Yes | No |
| Observations | 110 | 110 | 50 | 60 |
| $R^2$ | 0.034 | 0.378 | 0.512 | 0.518 |
| Adjusted $R^2$ | 0.025 | 0.202 | 0.336 | 0.187 |
| Department FEs | No | Yes | Yes | Yes |

Note: $*p < 0.1$; $**p < 0.05$; $***p < 0.01$. Provincial-level data. The independent variable is the percentage of the rural population living on haciendas as documented in the 1940 Census. The dependent variable is the number of Indigenous-peasant (hybrid) organizations in a given province. Labor conscription is coded as 1 if the province contained a portion of the Qhapaq Ñan and was thus eligible for conscription under Leguía's road-building program.
Sources: Melgar Bao (1988); Perez (1972); Regal (1936); Ministerio de Fomento (1930); Díez Canseco and Aguilar Revoredo (1929); Peru (1929); Portaro (1930).

hacienda population is associated with the formation of one additional hybrid organization ($p < 0.05$).

The hybrid organizations in this analysis pursued "Indigenist" claims, which generally correspond to what I call integration demands. *Indigenismo* was a powerful intellectual current between the 1940s and 1960s; advocates like José María Arguedas argued that bilingualism was the only way to ensure that Indigenous communities were incorporated into the Peruvian nation (Contreras 1996, 23). Indigenist intellectuals also embraced a larger set of integrationist demands that noted the importance of ethnicity, but—as was the case with the Kataristas and the CSUTCB in Bolivia—often subordinated Indigenous demands to class-based goals and ideologies. Coronado (2009) observes, "Even proposals that insisted on the integration of the indigenous population into the Peruvian nation . . . relied upon notions of these same people that stressed their existence first as the labor that would build the new nation" (168).

The earliest and strongest proponents of *Indigenismo* arose in the province of Cusco, which had been the capital of the Inca Empire. Artists and writers in the province sought to use *Indigenismo* and the symbolic importance of Cusco as a way to redefine "Peruvian nationalist discourse, jurisprudence, and domestic policy" (Poole 1997, 182). Pragmatic, provincial-level politicians also promoted this ideology as a way to contest their subordinate position vis-à-vis national elites (de la Cadena 2000, 45).

The uneasy relationship between class and ethnic claims that characterized *Indigenismo* persisted into the mid-twentieth century in Cusco. In one protest in 1962, Indigenous peasants made their demands in Quechua, associating the language "with political demands and even 'revolution.' . . . The uprising had a cultural identity, even if the leadership subordinated it to class rhetoric" (de la Cadena 2000, 190).

My theory predicts the prevalence of integrationist demands in the Cusco province (Table 7.4). In previous chapters, I demonstrated how high levels of early hacienda expansion in the provinces of Paucartambo, Paruro, and La Convención—also in the Cusco department—corresponded to long-term demands for assimilation. Conversely, lower levels of hacienda expansion and higher levels of state-led conscription in the provinces of Canas, Canchis, and Quispicanchi generally sparked demands for autonomy. Cusco's capital (the province of Cusco) differs from the other six cases I examined in the department: it experienced significant hacienda expansion *and* labor conscription. Its mid-twentieth-century Indigenist movements also embraced and promoted integration demands.

Demands for integration have ultimately been less enduring in Peru than in Bolivia. The weakness of integration demands in contemporary Peru may be attributed to the government's early adoption of integration and Indigenist policies, beginning in the 1920s under President Augusto Leguía and continuing under the leftist military government (1968–1975), which "made bilingual (Quechua/Spanish) education official and used indigenous symbols to promote their agrarian reform" (de la Cadena 2000, 325). The state's embrace of *Indigenismo* led societal groups—especially Indigenous communities—to seek alternative ways of formulating their demands. De la Cadena (2000) observes, "The absence of culturalist (or ethnic) political slogans among the people during that period, rather than a failure to incorporate anticolonial or ethnic rhetoric, represented both a historical shift and political strategy resulting from . . . the need to distance themselves from state-sponsored indigenismo" (326).

As such, Indigenous community demands in Peru have more often corresponded to either autonomy or assimilation and have been articulated

TABLE 7.4. Exposure to state-led and rural elite extraction, Peru

|  | Hacienda population (1876) | Hacienda population (1940) | Road conscription | Predicted demands |
| --- | --- | --- | --- | --- |
| La Convención | High: 80.1% | High: 54.1% | No | Assimilation |
| Paruro | High: 54.2% | Low: 20.7% | No | Assimilation |
| Paucartambo | High: 58.9% | High: 51.9% | Yes (very low) | Assimilation |
| Canas | Low: 0.6% | Low: 11.2% | Yes (high) | Autonomy |
| Canchis | Low: 2.5% | Low: 5.4% | Yes | Autonomy |
| Quispicanchi | Moderate: 37.2% | Low: 23.7% | Yes (high) | Autonomy |
| Cusco | Moderate: 41.2% | Moderate: 33.5% | Yes (high) | Integration |

*Note*: See Appendix E for more data on road conscription and hacienda expansion in these and other provinces in Cusco.
*Sources*: Díez Canseco and Aguilar Revoredo (1929); Macera (1976); Ministerio de Fomento (1930); Peru (1929); Perez (1972); Portaro (1930).

through either unions *or* ethnic organizations. The hybrid organizations that rose to prominence in the 1920s and thrived in later decades ceased to be relevant political actors, which caused a general decline in demands for integration. I demonstrate this by examining a dataset of over 600 Indigenous and peasant mobilizations between 1956 and 1964, documenting the actor responsible for organizing each event. I calculate the percentage of movements organized by unions, communities, and both unions and communities between 1956 and 1964.

As expected, I find relatively few examples of communities and unions jointly mobilizing to make demands on the state and large landowners. There is a bimodal distribution in the actor responsible for mobilization in almost every region of mid-twentieth-century Peru (Figure 7.4). Communities were the primary organizational force in all parts of the country except for the coast, where unions dominated. This finding is consistent with an extensive literature on powerful sugar and cotton unions, many of which arose on large coastal estates and became the basis of the populist APRA Party. Unions were also strong in the northern highlands which conforms with expectations, since Cajamarca, the largest department in this region, had many haciendas and a powerful union movement (Deere 1990, 24). This is also the area of Peru where, today, autonomy demands and Indigenous identities are the weakest (Carter 2024a).

Weak ties between communities and unions also explain—and indicate—the absence of integration demands. A 2012 census asked Peruvian Indigenous

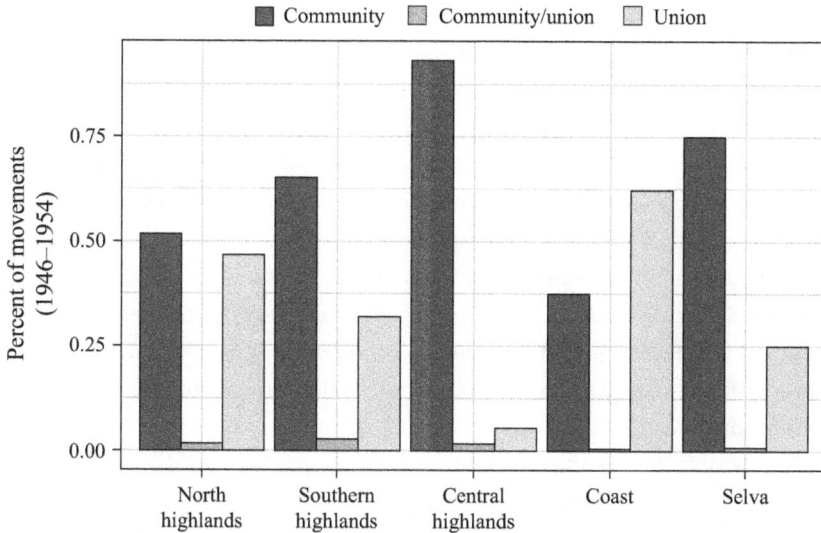

FIGURE 7.4. Organizer of Indigenous/peasant mobilization by region, 1956–1964
*Note*: The figure plots data classified by the author's coding of provincial-level mobilization (n = 662). Northern highlands: Cajamarca, Ancash, Cajamarca, Amazonas. Central highlands: Huánuco, Junín. Southern highlands: Cusco, Huancavelica, Puno, Ayacucho, Arequipa, Apurímac. Selva: San Martin, Madre de Dios. Coast: Lima, La Libertad, Piura, Moquegua, Lambayeque, Ica, Tumbes.
*Source*: Guzmán and Vargas (1981).

community leaders whether their communities belonged to any external organizations. Just over 6 percent of communities claimed membership in such organizations, many of which were local federations of Indigenous communities rather than unions. The data suggest that throughout Peru, unions have been powerful in certain areas, but they have rarely developed enduring linkages with Indigenous communities. As such, union and community mobilization appear to be substitutes. Communities have more often sustained Indigenous identities, institutions, and customs, while unions have driven class-based mobilization. Hybrid organizations and their demands for integration have been much less common.

## 7.3   Conclusion

This chapter has analyzed the effects of multiple forms of extraction on Indigenous communities' demand-making. Bolivia was more likely than Peru to experience state-led *and* rural elite extraction. These experiences generated integration demands: communities, often through hybrid organizations, called for bilingual education, anti-discrimination policies, and guaranteed political representation. These integration demands created mainstream ways of expressing ethnic identity, keeping Indigenous cultural practices and symbols salient even as governments attempted to force assimilation.

In Peru, hybrid organizations emerged with vigor in the 1920s and continued in certain southern regions, such as the province of Cusco and the department of Puno, into the mid-twentieth century. However, the integration demands these organizations advocated were quickly espoused by national politicians—including several presidents. The state's embrace (and co-optation) of integration encouraged societal groups, including Indigenous communities and unions, to mobilize instead for autonomy or assimilation.

These divergent paths in Bolivia and Peru have two critical implications. First, in Bolivia, both ethnic and class demands were often articulated by unions and political parties. On the one hand, this contributed to the persistence of Indigenous identities by establishing that ethnic and class identities did not need to compete with each other. On the other hand, Indigenous demands were ultimately subordinated to class-based claims. In Peru, conversely, class and ethnic demands were generally articulated separately and through distinct organizations. The community was the primary articulator of Indigenous demands, while unions mainly advocated peasant claims to the government. The absence of union-community linkages provided a challenge for Indigenous communities in earlier periods—when unions were the primary intermediary with corporatist and left governments—but created an opportunity for ethnic mobilization following the decline of labor organizations in recent decades.

Second, because Indigenous mobilization in Bolivia occurred through unions that had regional and national power, native groups have been better able to achieve national-level policy change. The 2009 Constitution, for example, contained a strong symbolic commitment to Indigenous rights, and the ethnopopulist Movement for Socialism (MAS) party has controlled the Bolivian presidency for almost 20 years. However, implementation and enforcement of Indigenous autonomy has been a challenge; local communities have varying levels of influence with the ethnic and non-Indigenous organizations that serve as critical intermediaries with the government.

Peru, by contrast, has no national-level ethnic political parties. Peruvian Indigenous communities that followed the union path were more likely to assimilate, reducing the size of an electoral base for an aspirant national-level ethnic party. Furthermore, the failure to integrate ethnic demands into more powerful and enduring class-based organizations has made it difficult to establish the inclusive, ethnopopulist parties that have experienced some electoral success in Latin America (Madrid 2008). Ethnic demands, particularly for autonomy, have arisen instead through individual communities' local-level lobbying efforts.

The analysis presented in this chapter offers a key addendum to previous work on class and ethnic mobilization in Latin America. The co-occurrence of both state-led labor conscription and rural elite extraction fostered hybrid forms of mobilization that stimulated future large-scale mobilization for Indigenous *identities* but not recognition of Indigenous *institutions* (integration). This mobilizational pattern dominated in Bolivia, where class-based organizations and Indigenous communities formed deep and enduring linkages. Communities subjected to only one form of extraction mobilized along either class or ethnic lines. The result, exemplified by Peru, was a bifurcated movement: traditional communities advocated protections for Indigenous institutions (autonomy), and unionized communities often lobbied for only workers' rights (assimilation).

Experiencing both forms of extraction has yielded similar outcomes in other Latin American countries. In Chiapas, Mexico, for example, communities were subjected to high levels of debt peonage and labor conscription—with the latter often preceding the former (Washbrook 2012). Consistent with my theory, Chiapas also had arguably the clearest example of a hybrid Indigenous-peasant movement, which "tied the reproduction of Indian culture to concrete material demands" (Mattiace 2003, 153). This movement eventually gave rise to the Zapatista Army of National Liberation, a powerful insurgent group that articulated both class and ethnic demands (Trejo 2012, 201–230).

# 8

# The Past, Present, and Future of Autonomy

[The peasant] stood up and went into the hut. A few minutes later, he came out carrying a black, battered old dispatch box, placed it before us, and opened it. With great care, he unfolded the almost golden sheets of paper. "These are our titles to the common lands of Tlaquiltenango. The land was ours in Indian times. The King of Spain recognized it as ours; we lost it to the planters and then Zapata fought and got it back. Here is Emiliano's own signature. They don't have these papers. We do. They prove our right to exist. And I will never lose them, even if it costs me my life."

—CARLOS FUENTES, *VIVA ZAPATA*

WHY DO SOME Indigenous communities eagerly embrace autonomy while others do not? This book has demonstrated that historical experiences with labor extraction at a critical juncture (the turn of the twentieth century) play an important explanatory role. This extraction was enduring, widespread, intense, and transformative. However, communities had very different experiences with it, which generated distinct and divergent legacies. The governments of Peru and Bolivia conscripted workers in some Indigenous communities to build roads, railways, and other infrastructure projects (*state-led* extraction). Other communities became trapped into debt peonage arrangements on large, agricultural estates (*rural elite* extraction). These two forms of extraction were often mutually exclusive, especially since large estate owners thwarted state efforts to conscript their workers. However, some communities experienced *both* types of extraction.

Communities that experienced state-led extraction developed a deep mistrust of the government and its institutions. As such, these communities often turned away from the state and toward their traditional Indigenous institutions to resist extraction. In Peru and Bolivia, for example, I showed that Indigenous leaders greatly increased their power during periods of state-led extraction, taking on new and more expansive roles. During these periods, ethnic identities also flourished, with Indigenous organizations arising and thriving in areas of labor conscription. Community investments in Indigenous institutions and identities continued through several mechanisms of persistence (collective memory, more powerful community leaders, and Indigenous organizations). Ultimately, these communities were more likely to demand protection for their long-standing institutions and identities (*autonomy*). Examples of these demands include community recognition, local self-government through traditional political institutions, and collectively held land titles.

Rural elite extraction had different effects, as large landowners frequently co-opted Indigenous institutions and leaders to seize native communities' land and gain access to their labor. Community members could not resist extraction through traditional, ethnic institutions and identities; instead, they turned to class-based organizations, mainly rural sector unions. These labor organizations sought to reduce the salience of ethnic identities and institutions, which they viewed as barriers to class-based mobilization. Community members accepted these changes because unions achieved key concessions through their organizational capacity and links to corporatist and left governments. Communities that mobilized in this way thus often abandoned Indigenous identities and institutions (*assimilation*), pursuing instead work-related demands, private land titles, and Spanish-only education.

Communities that experienced state-led extraction and *then* rural elite extraction represent a third path. During periods of government conscription, these communities invested in Indigenous institutions and identities. As such, when rural elite extraction occurred, Indigenous institutions and leaders were more likely to resist co-optation and retain their legitimacy within their communities. Labor organizations, which sought to mobilize Indigenous peasants, offered these powerful community leaders concessions in exchange for their collaboration. In Peru and Bolivia, for example, unions gave Indigenous authorities leadership positions and invoked Indigenous symbols and historical figures in their names and organizational imagery. Unions advocated recognizing Indigenous *identities* within existing state and market institutions

(*integration*); they demanded electoral quotas and reserved seats for Indigenous peoples, affirmative action programs, and bilingual education. Labor
organizations viewed the recognition of Indigenous *institutions*, however, as
too costly and a potential challenge to their authority.

The book's evidence, which draws on case studies, interviews, archival data,
surveys, and (natural) experiments in Bolivia and Peru, provides robust support for my theory. State-led extraction promoted demands for *autonomy*.
Rural elite extraction generated demands for *assimilation*. Experiencing both
forms of extraction sparked demands for *integration*.

This chapter further refines my argument by first considering scope conditions. It then explores communities' ability to sustain autonomy demands
over time, highlighting variation in two types of communities: those that
seek autonomy only under certain conditions ("selective demanders") and
those that call for it regardless of underlying structural and institutional factors ("universal demanders"). The book's findings bolster my assertion that
most communities are selective demanders. I conclude by considering how
the legacies of historical extraction have shaped contemporary outcomes for
Indigenous communities.

## 8.1   Scope Conditions

This section analyzes two cases that move beyond historical labor extraction:
the Navajo Livestock Reduction Act in the 1930s United States and contemporary land extraction in Bolivia's Chapare region. At first glance, the findings
do not seem to conform to my theory's predictions: state-led extraction in the
Navajo case led to an initial *rejection* (rather than embrace) of autonomy, and
rural elite extraction in Chapare has led to demands for autonomy (rather than
assimilation).

Upon closer examination, however, these cases refine rather than challenge
my argument. Unlike extractive efforts in Bolivia and Peru—where government officials bypassed Indigenous leaders and institutions—US government
extraction of the Navajo occurred *in coordination with* tribal leaders. In the near
term, this collaboration reduced Navajo peoples' faith in the tribal institutions
that autonomy would have protected. Soon, however, the Navajo replaced
these leaders with authorities opposed to stock reduction and redesigned their
tribal institutions to be more "representative" of tribal interests; subsequently,
autonomy demands emerged with vigor. This suggests that state-led extraction triggers autonomy demands only when community members believe

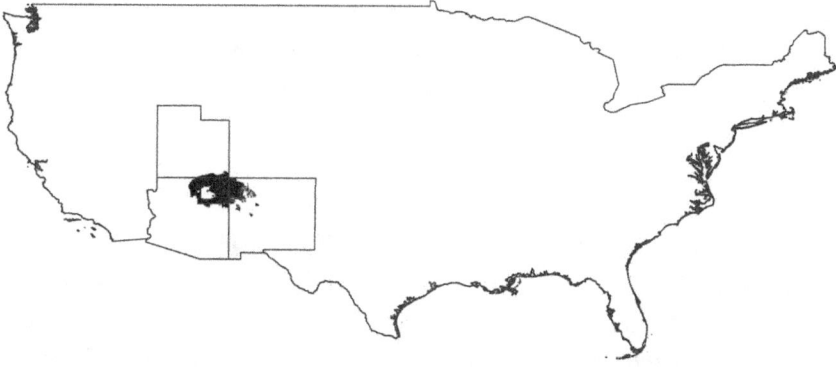

(a) Navajo Nation within Utah, Arizona, New Mexico (US)

(b) Chapare region within Cochabamba (Bolivia)

FIGURE 8.1. Location of Navajo Nation and Chapare

Indigenous leaders and institutions are acting independently of an extracting state.

Meanwhile, Chapare supports many of the core components of my theory. While rural elites were primarily responsible for extraction, Indigenous communities viewed the Bolivian government as facilitating this extraction. Trust in the state subsequently declined, and the predictions follow more closely those for state-led extraction: communities in the Chapare were more likely to demand autonomy.[1] Chapare demonstrates that *perceptions* of responsibility condition the theoretical expectations around extraction's effects.

### 8.1.1   Navajo Nation

In response to several factors, including "depleted vegetation, soil erosion, silt accumulation at the Hoover Dam, expanding herds, restrictions on off-reservation grazing, poor animal quality, and the faltering national economy," in 1933, the US federal government began seizing and slaughtering the Navajo's horses, goats, cows, and sheep (McPherson 1998, 6). Nearly 150,000 goats and 50,000 sheep were forcibly taken from the tribe in 1934 alone (Aberle 1982, 57). The Navajo mobilized to resist livestock reduction, including through violence (Weisiger 2007, 451).

Contrary to my theory's predictions, the Livestock Reduction Act (a case of state-led extraction) reduced trust in *tribal* institutions, particularly the Tribal Council, which "many Navajo now . . . viewed with disdain, believing it had aided and supported the federal government's stock reduction program" (Wilkins 2013, 22). Due to mistrust in tribal institutions and the federal government, the Navajo initially rejected autonomy; they were less likely than many other tribal groups to embrace the 1934 Indian Reorganization Act (IRA), which promised greater tribal authority and self-governance rights. Weisiger explains that the Navajo interpreted the vote on the IRA as "a referendum on stock reduction" and on Bureau of Indian Affairs Commissioner John Collier (Weisiger 2007, 447). He further notes that "in the eastern and northern jurisdictions of the reservation, where goat reduction had been especially devastating, people registered their anger by voting against the IRA" (Weisiger 2007, 447).[2] The policy generated "bitterness and anger among the Navajos" toward the federal government (Iverson 1983, 23). As Weisiger

---

1. This case thus differs from the historical instances of extraction analyzed earlier in the book, where states and rural elites competed for Indigenous resources—allowing communities to clearly and confidently assign blame for extraction.

2. At a meeting with Collier to discuss the IRA, one Navajo representative, Howard Gorman, argued, "This thing [the IRA], the thing you said that will make us strong, what do you mean by it? We have been told not once but many times this same thing, and all it is is a bunch of lies. What are we going to get in return for placing our votes in favor of the mark? What will become of the old treaties? You have not fulfilled those treaties yet!" (Roessel and Johnson 1974, 72).

(2011) describes, the "trauma of stock reduction [was] etched deeply into the collective memory of the Navajo" (8).

The rejection of autonomy was short-lived, and state-led extraction soon triggered my hypothesized investments in Indigenous institutions and identities. In 1936, the Navajo overhauled the Tribal Council and installed leaders who were openly hostile to Collier and stock reduction (Taylor 1980, 129). These actions mirror the evidence presented for Peru and Bolivia in Chapter 6; the experience of resisting state-led extraction led communities to not just invest in but also to *transform* existing Indigenous institutions. Stock reduction also reinforced the *ethnic* identity of the Navajo as a distinct and pastoralist people (Weisiger 2011, 66, 159, 180). Eventually, this reinvestment in Navajo identity and institutions promoted demands for autonomy. Sheridan (2012) argues that "one positive legacy of stock reduction was a growing demand for Navajo self-determination" (311). Thus, the initial opposition to autonomy under the IRA was not necessarily a rejection of the concept of autonomy per se. Instead, the Navajo likely wanted a stronger articulation of self-governance rights than what they trusted the government—or their existing tribal institutions—to provide.

### 8.1.2   Chapare

Chapare, in the northern region of Cochabamba, Bolivia, has historically been home to the Indigenous Yuracaré people. In recent decades, private actors—particularly coca growers and processors—have increasingly seized native land in the region. In the 1970s and 1980s, settlers from other regions of the country migrated to Chapare. These "colonists," as their supporters and opponents considered them, began to clear massive forest land for coca cultivation, eager to take advantage of the growing demand for cocaine in the United States. By 1985, between 40 and 45 percent of the world's coca leaf and coca paste production originated in Bolivia, and the small, tropical region of Chapare accounted for 70 percent of this output (Healy 1985). As occurred in the era of hacienda expansion, the influx of coca growers into the region resulted in both the loss of native land and the establishment of modern debt peonage between the *cocaleros* (coca growers) and Indigenous communities.[3]

---

3. Bjork-James (2020) describes, "Indigenous people are often dependent, landless laborers in their own land, earning around 20 bolivianos (less than US$3) to harvest a coca plot or selling their fish or wild meat to colonists for around 300 bolivianos ($\approx$ US$40) a month" (138).

My theory predicts that this rural elite extraction in Chapare would have increased calls for assimilation or integration, but demands for autonomy have emerged instead. In 2013, the Yurakaré Indigenous Council of the Chapare River (Consejo Indígena Yurakaré Rio Chapare, CONIYURA), comprised of 21 Indigenous communities in the region, began the process of converting to an autonomous Indigenous territory. Members of the Yurakaré nation voted unanimously in 2016 to pursue status as an AIOC, or Indigenous First Peoples' Peasant Autonomy (Pereyra 2016). The Yurakaré conception of autonomy included five main points: self-government; a statute consisting of self-defined rules and procedures; election of Yurakaré authorities according to traditional customs; use of justice under their own rules and procedures; and management, administration, and social control of natural resources on Yuracaré land (Ponce Vargas 2016, 53).[4]

The deep coordination between the Bolivian national government and coca growers might explain these autonomy demands. The 2005 election of President Evo Morales, a former general secretary of the main *cocalero* union, bolstered the colonists. The Morales government refused to enforce existing laws protecting much of the Indigenous territory. His administration likewise legalized coca production across a large swath of productive land in the region (Polygon 7), thereby incentivizing *cocalero* migrants to seize Indigenous land in this area for coca cultivation (Achtenberg 2012; Morales 2013, 84).[5] The *cocaleros* further monopolized control over local politics in the Chapare under the banner of Morales's Movement for Socialism (MAS) political party (Anria 2018, 82–85, 124; Crabtree and Chaplin 2013).

Chapare thus differs from the other cases discussed in this book. Whereas turn-of-the-twentieth-century labor extraction often pitted rural elites against the state (and viceversa), contemporary Chapare involves "joint" extraction: where rural elites extract with the government's active support. How can we explain the effects of this joint extraction, and why did it lead to autonomy demands in Chapare?

---

4. The adoption of AIOC is still pending, largely due to internal divisions over the charter's content and bureaucratic delays.

5. As one researcher noted following fieldwork in the region in 2016, "Currently . . . [the settlers] continue invading the lands of the indigenous people in general and the Yurakarés in particular, in search of natural resources and land suitable for growing coca. . . . For this reason, the Yurakarés say they live in times of the 'Colla [highland] colonizers'" (Ponce Vargas 2016, 24, author translation).

One possibility is that communities may have assigned particular blame to the Morales government for colonization and other extractive experiences, which could have generated effects closer to those I observed for state-led extraction. Indigenous communities have frequently noted the Morales administration's role in encouraging rural elites to take Indigenous land. In 2011, the Morales government launched a program to construct a highway originating in Villa Tunari (the capital of Chapare province) that would dissect the Isidoro Sécure National Park and Indigenous Territory (TIPNIS).[6] The 36 communities holding land in TIPNIS categorically rejected the project, arguing it "would be disastrous and devastating for our land, its ecosystems, and our ways of life as a people" (Sub Central de Pueblos Indígenas: Mojeños-Yurace-Chimane del TIPNIS 2012). Indigenous groups were also concerned that the road would make them more vulnerable to land extraction by Morales's *cocalero* allies (Fabricant and Postero 2015, 454; Kenner and Paz 2012; Laing 2018, 173).

Morales openly called on settlers to take Indigenous land to facilitate his construction of the highway. He reportedly said, "If I had time, I would go and make the Yuracaré women fall in love and convince them not to oppose [the road]. So, young men, you have instructions from the President to win over your compañeras [female friends] so that they do not oppose the construction of the road" (author translation).[7] In response, native leaders launched a series of marches demanding an end to the highway construction. Fabricant and Postero (2015) argue that these marches were partly driven by fear that a highway would lead to "increased invasion of the TIPNIS area by coca-growing colonizers living nearby" (454).[8]

The TIPNIS affair showed many Indigenous communities that "national interests in resource extraction would take precedence over locally based claims for indigenous autonomy" (Tockman and Cameron 2014, 60) and that the government had "limited ability—or willingness . . . to enact the promises it had made about representing and protecting indigenous peoples and their lands and customs" (Postero 2017, 131). Indigenous leader Rafael Quispe asserts that with the TIPNIS case, "the government has revealed

6. See, e.g., Achtenberg (2012).

7. See Infobae (2011, August 8).

8. These protests hardened Morales's resolve. Postero (2017) argues that "the controversy over the TIPNIS highway . . . made it clear that Morales was willing to sacrifice indigenous lands to extractivist development projects" (168).

its true identity, its indigenous mask has fallen and revealed its neoliberal face" (Orellana Candia 2011, 39, author translation). Communities directly affected by the road construction felt this betrayal by the Morales government most acutely; it appears to have shaped their decisions to pursue AIOC status. Delgado asserts that the TIPNIS conflict is inseparable from broader debates around Indigenous autonomy and self-determination (Delgado 2017, 375). More broadly, Indigenous leaders often note the importance of natural resource extraction and territorial loss when weighing the costs and benefits of pursuing autonomy (Augsburger and Haber 2018).

### 8.1.3   Discussion

These two analyses suggest it is important to exercise caution when applying the theory beyond the cases of Peru and Bolivia at the turn of the twentieth century. Timing, for example, is important in two ways. First, in the immediate term, state-led extraction reduced Navajo demands for autonomy. Over the long term, however, it increased them. The length of time it takes for autonomy demands to emerge is likely correlated with the extent to which state-led extraction co-opts Indigenous institutions—and the ease with which Indigenous peoples can replace colluding authorities.[9] Other factors can further delay the emergence of autonomy demands, including low trust in the state's willingness or capacity to respond faithfully to Indigenous mobilization.[10]

Timing also matters in a second way. New "critical junctures" of extraction can replace and undermine former ones. The Chapare case, for example, demonstrates that the effects of early rural elite extraction, which generally promoted demands for assimilation in Cochabamba (Chapter 5), may be eclipsed by later experiences of joint or state-led extraction. Consistent with the critical junctures framework, assessing the effects of historical extraction requires us to understand not only legacies but also when a legacy might end.

Beyond findings for the Navajo and Chapare cases, other scope conditions are also worth noting. For instance, I would not expect my predictions

9. Here, it is worth mentioning that Indigenous communities could not easily replace colluding authorities on large estates because, as described in Chapters 4 and 5, landowners (not community members) often appointed and dismissed Indigenous leaders.

10. The theory suggests that state-led extraction should erode confidence in the government, perhaps making such delays expected. This was the case, for example, for Peruvian labor conscription discussed in Chapter 6 (Figure 6.5).

regarding rural elite extraction to apply to the United States, as rural sector unions were much less prevalent, particularly on tribal reservations. Robust social organizations, as discussed in Chapter 1, are needed to mobilize and sustain resistance along class or ethnic lines over time.

The intensity of extraction also conditions the likelihood of observing my hypothesized effects. If extraction is too limited in impact or short-lived, it is unlikely to create enduring transformations (critical junctures) that shape long-term paths of political engagement. Conversely, if extraction is so strong that it destroys communities through death or out-migration, the theorized effects (which depend on preserving communal units) will not be observed. Thus, the predictions outlined in this book require extraction to be intense and enduring enough to generate resistance but not so severe that it tears communities apart.

Notwithstanding the scope conditions discussed above, the theory performs well beyond the cases of turn-of-the-twentieth-century labor extraction in Latin America. The analysis of the Navajo Livestock Reduction Act suggests that state-led extraction ultimately sparked resistance along ethnic lines, increased investments in Indigenous institutions, and promoted demands for autonomy. The Chapare case demonstrates that government involvement in land seizures is associated with increased ethnic mobilization and demands for autonomy. Further work should explore how communities assign blame for extraction—i.e., why the Bolivian government receives more blame for joint extraction than Chapare's colonists. Likewise, scholars might examine the conditions under which Indigenous communities remove colluding leaders. The Navajo replaced their Tribal Council with one that more faithfully represented tribal interests. Yet, communities' ability to punish colluding leaders likely varies in ways that have not been systematically analyzed.[11]

## 8.2   Universal vs. Selective Demanders

My theory represents a first effort to examine the historical foundations of demands for autonomy, assimilation, and integration. Yet, the likelihood that these legacies emerge—and the vigor with which they endure—depend on

11. Future research should also study how contemporary natural resource extraction affects mobilization for autonomy. Arce (2014) and Jaskoski (2022) examine important examples of contemporary Indigenous community responses to such extraction but devote less attention to enduring patterns of ethnic mobilization.

key institutional and structural conditions.[12] These factors might be considered comparative statics in my theoretical model. Some communities may express autonomy demands regardless of the political and economic environment, while in others, these demands may be latent and only activated in a favorable opportunity space. The relationship between state-led extraction and autonomy should be strongest under democracies, in post-conflict peace agreements (Van Cott 2001), where religious competition exists (Trejo 2012), and under neoliberal citizenship regimes (Yashar 2005). Integration demands may be more likely in democratic contexts because minoritized Indigenous groups can credibly obtain meaningful institutional representation. Finally, the relationship between rural elite extraction and assimilation should be strongest in closed political regimes; through corporatist arrangements and other forms of co-optation, autocratic governments reward demands that emphasize conformity (assimilation) over those that recognize diversity (autonomy and integration).

Factors beyond regime type might also shape the central state's willingness to respond to Indigenous groups' demands. In other work, I demonstrate how an extractive logic can also explain these supply-side government calculations. Rural elites in the nineteenth and early twentieth centuries often blocked central government efforts to recognize autonomy, which threatened their ability to extract Indigenous land, labor, and natural resources (Carter 2024b). Only when these rural elites experienced a sustained decline in their economic and political power, mainly due to import substitution industrialization policies and urbanization, did an enduring space open to recognize Indigenous autonomy. While not the primary focus of this book, these supply-side calculations shape Indigenous communities' willingness to make demands.

A similar logic can also explain the expression of nonautonomy demands. Communities that were subjected to rural elite extraction and then mobilized by unions and left parties may have been more willing to embrace peasant identities to obtain benefits from assimilationist administrations. Yet, even communities that otherwise preferred autonomy or integration may have strategically adopted class identities in response to these government incentives. In Chapter 7, I discussed such strategic behavior and established that

12. Díaz-Polanco (1998) notes, "The specific features of autonomy will be determined, on the one hand, by the historical nature of the collectivity that exercises it . . . and on the other, by the political orientation and degree of democracy in the state in which it acquires institutional and practical existence" (95).

the Peruvian government's embrace of "Indigenismo" caused many communities to eschew integrationist demands in favor of assimilation or autonomy. The above discussion suggests that labor extraction is not a deterministic predictor of Indigenous demands; national-level political and economic factors can influence which of the posited pathways is most likely to be observed.

The degree to which Indigenous demands translate into behavior also appears to vary. While some communities may consistently express their sincere demands (what I call "universal demanders"), others may be more strategic ("selective demanders"). More fine-grained distinctions can be made with respect to the degree to which communities are selective demand-makers, but I focus on a dichotomous distinction. I assume a community's demand-making type is a fixed characteristic determined prior to extraction. This type may reflect, for example, differences in risk aversion. Risk-averse communities are more likely to be selective demanders—advocating autonomy only when the structural and institutional conditions are favorable to its achievement. Risk-seeking communities are more likely to be universal demanders. These traits may themselves be legacies of historical discrimination and material deprivation.[13] Communities that have been more historically marginalized, for example, may more willingly take risks to change the status quo (i.e., universal demanders).[14]

There appear to be relatively few universal demanders. This book has established that most communities are at least somewhat selective about when they make demands. In Peru, for example, most communities that experienced state-led labor conscription initially rejected autonomy before taking up the cause later in the twentieth century. In the United States, the Navajo rejected autonomy when it was offered by an extractive government and a non-credible Tribal Council but became one of its most vocal proponents in subsequent decades. That demands are contingent and dynamic challenges a prevailing assumption in the literature: that autonomy is a universal (and relatively fixed) demand of Indigenous communities. This also provides

---

13. In this way, the sociocultural and distributive theories discussed in Chapters 1 and 2 can be instructive.

14. The alternative, however, is also plausible: they may be less willing to take risks that could cause further deprivation. For simplicity, I treat demander type as exogenous to historical experiences of extraction, but future theoretical work may explore the consequences of endogenizing these types.

an important contrast with the distributive and sociocultural approaches to ethnic autonomy discussed in Chapters 1 and 2.

Communities are thus not monoliths. Understanding their demands involves investigating three questions: (1) what communities prefer (and why), (2) when these preferences translate into political action, and (3) whether communities can sustain demands for autonomy over time. Claiming a right at a single moment in time, when accompanied by substantial mobilization of human or financial resources, may result in the adoption of a given policy. However, implementation and continued enforcement require sustained pressure and mobilization by those who benefit from the policy. Successfully demanding, achieving, and sustaining autonomy, therefore, involves a complex configuration of factors, some of which scholars have fully explored; others, including those highlighted in this book, have received less attention.

## 8.3   The Implications of Realized Autonomy Demands

It is impossible to separate the adoption of autonomy from its expected effects. Both states and Indigenous communities likely consider the potential implications of autonomy for welfare and governance before pursuing it. Prior empirical and theoretical work suggests opposing predictions. Some scholars might expect autonomy to jeopardize community welfare and reduce the prospects for democracy by creating alternative allegiances to non-state traditional institutions that can be exploitative or authoritarian (Popkin 1979). Indigenous autonomy may also reinforce ethnic identities or generate conflict among Indigenous peoples, both of which can undermine democracy and economic welfare (Eisenstadt 2007; Fontana 2022; Rabushka and Shepsle 1972; Recondo 2007).

However, there are also clear indications that autonomy strengthens both democratic consolidation and local welfare. On a number of domains, Indigenous institutions may promote better governance, serving as a valuable complement to otherwise low-capacity states. Greater collaboration between the government and traditional leaders—a necessary precondition for autonomy—can encourage state responsiveness and facilitate the provision of public goods (Baldwin 2015; Falleti and Riofrancos 2018; Honig 2022).[15] Recognizing Indigenous institutions has also been shown to

---

15. In my 2017 survey of Peruvian community presidents, 90 percent said they spoke with the mayor of their municipality at least once a month; over half said they spoke with the mayor

encourage historically marginalized Indigenous peoples to participate politically and engage with the state (McMurry 2022).[16]

Autonomy can likewise recognize and reinforce Indigenous institutions that *substitute* for an otherwise absent or ineffective state. In multiple contexts, scholars have found that formally recognizing chiefs,[17] tribal councils,[18] communal landholding arrangements,[19] and deliberative Indigenous assemblies[20] can have important and frequently positive welfare effects.[21] These improvements to local governance may preempt challenges to democracy that often arise in peripheral areas, including armed insurgent groups and populist, authoritarian politicians, who frequently use anti-establishment and anti-system appeals to build a support base among disaffected rural voters.

Despite the promise of autonomy, its effects heavily depend on the extent to which it is reliably enforced. State commitments to autonomy have been rightfully questioned. In Mexico, for instance, political parties frequently interfere in municipalities with purportedly autonomous Indigenous governments.[22] The Peruvian government recognized Indigenous communities in the 1920s but long retained the right to appoint communal authorities. The US government placed many limits on tribal authority in the wake of the 1934 IRA, which was supposed to offer tribes an unprecedented level of self-governance rights. Central governments in Bolivia and Panama have failed to provide

---

once a week. Fifty-six percent believed that a personal relationship between the mayor and community president was important for the community to receive assistance from the municipal government. Forty-two percent said the size of the community was important, and 24 percent said the community's distance from the district capital was important. Almost half (46 percent) said the mayor had come to them to learn about problems in their community.

16. The desire to preserve protections for Indigenous institutions may motivate this participation. Returning to my survey of Peruvian Indigenous community leaders, 63 percent said that if a community wanted assistance from the municipality, it was important to have community members in the local government. Over 50 percent of presidents said that the mayor during their term of office was from an Indigenous community. For a counterexample, see Hiskey and Goodman (2011).

17. See, e.g., Van der Windt et al. (2018); Baldwin (2013, 2015); Henn (2023).

18. See, e.g., Murtazashvili (2016); Washburn (1984); Kelly (1975); Mekeel (1944).

19. See, e.g., Cramb and Wills (1990); McMurry (2022); Sjaastad and Bromley (1997); cf. Place and Hazell (1993).

20. See, e.g., Díaz-Cayeros et al. (2014).

21. See, e.g., Honig (2022) demonstrates other important complementarities between state and traditional institutions.

22. See, e.g., Recondo (2007); Benton (2017); and Eisenstadt (2011).

adequate financial resources to autonomous Indigenous governments, which has thwarted the provision of key public goods and reduced grassroots support for autonomy (Carter 2022).[23] A prevailing theory among practitioners with whom I have spoken is that governments often undermine autonomy, viewing it as creating a potential competitor for legitimacy and authority and a more difficult set of institutions to manipulate. A high-ranking official in Bolivia explained to me that the municipality of Huacaya had experienced numerous delays in its autonomy application, largely because the central government did not want to replace a copartisan MAS mayor with an Indigenous assembly.[24]

While governments may actively undermine Indigenous autonomy, a lack of capacity may also prevent faithful implementation and enforcement of autonomy frameworks. In some cases, overburdened bureaucracies simply cannot efficiently process autonomy requests. Several officials and Indigenous leaders in Bolivia mentioned that the lengthy bureaucratic review associated with applying for political autonomy hinders its implementation; too few employees and too little information can delay final government approval by a decade.

The effects of autonomy also depend on the nature of traditional Indigenous institutions. The basic principles underlying these institutions—such as direct democracy, reciprocity, and redistribution—may remain constant, but their institutional form has often shifted, leading to variation in institutional strength (Baldwin and Ricart-Huguet 2023; Honig 2022). Hierarchical institutions are often more effective at interfacing with the state and overcoming some of the issues of resource distribution described above.[25] A single point of contact with substantial power within a community (e.g., a chief) can become a valuable ally for government officials. At the same time, however, these leaders may be vulnerable to state co-optation, reducing their responsiveness to community member demands.

23. See also Falleti (2005).

24. Interview with Bolivian government official, La Paz, July 2023.

25. A key contribution of this book is demonstrating one important source of this variation in institutional strength, by examining pivotal experiences with extraction. Under state-led conscription, power relations within communities became more vertically structured with leaders taking on more powerful roles. Where conscription and debt peonage were both experienced, Indigenous institutions were integrated into unions: many Indigenous leaders became union officials, and some unions in Bolivia even adopted the structure of Indigenous communities, or *ayllus* (see Chapter 7).

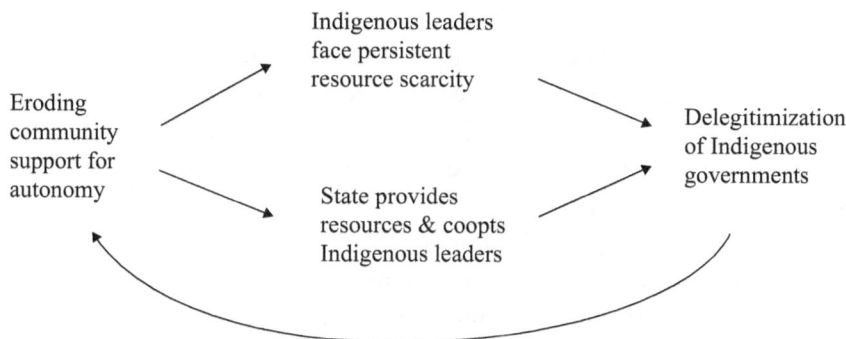

FIGURE 8.2. Autonomy-eroding spiral

Autonomy's impact on welfare shapes communities' likelihood of pursuing and preserving it. If it does not improve outcomes—due to government failures in enforcement or poor performance by traditional institutions—this can generate an *autonomy-eroding spiral* through one of two paths (Figure 8.2). First, a persistent lack of resources—due to willful or involuntary government action—can prevent Indigenous leaders from fulfilling the responsibilities that constituents (i.e., community members) increasingly assign to autonomous governments. This may delegitimize Indigenous leaders and traditional institutions and increase local demand for a return to governance through state institutions, as has occurred in some parts of Bolivia (Stauffer 2018). In the second path, Indigenous leaders accept greater state control (i.e., co-optation) in exchange for more access to government resources.[26] If Indigenous leaders are viewed as extensions of the central state (rather than independent decision-makers), Indigenous community members may lose their confidence in autonomous governments. Both of these paths, therefore, threaten to erode support for autonomy.

Consistent with this book's argument, Indigenous mobilization to demand resources and meaningful autonomy can prevent the emergence of these

---

26. Indigenous leaders must constantly balance what has—in scholarship on trade unions—been labeled an autonomy-control dilemma (Dahl 1982). Returning to the points raised in Chapter 3, Indigenous leaders and the state have misaligned interests. State officials seek to offer as little policy and financial support as they can to exert control over Indigenous communities and their leaders. Indigenous leaders, on the other hand, seek to maximize the support they receive from the state while minimizing government control. Given historical power imbalances, Indigenous leaders, where they have had bargaining power at all, have often had to accept greater state control in exchange for resources.

spirals—but only in the context of sustained autonomy demands. Communities that developed a historical capacity to mobilize on behalf of autonomy demands should be more likely to do so to promote autonomy's faithful implementation and enforcement (even if the state has low capacity or otherwise lacks credibility).[27] In fact, in other work, I show that this is very often the case (Carter 2024a).[28]

Achieving meaningful and enduring government protection can generate a more virtuous cycle of Indigenous autonomy (and prevent the autonomy-eroding spiral). Communities that receive rights in one period are especially likely to mobilize if those rights are removed or revoked in the future. In Latin America, the initial recognition of rights in the mid-twentieth century set an expectation among Indigenous groups about access to both the state and government protections for workers and ethnic collectives (Yashar 1998). Indigenous communities had acquired a sense of what the state could, and perhaps should, provide. States that reneged on their commitment to autonomy provoked further mobilization for government protection of ethnic institutions and rights.[29] Autonomy may be self-reinforcing even if not threatened or revoked. Recognizing traditional Indigenous political institutions increases the legitimacy and power of ethnic leaders, expanding their ability to mobilize their communities to achieve and defend autonomy. Issuing collectively held titles to Indigenous lands has similar effects; since Indigenous elites mediate access to collectively held land, they can withdraw access to it if community members do not participate in collective action.[30]

Thus, while the welfare effects associated with autonomy are generally thought to be positive, they depend on the government's willingness or ability to enforce existing protections for Indigenous institutions. Indigenous groups

27. In Latin America, for example, states' inability (O'Donnell 1996) or unwillingness (Holland 2017) to implement and enforce the law—particularly in the peripheral areas where Indigenous populations are likely to reside—raises serious questions about the effective recognition of Indigenous rights.

28. Communities that did *not* develop the capacity to collectively mobilize (or that lost it) are more likely to view autonomy under non-credible governments as a lost cause; they are more likely to pursue integration or assimilation instead.

29. The repeal of the Indian tribute, for example, threatened Indigenous groups' long-standing rights to communal land and political self-governance, provoking rebellions in Peru and other parts of Latin America.

30. Mexican Indigenous leaders often said this was how they compelled participation in unpaid labor (Author interviews, Oaxaca, February 2017).

(especially those with a history of sustained ethnic mobilization) may mobilize to ensure that the state respects and protects their autonomy.[31]

## 8.4 Rethinking Indigenous Mobilization

Debates over the relative importance of class and ethnicity as alternative strategies of political mobilization have been a defining feature of political life in contemporary societies. In urban areas of Sub-Saharan Africa, individuals in some neighborhoods are more likely to vote along a class identity, while ethnic ties determine others' vote choice (Nathan 2019). In Malaysia, ethnic divisions—particularly between Chinese and Malays—have inhibited the emergence of robust, multiethnic political coalitions based on common class interests (Bertrand 2013, 119). And in the United States, *The New York Times* has run headlines that read, "Should Biden Emphasize Race or Class or Both or None of the Above?" and "An End to the Class vs. Race Debate."[32] Studies of when marginalized groups mobilize along class as opposed to ethno-racial lines—and which strategy is more likely to inspire enduring change—thus remain central to modern politics.

Yet, class and ethnic identities have often been complementary forms of mobilization—as in the case of integration demands. While this book is not the first to highlight such complementarities, it is among the first to analyze the conditions under which these two forms of organizing are substituting versus complementary. It has also demonstrated that complementarity is more likely to occur on clearly defined domains: unions and left parties are more likely to incorporate demands for ethnic cultural rights (e.g., Indigenous languages) over those that advocate broader political and economic transformations (e.g., self-governance rights for Indigenous communities or collective landholding).

The form that mobilization takes (class, ethnic, or a hybrid of the two) ultimately shapes policy outputs and outcomes. Aggregating Indigenous groups' demands into large-scale organizations has resulted in national-level policy change (Jackson and Warren 2005; Van Cott 2005; Yashar 2005). Yet,

---

31. Other institutional and structural factors can also facilitate a climate in which communities can achieve and maintain autonomy, including those mentioned above: the existence of pluricultural constitutions and peace agreements (Van Cott 2001), religious competition (Trejo 2012), and favorable citizenship regimes (Yashar 2005).

32. See, e.g., Banks (2018); Edsall (2021).

local Indigenous communities must often mobilize by themselves to demand and achieve implementation and enforcement. In the cases I have examined, there appears to be a trade-off between the large-scale movements that promote *adopting* autonomy and the more local-level organization necessary to implement and enforce it. Peruvian communities' ability to organize has allowed most of them to achieve recognition and collective titles first offered in the 1920s; yet, the failure of these communities to aggregate into large-scale Indigenous organizations has likely thwarted further extensions of Indigenous rights in subsequent decades. In contrast, Bolivian Indigenous groups have achieved several key national-level policy concessions, including collective land titles and political autonomy; yet, these reforms have, to date, benefited a relatively small proportion of the country's Indigenous communities. Whether or not large-scale mobilization crowds out more local forms of organizing—and viceversa—might serve as fruitful ground for future research.

Indigenous communities' achievements have expanded the universe of groups demanding and receiving autonomy. For instance, Afro-descendant populations in Honduras and Nicaragua have nominally obtained political autonomy, and Colombia's 1991 Constitution provided a legal means to recognize and title communal land for the country's Afro-descendant communities.[33] Conversations around Indigenous autonomy have also arisen in Sub-Saharan Africa, where a host of minoritized ethnic groups that did not historically identify as Indigenous are now using the language of Indigeneity to demand rights from the state, including autonomy (Ndahinda 2011, 6–7).

The successes of Indigenous rights movements have kept ethnic identities and institutions salient despite deep structural changes. Indigenous groups in cities are increasingly mobilizing around ethnic identities and articulating their demands through neighborhood associations and school boards (Horn 2022, 43). These organizations may become new spaces through which Indigenous communities—which have been increasingly transplanted into urban and peri-urban areas—can communicate autonomy demands.

---

33. Yet, as with Indigenous communities in Latin America, governments have erected barriers to this autonomy. As Katerí Hernández observes, "Afro-Colombians have been dissuaded from pursuing the land title process. . . . Afro-Colombian community organizers seeking collective ownership have seen themselves labeled as guerrillas or terrorists and then targeted for violence by a government interested in controlling resource-rich Afro-Colombian areas" (Hernández 2013, 116).

While recent decades have ushered in new and expanded patterns of Indigenous mobilization, ethnic organizations are nothing new to Latin American history. In fact, examining the past 500 years, the class-based mobilization that has occupied much scholarly attention appears to be a relatively new phenomenon when analyzed alongside the Indigenous revolts of the colonial period; the postcolonial ethnic uprisings throughout the Andes, Central America, and Mexico; the important Indigenous organizations in early twentieth-century Peru, Bolivia, and Chile; and the contemporary rise of Indigenous movements throughout the region.

Understanding the evolution and transformation of ethnic mobilization provides insight into contemporary Indigenous organizations, communities, and movements, which have complex and multifaceted demands. Some prioritize autonomy, while others want integration—or even assimilation.[34] Exploring and explaining this heterogeneity has been the central goal of my book. The findings challenge a fundamental assumption underlying most previous work on Indigenous mobilization: that Indigenous groups uniformly want autonomy. They also highlight that Indigenous groups' present-day preferences are a dynamic legacy of prior patterns of mobilization.

********

This book has demonstrated how historical extraction by the state and rural elites influenced future Indigenous-state relations. Such extraction generated distinct patterns of initial resistance. It conditioned how Indigenous communities invested in different identities and institutions. And, ultimately, it shaped demands for autonomy, assimilation, and integration—with important implications for community welfare.

These observations do not suggest, however, that the current state of native communities was an inevitable outcome of past exploitation. Other factors may have also shaped Indigenous groups' institutional investments and demands, including levels of market integration and exposure to non-extractive forms of state repression. Some communities may also have valued Indigenous institutions more than others—for idiosyncratic or systematic reasons, including, perhaps, extraction. My explanation is not intended to provide a definitive account but rather to offer a first effort to explore variation

---

34. Even this characterization is likely too coarse, as many communities advocate a set of demands that include claims that fall into each of these three categories.

in when communities demand autonomy as opposed to other forms of inclusion.[35]

This book has established that Indigenous peoples do not simply accept exploitation, whether this consists of acute experiences of labor extraction or more enduring (and perhaps subtler) forms of exclusion and marginalization. They have mobilized and resisted—to protect their short-term well-being and promote the long-term welfare of their communities. Through this mobilization, native communities—as peasants and as Indigenous peoples, through unions and ethnic organizations—have debated, shaped, and redefined what it means to be included in the postcolonial nation-states that have so often sought to exclude them.

35. An investigation of the effects of other, potentially complementary factors is left for future research.

# Discussion of Chapter 6
# Research Design

CHAPTER 6 analyzes a regression-discontinuity design (RDD) in Peru, where a community's proximity to a border dividing conscription from non-conscription provinces serves as a measure of exposure to state-led extraction under President Augusto Leguía. This appendix provides supplementary materials to discuss the design, data, and potential limitations.

## A.1   Tests of RDD Assumptions

To test the main identifying assumption of the RDD—continuity of potential outcomes across treat-control borders—I perform a series of balance tests. I analyze six municipal-level covariates for which pre-treatment data is available. These include measures of ethnic and economic composition, taken from an 1876 census: number of haciendas, total population, number of Indigenous communities, rural population, and Indigenous population. I also analyze the percentage of residents of each municipality with primary education, which is taken from a 1902 education census. Balance tests show that municipalities on either side of the border did not exhibit significant pre-treatment differences on potentially important covariates.[A1] Sorting may also pose a threat to inference if municipalities select into or out of Qhapaq Ñan provinces, but there is no evidence of this from a conditional density (McCrary) test ($p = 0.23$).[A2]

---

A1. There are no extant pre-treatment measures of the outcome; however, Figure A.1 shows balance on a proxy measure of bilingualism: percent of individuals in 1902 with primary education.

A2. See Figure A.2.

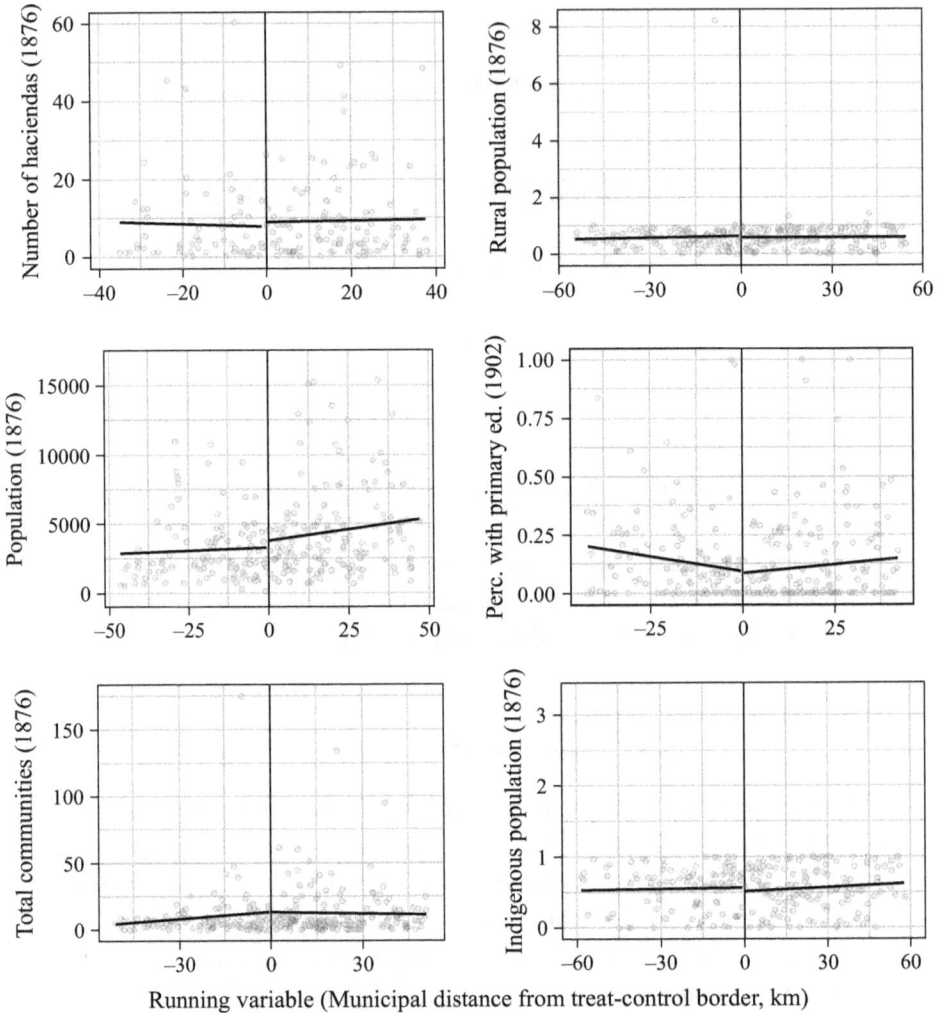

FIGURE A.1. Test of balance on available pre-treatment covariates
*Note*: Data taken from 1876 National Population Census and 1901 Census of
Schools. None of the above tests are significant at $p < 0.1$. The data has been
binned, and shading of points indicates the density of observations at each value
of the running variable.

A second assumption requires that a municipality's potential outcomes
depend only on whether it is in a Qhapaq Ñan province and not on whether
other municipalities are "assigned" to a Qhapaq Ñan province. The particular
concern in this case is that one municipality's exposure to labor conscription
may generate mobilization that spills over to other communities that are not

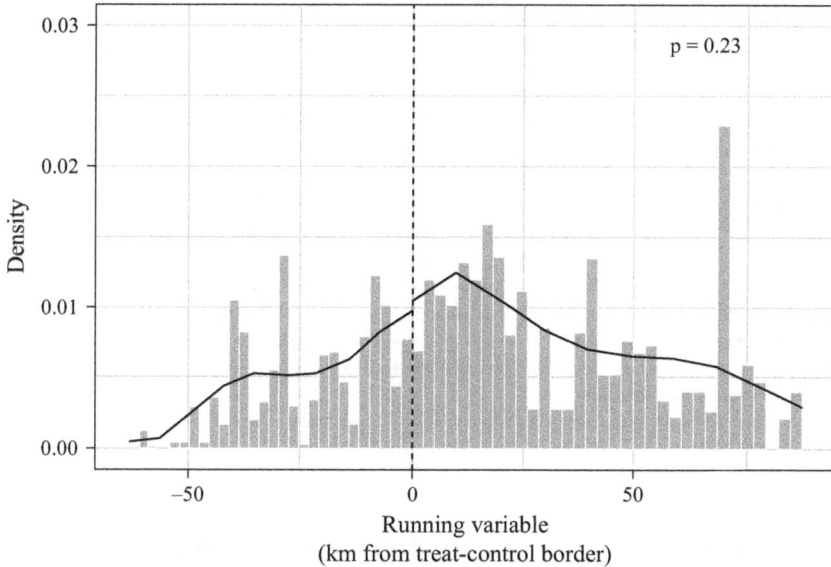

FIGURE A.2. Test of sorting around cut point

exposed to labor conscription. As I discuss in the next section, I find no evidence of this.[A3] Individual movement out of communities would not represent a concern for spillovers as individuals must be born in a community to achieve membership. Any movement out of a community is thus part of the treatment but not a threat to the noninterference assumption as individuals cannot easily relocate from one community to another.[A4]

A further concern involves bundling of the treatment; those provincial officials exposed to the treatment—and who have access to Leguía's roads— may have adopted different policies toward Indigenous communities than governments in control provinces. However, in the Peruvian case, provincial governments control neither recognition nor Indigenous policy more generally, making this unlikely to account for the differences I observe for autonomy and assimilation.[A5]

A3. Furthermore, if such spillovers did occur in a widespread way, we would expect no significant effect of conscription on mobilization.

A4. Table A.1 refutes the out-migration theory; communities that experienced conscription were larger in 2012 than those that did not.

A5. Provincial governments could have altered their behavior—due to conscription—in ways that shaped Indigenous collective action. While I do not find evidence supporting this, it cannot be completely dismissed.

TABLE A.1. Effect of conscription on community size and year of recognition

|  | Comm. size | Comm. size | Year of rec. | Year of rec. |
|---|---|---|---|---|
| QN Province | 53.850*** (13.601) | 45.351*** (14.584) | 14.483*** (3.949) | 11.794*** (3.159) |
| BW selector | CER | MSE | CER | MSE |
| BW | 19 | 23 | 17 | 22 |
| N | 2778 | 2778 | 2332 | 2332 |

Note: *p < 0.1; **p < 0.05; ***p < 0.01. Estimates taken from a local linear regression-discontinuity analysis. The running variable is the municipality's distance from a border dividing a treated (i.e., Qhapaq Ñan) province from a control one. SEs clustered at province level. Dependent variable is community size and year of community recognition.

Sources: Instituto Nacional de Estadística e Informática (2014); Ministerio de Vivienda, Construccion, y Saneamiento (2009).

To test for a causal relationship between conscription and increased Indigenous mobilization, I use the regression-discontinuity design and the aforementioned database of Indigenous movements against municipal and provincial officials that occurred between 1920 and 1930. The movements are documented at the municipal level.[A6] Importantly, for noninterference concerns, there is no evidence of cross-provincial mobilization in response to conscription.[A7]

## A.2 Data and Coding of Variables

This section outlines the coding of the main independent and dependent variables used in this study. I also detail the main data sources used in the analyses. Below, I address potential issues that may arise with these data sources.

A6. Data on each movement is generally limited; most entries contain only the names of the communities that mobilized, the target of mobilization (e.g., a landowner, municipal prefect), and a general statement of the complaint (e.g., abuses, land seizures).

A7. None of the movements I analyzed involved cross-provincial mobilization against conscription. This is likely because provincial governments were the primary target of Indigenous demands and an important intermediary with the national government. There were other instances, however, of cross-provincial mobilization, particularly when there was a national-level threat that almost uniformly threatened all communities (e.g., the nineteenth-century Indigenous head tax).

## A.3 Calculation of Running Variable

Data collection on the running and treatment variables involved an extensive review of primary and secondary sources. To calculate the distance to borders dividing treatment from control provinces, I first reconstructed the map of provincial borders in 1920. I used evidence from Kubler (1952), as well as an analysis of government laws mandating the creation of new provinces. I defined a study group as all provinces located in Peru's mountainous Andean region. Alberto Regal's *Los Caminos del Inca*, which compiles information from sixteenth-century travel documents, provided information on the location of the Qhapaq Ñan (Regal 1936). Based on my archival research, this was the source that reflects best what Leguía thought to be the location of the Inca Road in the 1920s. I used this information to code provinces in the Andes as containing a portion of the Inca Road or not. I also collected data on Leguía-era road construction from sources published at the end of Leguía's term.[A8]

I then used a straight-line distance measure to determine how far each municipality (the lowest level of administration in Peru) was from a border dividing a treatment from a control province. I calculated distances of municipalities to provincial borders using a variety of official, government-issued maps from the period. All communities can be considered cluster-assigned to their distance from a treat-control border. Communities inside a control province are given negative value on the running variable (in km), and those inside a treated province are given a positive value (in km).

### Data on Conscripted Workers

To my knowledge, no systematic data exists at any level—national or subnational—on road conscription in Peru. Partial sources exist. These include Araujo Antonio (1991); Dirección de Vías de Comunicación (1928); Peru Dirección Nacional de Estadistica y Censos (1944). In some provinces, almost all male community members were forced to work, regardless of age. In the province of Lima, 44,800 workers were conscripted in just the first half of 1928 (Dirección de Vías de Comunicación 1928, 217); the 1940 Census

---

A8. The main source was Ministerio de Fomento (1930), a government source that documented the kilometers of road planned and constructed in each province under Leguía. I further cross-checked the data in this volume with two non-government sources: Díez Canseco and Aguilar Revoredo (1929) and Portaro (1930).

calculates that there were just over 67,000 Indigenous males in the entire province. In the province of Pallasca, about half of the Indigenous male population in 1940 (5,514 people) worked on a single project in 1928, and a much larger percentage (5,392) was included in the conscription rolls (Dirección de Vías de Comunicación 1928, 100). At this point, it is important to note that not all communities worked on every project; in the first half of 1928, for example, communities in a few districts in Pallasca sent more than two-thirds of their conscripts to work (Cabana, Tauca, and Llapo) while others sent fewer than 30 percent of their conscripts (Yupán and Cajamala).[A9] However, there is no evidence that these differences were correlated across time; in other words, even if a community avoided conscription in one period, there is no evidence that it also avoided conscription in future periods. For road conscription in Bolivia, slightly more comprehensive data is available at a lower level of analysis in Ministro del Ramo (1908); Prefecto de Cochabamba (1915); Prefecto de Oruro (1911) and Prefecto de Potosí (1916).

### The 2012 Agrarian Census

For all but one of the dependent variables, I draw on evidence from a 2012 census of agrarian communities. The census covered over 70 percent of Indigenous-peasant communities. There was one response from each community; the community leader was responsible for responding. Generally, there was a close correspondence between the responses to the community census and a survey I conducted of Indigenous community leaders in Cusco, Peru in 2017.

## A.4   DV: Community Recognition and Communal Land Titles

Each community leader was asked in the census if her community is registered with the central government. Community registration is an important Indigenous right in and of itself, as it entails governments recognizing the basic unit of Indigenous social, economic, and political organization: the community. This variable is thus coded as 0 or 1, where 0 indicates no recognition and 1 indicates recognition.

Community leaders were also asked if they have a completed title to their communal land. Some communities have incomplete titles because of

A9. See Dirección de Vías de Comunicación (1928, 99).

administrative delays or their failure to produce the required documentation. During my fieldwork, I learned that the best predictor of having a completed title is community effort. In other words, communities can achieve a communal title if they can produce the needed documentation and pressure the government to recognize their communal land. Thus, a completed title provides a measure of revealed preferences for autonomy. I use the question around having a completed title and code communities that have a completed title as 1 and all others as 0.

## A.5    DV: Indigenous Institutions Index

The census also asks about several Indigenous institutions. Using the available questions and information I learned during interviews and through an original survey, I construct an index of a series of yes/no questions that community leaders were asked (Table A.2). The first question asks whether traditional leaders remain in power in Indigenous communities. This is an important measure of the persistence of Indigenous political institutions. The second question asks whether members of the community council comply with their requirements to provide unpaid services to their community. This can require organizing and funding festivals for the community or serving as justice of the peace. This *cargo* system is common throughout Indigenous communities in Latin America. I then examine two questions around economic institutions: whether community members participate in communal work and whether there is communal farming. These are Indigenous institutions traditionally associated with subsistence agriculture and the moral—as opposed to market—economy (Scott 1977).

I then analyze a series of questions around social institutions, namely *ayni*, *minka*, and *mita*. While these terms are sometimes used interchangeably, they, in fact, have distinct meanings. Ayni involves the reciprocal exchange of labor between members of a community. For example, if one community member cannot harvest his crops because of illness, others in the community will come to help him, with the expectation that that assistance will be repaid in kind, if needed, at a later date. While ayni involves reciprocity among individual community members, minka and mita both involve community member obligations to the broader community. Minka often entails short-term work to build or repair infrastructure, such as roads, community centers, or schools— within the community. Mita involves unpaid labor that is provided for public

TABLE A.2. Components of index of Indigenous institutions

| Type of institution | Question in 2012 Cenagro |
| --- | --- |
| Political | 1) Are there traditional authorities in power? <br> 2) Do the members of the community council comply with the cargo system (unpaid, temporary service in community posts)? |
| Economic | 3) Do community members participate in communal work? <br> 4) Is there communal farming? |
| Social | 5) Do community members preserve ayni? <br> 6) Do community members preserve minka? <br> 7) Do community members preserve mita? |

works projects, often outside of the community. I sum the dummy variable values for each item to construct an index that can take on values from 0 to 7. An Item Response Theory (IRT) model of the index suggests a high correlation among the index components. The standardized root mean square residual (SRMSR) is 0.025, far less than the conventional benchmark of 0.08.

## A.6 Mechanism: Indigenous-Peasant Movements (1920–1930)

For the community collective mobilization outcome, I have compiled data from several primary and secondary sources. For the main outcome presented in the book, I use data from the Boletínes de Asuntos Indígenas, which include around five hundred Indigenous denunciations and movements that occurred between 1922 and 1930. I focus on Indigenous movements explicitly targeted at the road conscription law or abuses by local authorities; I do not include either denouncements by individuals or movements against large landowners. I supplement this analysis with data from secondary sources: Kammann (1982), Kapsoli and Reátegui (1987), and Kapsoli (1982). Kammann (1982) draws primarily on media and secondary sources for a subset of departments in the southern Andean region, and documents 104 Indigenous-peasant movements between the late 1800s and 1964; I focus on those against local authorities that occurred between 1920 and 1930. Kapsoli and Reátegui (1987) document hundreds of complaints filed in the Actas de la Patronato de la Raza Indígena by Indigenous communities between 1922 and 1930; I focus on those that concerned abuses by local authorities. I also include in the analysis a small number of movements documented as case studies in Kapsoli (1982, 68–79).

Many movements occurred within municipalities, and, thus, data is coded at that level. However, some movements occurred at the provincial level. In those cases, I code all municipalities within a province as having experienced an Indigenous movement, as more fine-grained data—which would allow for coding at the municipal level—is unavailable, and it is likely that many communities within the province were in fact part of the movement.

## A.7   Data Concerns and Limitations

The analysis in Chapter 6 relies primarily on evidence from a community census. The broad coverage of this census is a feature; to my knowledge, no other comprehensive, national-level dataset on Indigenous communities exists in Latin America. However, two issues arise from it, which could each threaten inference. First, about 30% of Indigenous communities are not included in the dataset, as census takers could not contact them. However, among the Andean subset used in my analysis, response rates are nearly 95%. Second, communities not affected by labor conscription could have been more likely to disband and disappear; this selective attrition could bias estimates, if, for example, the control group used in the analysis is a non-random subset of the true control group. I address the latter concern in Carter (2024a). Comparing data on communities in 1876 and 2009, I show that there is no difference in the survival of communities based on exposure to conscription.

A second issue also may be present in the census data. The outcomes are measured using self-reported data from Indigenous community leaders, who may overstate the prevalence of Indigenous languages and institutions. This is primarily an issue for determining the magnitude of effects. For example, the majority of leaders report preserving between three and five Indigenous institutions. Based on a survey I conducted with Indigenous community leaders and an interviews, there should be far more communities on the lower range of this index. In many communities in Cusco, for example, leaders in my survey reported not mobilizing any social institutions; yet, in the data, almost all communities in Cusco (> 97%) report doing so. This overreporting may explain the relatively low magnitude of the observed effect in Figure 6.4—an increase of about 0.3 items out of 7.

A third issue arises from the treatment. Here, I use an ITT analysis based on the location of the Inca Road because there is no comprehensive measure of the number of conscripts at any level—national or subnational. Partial estimates exist, such as the ones detailed in this appendix, but full data does not. I instead rely on *eligibility* for labor conscription, a weaker treatment than the *experience* of conscription. Archival and secondary sources suggest that communities generally knew about the road conscription program—and importantly their eligibility for it—even if they ultimately did not experience conscription. Many communities, as I discuss in the main text, that were eligible for conscription did, in fact, experience it.

A fourth issue may arise around the mobilization outcome. Districts coded as "0" in my compiled dataset may have experienced Indigenous mobilizations that were not covered or reported by any of the sources that have survived to the present. This concern is perhaps less problematic than it initially appears, as most community mobilizations involved communities traveling to the offices of provincial authorities—which were located in more populous provincial capitals. Therefore, even mobilization events by small communities were likely to be detected by newspapers, observers, or outposts of government agencies located in provincial capitals, where the revolts took place. Nevertheless, I attempt to address this issue through imputation. For all provinces where documentation on mobilizations is comparatively weak (i.e., the Northern and Central Sierra), I code all areas that did not have a documented mobilization—coded as not having had a mobilization in the main text—as having had a mobilization. The results remain strong and significant; the results are also robust to including only the municipalities that are present in the autonomy dataset.[A10]

A fifth issue could emerge from the use of the Kapsoli and Reátegui (1987) and Kapsoli (1982) data on Indigenous movements. One might be concerned that there is ideological bias in the reporting of movements, as Kapsoli was closely linked to Peru's peasant movement and had a stated interest in promoting a peasant revolution (de la Cadena 2000, 121). This does not seem to be the case. Kapsoli and Reátegui (1987) draw directly from 154 complaints in the Patronato de la Raza Indígena. While I could not verify all the sources

---

A10. Both analyses are included in Carter (2024a), along with an analysis to address missingness in the autonomy measure. NAs in the measure arise from missingness in the communal title component. I replace missing values with the mean of the communal title measure and perform the analyses described in the main text.

they consulted, the ones I could verify did not indicate selective reporting. Concerning the Kapsoli (1982) piece, I draw on a small collection of Indigenous movement case studies he conducts. I could verify from other sources that the movements documented in Kapsoli (1982) did, in fact, occur, and other accounts of these movements do not significantly diverge from his. More broadly, I have also not found any evidence or secondary sources to suggest that Kapsoli selectively reported data to promote his ideological goals.

A further point of discussion involves the design itself. I have noted some of the weaknesses of the design in the main text and specifically that it relies on an untestable assumption (continuity of potential outcomes) that is particularly hard to evaluate—with quantitative data—in this empirical case, given the relative lack of pre-treatment data. Despite this, the design generally performs well on the criteria highlighted by Dunning (2012) for a strong natural experiment. Based on the available data and first- and secondhand accounts of the road conscription program, the assumptions generally hold. The relevance of the intervention is also high; as I discuss in the main text, labor conscription was a moment of significant change that shaped the long-term evolution of Indigenous-state relations in Latin America. One concern on this domain involves a potential lack of external validity: can findings around a specific instance of labor conscription generalize to other cases and time periods? I address these points in the conclusion section of the main text. Finally, Dunning (2012) argues that the credibility of statistical models should be high in a strong natural experiment. While I do not rely on a difference-in-means in this case—as Dunning recommends—I use a nonparametric estimation strategy, which makes weaker assumptions than parametric estimation strategies.

Altitude presents another concern and could confound the results observed in this chapter. Altitude can only be calculated at the district level, preventing us from measuring differences in altitude across communities. Nevertheless, Carter (2024a) demonstrates that the results are observed across the different quartiles of municipal altitude.

Finally, a small collection of treated provinces—Huaraz, Huaylas, and Yungay in Ancash; Pachitea in Huanuco; and Ayabaca and Huancabamba in Piura—do not have a contiguous control province. I show in Carter (2024a) that the main results are robust to excluding these provinces.

# Relationship between Communal Landholding and Communal Labor

EXAMINING THE 2012 Census of Peruvian Indigenous and Peasant Communities, the relationship between communal landholding and the maintenance of traditional institutions of communal labor is robust. Indigenous leaders were asked which traditional institutions of reciprocity persist in their community: ayni, minka, and mita. They were also asked—more generally—whether the tradition of communal labor continues in their communities. Finally, they were asked whether lands within their communities are collectively held. Running a simple OLS regression of these different labor institutions on an indicator for whether a community maintains collectively held land suggests a strong, positive relationship (Table B.1).

However, leaders have also had to confront the fact that increased integration into external markets has raised the opportunity cost to community members of participating in these traditional institutions of unpaid communal labor. Several community presidents in Peru and Bolivia told me that the decline in the use of communal labor arose from an increased expectation of payment from community members.

In the survey I conducted in Cusco, I included questions that measure community presidents' self-perceptions of their power vis-à-vis state officials. Presidents were given a scenario in which their community needed a public good that would be provided with the unpaid labor of community members. They were first asked what percentage of their community's members would participate if the mayor organized the unpaid labor event; they were then asked what percentage would join if *they* organized the event. The difference in these estimates provides a measure of Indigenous leaders' perceptions of their own power vis-à-vis community members and state officials (Figure B.1). Just

TABLE B.1. Indigenous communal land and labor institutions, 2012 Peru

| | Dependent variable: | | | |
|---|---|---|---|---|
| | Ayni (1) | Minka (2) | Mita (3) | Communal labor (4) |
| Communal land | −0.005 | 0.084*** | 0.007** | 0.196*** |
| | (0.015) | (0.015) | (0.003) | (0.010) |
| Constant | 0.594*** | 0.507*** | 0.004 | 0.743*** |
| | (0.013) | (0.013) | (0.002) | (0.008) |
| Observations | 4,993 | 4,994 | 4,993 | 4,993 |
| $R^2$ | 0.00002 | 0.006 | 0.001 | 0.077 |
| Adjusted $R^2$ | −0.0002 | 0.006 | 0.001 | 0.077 |

Note: $^*p < 0.1$; $^{**}p < 0.05$; $^{***}p < 0.01$. Results are from an OLS regression of dependent variables on an indicator of communal landholding. The dependent variable in the fourth column is a three-item index that sums the binary indicators in each of the first three columns.
Source: Instituto Nacional de Estadística e Informática (2014).

over half of community presidents reported they had the same power as the mayor: there was no difference in the president's estimate based on whether they or the mayor organized the communal labor event. About 27 percent estimated they had more mobilizational power within their communities than the mayor. Eighteen percent suggested they had less mobilizational power than the mayor.

A notable observation from the above findings is that there has been a general decline in the power of Indigenous community leaders. Many believe that even on a central domain of their authority—the organization and mobilization of communal labor—they do not have a clear, competitive advantage over mayors. That a plurality also claim that communal labor institutions have declined is further evidence of an erosion of the authority of community leaders. These findings are particularly notable given that they are derived from the responses of community presidents, who might be incentivized to overstate their power.

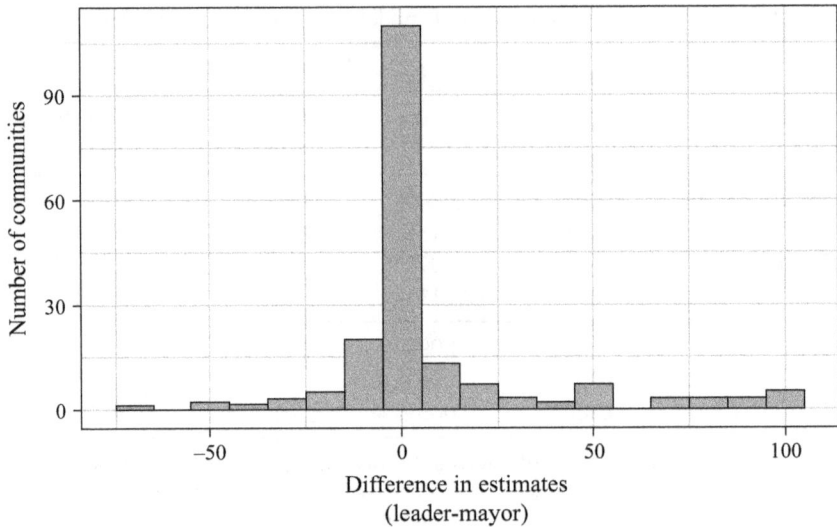

FIGURE B.1. Community leaders' self-assessment of power
*Note*: Data taken from a 2017-survey conducted by the author with current and former community presidents in Cusco, Peru. Community presidents were asked to estimate the percentage of community members they could mobilize for unpaid labor on a public good. They were then asked to estimate the percentage of community members the *mayor* could mobilize for the same unpaid labor event. A histogram of the differences in these estimates is plotted here. $N = 314$.

APPENDIX C

# Ethical Considerations of Interview Research

AS PART of the broader project of which this book is a part, I conducted semi-structured interviews with over seventy local officials, including bureaucrats, Indigenous leaders, and mayors. Because this research was conducted with elected authorities, it was reviewed by human subjects at UC Berkeley and deemed exempt from further review "as it satisfies the Federal and/or [university] requirements under category(ies) 2, 3" (IRB Protocol 2016-09-9126).

Every effort was taken to ensure that the highest ethical standards were maintained. Before beginning the interviews, the purpose of the research was explained—i.e., to understand dynamics of governance in Peruvian and Bolivian Indigenous communities—and verbal consent was obtained. Recordings were taken only with the consent of the community president or the mayor. Upon completion of fieldwork, recorded interviews were transcribed, identifying information was removed, and the recordings were destroyed to preserve anonymity. The research adheres to the 2020 APSA Principles and Guidance document submitted by the Ad Hoc Committee on Human Subjects Research.

APPENDIX D

# Information for Author-Conducted Surveys

TABLE D.1. Respondent traits: 2017 Peruvian Indigenous leader survey

| Variable | Mean |
| --- | --- |
| Head of household | 0.98 |
| Income (Less than S./100) | 0.27 |
| Income (between S./100 and S./600) | 0.42 |
| Income (More than S./600) | 0.31 |
| Male | 0.95 |
| Age | 48.34 |
| Education (Primary) | 0.72 |
| Education (Secondary) | 0.39 |
| Literate | 0.97 |
| Farmer | 0.64 |
| Business/sales | 0.06 |
| Laborer (other) | 0.06 |
| Construction | 0.10 |
| Current president | 0.59 |
| Private landholder | 0.79 |
| Resident of communal land | 0.16 |
| Previous municipal official | 0.41 |
| Distance to district capital ( < 1 hour) | 0.67 |

*Note*: All variables are binary except age ($N = 318$).

TABLE D.2. Respondent traits: 2020 Bolivian
Indigenous citizen survey

| Variable | Mean |
|---|---|
| Education (Primary) | 0.83 |
| Education (Secondary) | 0.66 |
| Income (sufficient to cover expenses) | 0.36 |
| Rural | 0.33 |
| Speaks Indigenous language | 0.70 |
| Member of Indigenous community | 0.33 |
| Member of Indigenous organization | 0.05 |
| Age | 35.24 |
| Female | 0.46 |
| Supporter of MAS political party | 0.50 |
| Self-employed | 0.42 |
| Public employee | 0.09 |

*Note*: All variables are binary except age ($N = 1,006$).

# Extraction Data for All Cusco Provinces

TABLE E.1. Extraction data for Cusco provinces

| Province | Road finished (kms) | Hacienda population (1876) | Hacienda population (1940) |
|---|---|---|---|
| Espinar | 0 | – | 10.4% |
| Chumbivilcas | 0 | 21.8% | 17.2% |
| **Paruro** | 0 | 54.2% | 20.7% |
| **La Convención** | 0 | 80.1% | 54.1% |
| **Paucartambo** | 8,500 | 58.9% | 51.9% |
| Calca | 12,000 | 24.8% | 33.1% |
| Urubamba | 32,000 | 42.8% | 23.5% |
| Acomayo | 35,000 | 9.1% | 8.2% |
| Andahuaylas | 37,000 | 34.7% | 15.5% |
| Anta | 40,000 | 19.6% | 35.7% |
| **Canas** | 136,000 | 0.6% | 11.2% |
| **Canchis** | 150,000 | 2.5% | 5.4% |
| **Quispicanchi** | 192,000 | 37.2% | 23.7% |
| **Cusco** | 217,000 | 41.2% | 33.5% |

*Note*: Road building data indicates exposure to state-led extraction. The hacienda data measure exposure to rural elite extraction in early (1876) and later (1940) periods. Bolded provinces are those included as case studies in the book.
*Sources*: Perez (1972); Macera (1976); Ministerio de Fomento (1930).

# BIBLIOGRAPHY

Abercrombie, T. A. (1998). *Pathways of Memory and Power: Ethnography and History Among an Andean People*. University of Wisconsin Press, Madison, WI.

Aberle, D. F. (1982). *The Peyote Religion Among the Navaho*. University of Oklahoma Press, Norman, OK.

Acemoglu, D., Johnson, S., and Robinson, J. A. (2001). The Colonial Origins of Comparative Development: An Empirical Investigation. *American Economic Review*, 91(5):1369–1401.

Achtenberg, E. (2012). Bolivia: TIPNIS Communities Divided As Road Consultation Begins.

Ackerman, E. F. (2021). *Origins of the Mass Party: Dispossession and the Party-Form in Mexico and Bolivia in Comparative Perspective*. Oxford University Press, Oxford, England.

Agencia de Noticias Fides. (2022, September 23). Foro expone las dificultades para acceder a la autonomía indígena y trámites que demoran más de 10 años. *Noticias Fides*.

Ahlquist, J. S. and Levi, M. (2013). *In the Interest of Others: Organizations and Social Activism*. Princeton University Press, Princeton.

Albiez-Wieck, S. (2022). *Taxing Difference in Peru and New Spain (16th–19th Century): Negotiating Social Differences and Belonging*. Brill, Middletown.

Albó, X. (1987). From MNRistas to Kataristas to Katari. In Stern, S., editor, *Resistance, Rebellion, and Consciousness in the Andean Peasant World, 18th to 20th Centuries*, pages 379–419. University of Wisconsin Press, Madison, WI.

Albó, X. (1999). Andean People in the Twentieth Century. In Salomon, F. and Schwartz, S. B., editors, *The Cambridge History of the Native Peoples of the Americas*, volume 3, pages 761–871. Cambridge University Press, Cambridge.

Albó, X. (2002a). Bolivia: From Indian and Campesino Leaders to Councillors and Parliamentary Deputies. In Sieder, R., editor, *Multiculturalism in Latin America: Indigenous Rights, Diversity and Democracy*, pages 74–103. Springer, New York.

Albó, X. (2002b). *Pueblos indios en la política*. CIPCA, La Paz.

Alejo, E. T., Ortuste, G. R., and Albó, X. (1994). *Votos y Wiphalas: campesinos y pueblos originarios en democracia*. Fundación Milenio, La Paz.

Alexander, R. J. (1972). Chilean Agricultural Workers' Unionization during the Frei Administration. *Journal of Economic Issues*, 6(2/3):15–28.

Andolina, R. (2003). The Sovereign and Its Shadow: Constituent Assembly and Indigenous Movement in Ecuador. *Journal of Latin American Studies*, 35(4):721–750.

Anria, S. (2018). *When Movements Become Parties: The Bolivian MAS in Comparative Perspective*. Cambridge Studies in Comparative Politics. Cambridge University Press, Cambridge.

Araujo Antonio, A. P. (1991). *El trabajo indígena gratuito en Junín y en Huamanga: 1890–1930.* Thesis, Universidad Nacional San Cristóbal de Huamanga, Ayacucho.

Arce, M. (2014). *Resource Extraction and Protest in Peru.* University of Pittsburgh Press.

Ari, W. (2014). *Earth Politics: Religion, Decolonization, and Bolivia's Indigenous Intellectuals.* Duke University Press, Durham.

Arias, A. (1990). Changing Indian Identity: Guatemala's Violent Transition to Modernity. In Smith, C., editor, *Guatemalan Indians and the State, 1540–1988,* pages 230–257. University of Texas Press, Austin.

Arroyo, C. (2004). La experiencia del Comité Central Pro-Derecho Indígena Tahuantinsuyo. *Estudios Interdisciplinarios de América Latina y el Caribe,* 15(1):185–208.

Augsburger, A. and Haber, P. (2018). Visions in conflict: State hegemony versus plurinationality in the construction of indigenous autonomy in Bolivia. *Latin American and Caribbean Ethnic Studies,* 13(2):135–156.

Ayala Mercado, E. (1955). *Qué sucede con la reforma agraria?* Publicaciones S.P.I.C. Subsecretaría de Prensa, Informaciones y Cultura, La Paz, Bolivia.

Baldwin, K. (2013). Why Vote with the Chief? Political Connections and Public Goods Provision in Zambia. *American Journal of Political Science,* 57(4):794–809.

Baldwin, K. (2015). *The Paradox of Traditional Chiefs in Democratic Africa.* Cambridge University Press, Cambridge, UK.

Baldwin, K. and Ricart-Huguet, J. (2023). Does Land Quality Increase the Power of Traditional Leaders in Contemporary Africa? *The Journal of Politics,* 85(1):334–339.

Banks, R. R. (2018). Opinion | An End to the Class vs. Race Debate. *The New York Times.*

Bao, R. M. and Indacochea, C. R. (2002). Los nuevos escenarios de los movimientos indígenas en el Perú. *Araucaria,* 4(8):92–108.

Basadre, J. (2014). *Historia de la República del Perú, 1822–1933,* volume 14. Producciones Cantabria, Lima.

Bates, R. H. (1983). Modernization, Ethnic Competition, and the Rationality of Politics in Contemporary Africa. In *State versus Ethnic Claims.* Routledge.

Baud, M. (2007). Liberalism, Indigenismo, and Social Mobilization in Late Nineteenth-Century Ecuador. In Becker, M. and Clark, A. K., editors, *Highland Indians and the State in Modern Ecuador,* pages 72–88. University of Pittsburgh Press, Pittsburgh.

Becker, M. (2008). *Indians and Leftists in the Making of Ecuador's Modern Indigenous Movements.* Duke University Press, Durham, NC.

Benton, A. L. (2017). Configuring Authority over Electoral Manipulation in Electoral Authoritarian Regimes: Evidence from Mexico. *Democratization,* 24(3):521–543.

Bernstein, H., Crow, B., and Johnson, H. (1992). *Rural Livelihoods: Crises and Responses.* Oxford University Press, Oxford, England.

Bertrand, J. (2013). *Political Change in Southeast Asia.* Cambridge University Press, Cambridge, UK.

Bjork-James, C. (2020). When Plurinational States Undermine Indigenous Territories: TIPNIS in Bolivia. In Robins, N. A. and Fraser, B. J., editors, *Landscapes of Inequity: Environmental Justice in the Andes-Amazon Region,* pages 127–166. University of Nebraska Press, Lincoln.

Bolivia (1902). *Prestación vial: ley de diciembre de 1901 y decreto reglamentario de 10 de abril de 1902.* Imp. del estado, J. Calasanz Tapia, La Paz.

Bolivia Congreso Nacional Cámara de Diputados (1902). *Redactor de la H. Cámara de Diputados (Sesiones reservadas)*. Escuela Tip. Salesiana., La Paz.

Bolivia Congreso Nacional Cámara de Senadores (1909). *Redactor del H. Senado Nacional*. Gobierno de Bolivia, La Paz.

Bolivia Dirección General de Estadística y Censos (1956). *Censo Agropecuario, 1950*. Gobierno de Bolivia, La Paz.

Bonilla, H. (1985). Peru and Bolivia from Independence to the War of the Pacific. In Bethell, L., editor, *The Cambridge History of Latin America*, pages 539–582. Cambridge University Press, Cambridge, UK.

Bourricaud, F. (1967). *Cambios en Puno: estudios de sociología andina*. Instituto Indigenista Interamericano, Mexico.

Brubaker, R., Feischmidt, M., Fox, J., and Grancea, L. (2018). *Nationalist Politics and Everyday Ethnicity in a Transylvanian Town*. Princeton University Press, Princeton.

Brysk, A. (2000). *From Tribal Village to Global Village: Indian Rights and International Relations in Latin America*. Stanford University Press, Stanford, CA.

Bulmer-Thomas, V. (1987). *The Political Economy of Central America since 1920*. Cambridge University Press.

Bureau of Indian Affairs. (n.d.). What is Fractionation? U.S. Department of the Interior. https://www.bia.gov/bia/ots/dtlc/fractionation

del Busto Duthurburu, J. A., Rosales Aguirre, J., and Gutiérrez, Y. C. (2004). *Historia de Piura*. Universidad de Piura, Piura.

de la Cadena, M. (2000). *Indigenous Mestizos: The Politics of Race and Culture in Cuzco, Peru, 1919–1991*. Duke University Press, Durham.

Calisto, M. M. (1993). *Peasant Resistance in the Aymara Districts of the Highlands of Peru, 1900–1930: An Attempt at Self-Governance*. PhD thesis, University of California, San Diego.

Canessa, A. (2000). Contesting Hybridity: Evangelistas and Kataristas in Highland Bolivia. *Journal of Latin American Studies*, 32(1):115–144.

Cant, A. (2012). 'Land for Those Who Work It': A Visual Analysis of Agrarian Reform Posters in Velasco's Peru. *Journal of Latin American Studies*, 44(1):1–37.

Cant, A. (2021). *Land Without Masters: Agrarian Reform and Political Change under Peru's Military Government*. University of Texas Press, Austin.

Caplan, K. D. (2009). *Indigenous Citizens: Local Liberalism in Early National Oaxaca and Yucatán*. Stanford University Press, Redwood City.

Cárdenas, M. (2010). State Capacity in Latin America. *Economía*, 10(2):1–45.

Carter, C. L. (2021). The Representational Effects of Communal Property: Evidence from Peru's Indigenous Groups. *Comparative Political Studies*, 54(2):2191–2225.

Carter, C. L. (2022). The Autonomy-Representation Dilemma: Indigenous Groups and Distributive Benefits in the Americas. *Journal of Race, Ethnicity, and Politics*, 7(2):294–315.

Carter, C. L. (2024a). Extraction, Assimilation, and Accommodation: The Historical Foundations of Indigenous-State Relations in Latin America. *American Political Science Review*, 118(1):38–53.

Carter, C. L. (2024b). A Space for Autonomy: Indigenous Rights in Post-independence Latin America.

Carter, W. E. (1965). *Aymara Communities and the Bolivian Agrarian Reform*. University of Florida Press, Gainesville, FL.

Casen, C. (2012). Bolivian Katarism: The Emergence of an Indian Challenge to the Social Order. *Critique internationale*, 57(4):23–36.

Chandra, K. (2004). *Why Ethnic Parties Succeed: Patronage and Ethnic Head Counts in India*. Cambridge Studies in Comparative Politics. Cambridge University Press, Cambridge.

Chaplin, D. (2015). *The Peruvian Industrial Labor Force*. Princeton University Press, Princeton.

Chesterton, B. M. (2016). *The Chaco War: Environment, Ethnicity, and Nationalism*. Bloomsbury Publishing, London, UK.

Chilton, A. and Versteeg, M. (2020). *How Constitutional Rights Matter*. Oxford University Press, Oxford, England.

Choque Canqui, R. and Ticona Alejo, E. (1996). *Jesús de Machaca: la marka rebelde*. CEDOIN, La Paz.

Clark, K. (2007). Shifting Paternalisms in Indian-State Relations. In Clark, A. K. and Becker, M., editors, *Highland Indians and the State in Modern Ecuador*, pages 89–104. University of Pittsburgh Press, Pittsburgh, PA.

Clark, R. J. (1968). Land Reform and Peasant Market Participation on the North Highlands of Bolivia. *Land Economics*, 44(2):153–172.

Coates, K. (2022). The Heavy Hand of Canadian Paternalism is Still Disrupting Indigenous Communities. *Toronto Star*.

Collier, R. B. and Collier, D. (2002). *Shaping the Political Arena: Critical Junctures, the Labor Movement, and Regime Dynamics in Latin America*. University of Notre Dame Press, Notre Dame, Indiana.

Comisión Verdad Histórica y Nuevo Trato con los Pueblos Indígenas (2009). *Informe de la Comisión Verdad Histórica y Nuevo Trato con los Pueblos Indígenas*. Gobierno de Chile. Ministerio de Planificación, Santiago, Chile.

Condarco Morales, R. (1983). *Zárate, el "temible" Willka: historia de la rebelión indígena de 1899 en la República de Bolivia*. Imprenta y Librería Renovación, La Paz, Bolivia.

Contreras, C. (1996). Maestros, mistis y campesinos en el Perú rural del siglo XX.

Contreras, C. and Zuloaga, M. (2014). *Historia mínima de Perú*. El Colegio de Mexico AC, Mexico.

Cook, N. D. (2003). The Corregidores of the Colca Valley, Peru: Imperial Administration in an Andean Region. *Anuario de Estudios Americanos*, 60(2):413–439.

Coronado, J. (2009). *The Andes Imagined: Indigenismo, Society, and Modernity*. University of Pittsburgh Press, Pittsburgh.

Corres, M. J. B., Polo, C. J. S., and Eisenstadt, T. A. (2016). *Democracia, derechos humanos y derechos indígenas en municipios de usos y costumbres: resultados de una encuesta*. Instituto Estatal Electoral y de Participación Ciudadana de Oaxaca (IEEPCO), Oaxaca, Mexico.

Cotler, J. (1970). Traditional Haciendas and Communities in a Context of Political Mobilization in Peru. In Stavenhagen, R., editor, *Agrarian Problems and Peasant Movements in Latin America*, pages 533–558. Doubleday Anchor, Garden City, NY.

Cotler, J. (1976). Haciendas y comunidades tradicionales en un contexto de movilización política. In Mar, J. M., editor, *Hacienda, comunidad y campesinado en el Perú*, pages 311–342. Instituto de Estudios Peruanos, Lima.

Cozzaglio, P. and Abramovic, P. (2022). Plurinacionalidad indígena en nueva Constitución divide aguas en Chile.

Crabtree, J. and Chaplin, A. (2013). *Bolivia: Processes of Change.* Zed Books, London, UK.

Craig, W. (1972). Peru: The Peasant Movement of La Convención. In Landsberger, H. A., editor, *Latin American Peasant Movements*, pages 274–296. Cornell University Press, Ithaca.

Cramb, R. A. and Wills, I. R. (1990). The Role of Traditional Institutions in Rural Development: Community-Based Land Tenure and Government Land Policy in Sarawak, Malaysia. *World Development*, 18(3): 347–360.

Crow, J. (2010). Negotiating Inclusion in the Nation: Mapuche Intellectuals and the Chilean State. *Latin American and Caribbean Ethnic Studies*, 5(2):131–152.

Crow, J. (2022). *Itinerant Ideas: Race, Indigeneity and Cross-Border Intellectual Encounters in Latin America (1900–1950).* Springer Nature, Cham, Switzerland.

Cueto, M. (2017). *The Return of Epidemics: Health and Society in Peru During the Twentieth Century.* Taylor & Francis, London.

Cusicanqui, S. R. (1990). Liberal Democracy and Ayllu Democracy in Bolivia: The Case of Northern Potosí. *The Journal of Development Studies*, 26(4):97–121.

Cusicanqui, S. R. (2012). Ch'ixinakax Utxiwa: A Reflection on the Practices and Discourses of Decolonization. *South Atlantic Quarterly*, 111(1): 95–109.

Cussi, S., Calle, D., and Mamani, A. (1999). Nayaruxa chuymaxa ususkakituwa: Historia de la Federación de Ayllus y Comunidades Originarias de la Provincia Ingavi. In Parga, J. S., editor, *Cultura política en la sociedad ecuatoriana*, pages 37–58. Editorial Abya Yala, Quito.

Dahl, R. A. (1982). *Dilemmas of Pluralist Democracy: Autonomy vs. Control.* Yale University Press, New Haven.

Dandler, J. and Torrico A., J. (1987). Bolivia, 1945–1947. In Stern, S., editor, *Resistance, Rebellion, and Consciousness in the Andean Peasant World, 18th to 20th Centuries*, pages 334–378. University of Wisconsin Press, Madison, WI.

Davies, T. M. (1974). *Indian Integration in Peru: A Half Century of Experience, 1900–1948.* University of Nebraska Press, Lincoln.

Dawson, A. S. (2020). *Indian and Nation in Revolutionary Mexico.* University of Arizona Press, Tucson.

Deere, C. D. (1990). *Household and Class Relations: Peasants and Landlords in Northern Peru.* Univ of California Press, Berkeley.

Delgado, A. C. (2017). The TIPNIS Conflict in Bolivia. *Contexto Internacional*, 39(2):373–392.

Dell, M. (2010). The Persistent Effects of Peru's Mining Mita. *Econometrica*, 78(6):1863–1903.

Deloria, V. (2002). *The Indian Reorganization Act: Congresses and Bills.* University of Oklahoma Press, Norman, OK.

Diaz-Cayeros, A., Estévez, F., and Magaloni, B. (2016). *The Political Logic of Poverty Relief: Electoral Strategies and Social Policy in Mexico.* Cambridge University Press, Cambridge.

Díaz-Cayeros, A., Magaloni, B., and Ruiz-Euler, A. (2014). Traditional Governance, Citizen Engagement, and Local Public Goods: Evidence from Mexico. *World Development*, 53:80–93.

Díaz Martínez, A. (2016). Capítulo VI: ensayo de conclusión (1985). In Tanaka, M., editor, *Antología del pensamiento crítico peruano contemporáneo*, pages 409–430. CLACSO, Buenos Aires.

Díaz-Polanco, H. (1998). La Autonomía, Demanda Central de los Pueblos Indígenas: Signifi-
cado e Implicaciones. In Alta, V., Iturralde, D., and López Bassola, M., editors, *Pueblos
Indígenas y Estado En América Latina*, pages 213–220. Editorial Abya Yala, Quito.

Díez Canseco, E. and Aguilar Revoredo, J. F. (1929). *La Red Nacional de Carreteras*. Imprenta
Torres Aguirre, Lima, Perú, 2 edition.

Dirección de Vías de Comunicación (1928). *Primera Conferencia Técnica Nacional de Carreteras:
programa y cuestionario*. Ministerio de Fomento, Lima.

Dobyns, H. F. (1964). *The Social Matrix of Peruvian Indigenous Communities*. Department of
Anthropology, Cornell University, Ithaca.

Drinot, P. (2000). Peru, 1884–1930: A Beggar Sitting on a Bench of Gold? In Cárdenas, E.,
Ocampo, J. A., and Thorp, R., editors, *An Economic History of Twentieth-Century Latin
America: Volume 1 The Export Age: The Latin American Economies in the Late Nineteenth
and Early Twentieth Centuries*, St Antony's Series, pages 152–187. Palgrave Macmillan UK,
London.

Drzewieniecki, J. E. (1996). *Indigenous Politics, Local Power, and the State in Peru, 1821–1968*. PhD
thesis, State University of New York at Buffalo.

Dubertret, F. and Alden Wily, L. (2015). Percent of Indigenous and Community Lands. In
*LandMark: The Global Platform of Indigenous and Community Lands*.

Dunn, W. E. (1925). *Peru: A Commercial and Industrial Handbook*. 25. United States Department
of Commerce, Washington, D.C.

Dunning, T. (2012). *Natural Experiments in the Social Sciences: A Design-Based Approach*. Cambridge University Press, Cambridge, UK.

Dunning, T. and Harrison, L. (2010). Cross-Cutting Cleavages and Ethnic Voting: An Experimental Study of Cousinage in Mali. *American Political Science Review*, 104(1):21–39.

Eberhart, T. M. (1977). The Socio-political Dimensions of Latin American Peasant Movements: A Comparative Analysis of the Bolivian Syndicates Following the 1952 Revolution
and the La Convencion Valley Peasant Movement of Peru. Master's thesis, American
University, District of Columbia.

Edsall, T. B. (2021). Opinion | Should Biden Emphasize Race or Class or Both or None of the
Above? *The New York Times*.

Edwards, A. D. and Jones, D. G. (2019). *Community and Community Development*. Walter de
Gruyter, Berlin.

Egan, N. E. (2019). *Infrastructure, State Formation, and Social Change in Bolivia at the Start of the
Twentieth Century*. PhD thesis, UC San Diego.

Eisenstadt, T. A. (2007). Usos y Costumbres and Postelectoral Conflicts in Oaxaca, Mexico, 1995–2004: An Empirical and Normative Assessment. *Latin American Research Review*,
42(1):52–77.

Eisenstadt, T. A. (2011). *Politics, Identity, and Mexico's Indigenous Rights Movements*. Cambridge
University Press, Cambridge, UK.

Escárzaga Nicté, F. (1999). La sublevación de Ancash. Proyecto nacional y guerra de razas.
*Política y Cultura*, 12:151–176.

Escobar, A. (1972). Lingüística y política. In Escobar, A., editor, *El reto del multilingüismo en el
Perú*, pages 15–34. Instituto de Estudios Peruanos, Lima.

Esquivel, A. B. (2013). Afectaciones históricas a la red vial inca y la necesidad del estudio documentario de carreteras para la investigación y el registro de caminos prehispánicos. *Cuadernos del Qhapaq Ñan*, 1(1):32–51.

Evans, L. E. (2011). Expertise and Scale of Conflict: Governments as Advocates in American Indian Politics. *American Political Science Review*, 105(4):663–682.

Ewen, A. (2016). Mexico: The Crisis of Identity. In Lobo, S., Talbot, S., and Carlston, T. M., editors, *Native American Voices*, pages 81–89. Routledge, London, UK.

Fabricant, N. and Postero, N. (2015). Sacrificing Indigenous Bodies and Lands: The Political-Economic History of Lowland Bolivia in Light of the Recent TIPNIS Debate. *The Journal of Latin American and Caribbean Anthropology*, 20(3):452–474.

Fallaw, B. (2001). *Cárdenas Compromised: The Failure of Reform in Postrevolutionary Yucatán*. Duke University Press, Durham, NC.

Falleti, T. G. (2005). A Sequential Theory of Decentralization: Latin American Cases in Comparative Perspective. *American Political Science Review*, (03):327–346.

Falleti, T. G. and Riofrancos, T. N. (2018). Endogenous Participation: Strengthening Prior Consultation in Extractive Economies. *World Politics*, 70(1):86–121.

Favre, H. (1976). Evolución y Situación de la Hacienda Tradicional de la Región de Huancavelíca. In Matos Mar, J., editor, *Hacienda, Comunidad y Campesinado En El Perú*, pages 105–138. Instituto de Estudios Peruanos, Lima.

Finkel, E. (2015). The Phoenix Effect of State Repression: Jewish Resistance during the Holocaust. *American Political Science Review*, 109(2):339–353.

Flores Galindo, A. (1977). *Arequipa y el sur andino: ensayo de historia regional (siglos XVIII-XX)*. Editorial Horizonte, Lima.

Flores Galindo, A. (1993). *Buscando un inca: identidad y utopía en los Andes*. Consejo Nacional para la Cultura y las Artes, Lima.

Foerster, R. and Montecino Aguirre, S. (1988). *Organizaciones, líderes y contiendas mapuches, 1900-1970*. Ediciones CEM, Santiago, Chile.

Fonseca Martel, C. and Mayer, E. (1991). De hacienda a comunidad: El impacto de la reforma agraria en la provincia de Paucartambo-Cuzco, Perú. In *Reproducción y Transformación de Las Sociedades Andinas Siglos XVI–XX*, volume 2, pages 349–400. Abya-Yala, Quito.

Fontana, L. B. (2022). *Recognition Politics: Indigenous Rights and Ethnic Conflict in the Andes*. Cambridge University Press, Cambridge, UK.

Forment, C. A. (2013). *Democracy in Latin America, 1760–1900: Volume 1, Civic Selfhood and Public Life in Mexico and Peru*. University of Chicago Press, Chicago.

Franco, A. P., Galiani, S., and Lavado, P. (2021). Long-Term Effects of the Inca Road. Working Paper 28979, NBER.

Fundación TIERRA (2009). *Censo Agropecuario 1950*. Fundación Tierra, La Paz.

Galindo, A. F. (2010). *In Search of an Inca: Identity and Utopia in the Andes*. Cambridge University Press, Cambridge, UK.

Ghai, Y. (2000). Ethnicity and Autonomy: A Framework for Analysis. In Ghai, Y., editor, *Autonomy and Ethnicity: Negotiating Competing Claims in Multi-ethnic States*, pages 1–26. Cambridge University Press, Cambridge, UK.

Gleijeses, P. (1989). The Agrarian Reform of Jacobo Arbenz. *Journal of Latin American Studies,* 21(3):453–480.

Gonzáles, C. W. A. (2011). The Concept of Inca Province at Tawantinsuyu. *Indiana,* 28: 79–107.

Gotkowitz, L. (2008). *A Revolution for Our Rights: Indigenous Struggles for Land and Justice in Bolivia, 1880–1952.* Duke University Press, Durham, NC.

Gourevitch, P. A. (1979). The Reemergence of "Peripheral Nationalisms": Some Comparative Speculations on the Spatial Distribution of Political Leadership and Economic Growth. *Comparative Studies in Society and History,* 21(3):303–322.

Grieshaber, E. P. (1977). *Survival of Indian Communities in Nineteenth-Century Bolivia.* PhD thesis, University of North Carolina at Chapel Hill.

Grieshaber, E. P. (1979). Hacienda-Indian Community Relations and Indian Acculturation: An Historiographical Essay. *Latin American Research Review,* 14(3):107–128.

Grieshaber, E. P. (1980). Survival of Indian Communities in Nineteenth-Century Bolivia: A Regional Comparison. *Journal of Latin American Studies,* 12(2):223–269.

Grieshaber, E. P. (1990). La expansión de la hacienda en el departamento de La Paz, Bolivia, 1850–1920, una versión cuantitativa. *Andes, Antropología e historia,* 2–3:33–83.

Guardado, J. (2018). Office-Selling, Corruption, and Long-Term Development in Peru. *American Political Science Review,* 112(4):971–995.

Gurr, T. R. (1994). Peoples against States: Ethnopolitical Conflict and the Changing World System. 1994 Presidential Address. *International Studies Quarterly,* 38(3):347–377.

Gutiérrez Aguilar, R. (2014). *Rhythms of the Pachakuti: Indigenous Uprising and State Power in Bolivia.* Duke University Press, Durham, NC.

Guzmán, V. and Vargas, V. (1981). *Cronología de los movimientos campesinos, 1956–1964.* Investigación, Documentación, Educación, Asesoría, Servicios, Lima.

Hale, C. R. (2002). Does Multiculturalism Menace? Governance, Cultural Rights and the Politics of Identity in Guatemala. *Journal of Latin American Studies,* 34(3):485–524.

Handelman, H. (1974). *Struggle in the Andes: Peasant Political Mobilization in Peru.* University of Texas Press, Austin.

Handy, J. (1994). The Corporate Community, Campesino Organizations, and Agrarian Reform: 1950–1964. In Smith, C. A. and Moors, M. M., editors, *Guatemalan Indians and the State: 1540 to 1988,* Symposia on Latin America Series, pages 163–182. University of Texas Press, Austin.

Hannum, H. (1996). *Autonomy, Sovereignty, and Self-Determination: The Accommodation of Conflicting Rights.* University of Pennsylvania Press.

Hartle, D. G. and Bird, R. M. (1971). The Demand for Local Political Autonomy: An Individualistic Theory. *The Journal of Conflict Resolution,* 15(4):443–456.

Healy, K. (1985). The Cocaine Industry in Bolivia—Its Impact on the Peasantry. *Cultural Survival Quarterly Magazine.*

Hechter, M. (2000). *Containing Nationalism.* Oxford University Press, New York.

Heilman, J. (2010a). *Before the Shining Path: Politics in Rural Ayacucho, 1895–1980.* Stanford University Press, Stanford, CA.

Heilman, J. (2010b). Under Civilian Colonels: Indigenous Political Mobilization in 1920s Ayacucho, Peru. *The Americas,* 66(4):501–526.

Heilman, J. (2018). Por un imperio de ciudadanos: El movimiento "Tahuantinsuyo" en el Ayacucho de los años 1920. In Drinot, P., editor, *La Patria Nueva: Economía, Sociedad y Cultura En El Perú, 1919–1930*, pages 169–198. UNC Press, Chapel Hill.

Heilman, J. P. (2015). Yellows against Reds: Campesino Anticommunism in 1960s Ayacucho, Peru. *Latin American Research Review*, 50(2):154–175.

Henderson, P. (1997). Cocoa, Finance and the State in Ecuador, 1895–1925. *Bulletin of Latin American Research*, 16(2):169–186.

Henn, S. J. (2023). Complements or Substitutes? How Institutional Arrangements Bind Traditional Authorities and the State in Africa. *American Political Science Review*, 117(3):871–890.

Hernández, T. K. (2013). *Racial Subordination in Latin America: The Role of the State, Customary Law, and the New Civil Rights Response*. Cambridge University Press, Cambridge, UK.

Hirsch, S. (2010). Peruvian Anarcho-Syndicalism. In Hirsch, S. and van der Walt, L., editors, *Anarchism and Syndicalism in the Colonial and Postcolonial World, 1870–1940: The Praxis of National Liberation, Internationalism, and Social Revolution*, pages 225–271. Brill, Boston.

Hirsch, S. J. (2020). Anarchists and "the Indian Problem" in Peru, 1898–1927. *Anarchist Studies*, 28(2):54–76.

Hiskey, J. T. and Goodman, G. L. (2011). The Participation Paradox of Indigenous Autonomy in Mexico. *Latin American Politics and Society*, 53(2):61–86.

Hobsbawm, E. J. E. (1969). A Case of Neo-feudalism: La Convencion, Peru. *Journal of Latin American Studies*, 1(1):31–50.

Holland, A. C. (2017). *Forbearance as Redistribution: The Politics of Informal Welfare in Latin America*. Cambridge Studies in Comparative Politics. Cambridge University Press, Cambridge.

Holzinger, K., Haer, R., Bayer, A., Behr, D. M., and Neupert-Wentz, C. (2019). The Constitutionalization of Indigenous Group Rights, Traditional Political Institutions, and Customary Law. *Comparative Political Studies*, 52(12):1775–1809.

Honig, L. (2022). *Land Politics: How Customary Institutions Shape State Building in Zambia and Senegal*. Cambridge University Press, Cambridge.

Horn, P. (2022). Diverse Articulations of Urban Indigeneity among Lowland Indigenous Groups in Santa Cruz, Bolivia. *Bulletin of Latin American Research*, 41(1):37–52.

Horowitz, D. L. (1981). Patterns of Ethnic Separatism. *Comparative Studies in Society and History*, 23(2):165–195.

Horowitz, D. L. (1985). *Ethnic Groups in Conflict*. University of California Press, Berkeley, CA.

Htun, M. (2016). *Inclusion without Representation in Latin America: Gender Quotas and Ethnic Reservations*. Cambridge University Press, Cambridge, UK.

Huillca, S. and Samanez, H. N. (1975). *Huillca, habla un campesino peruano*. Ediciones Corregidor.

Hunefeldt, C. (2010). The Rural Landscape and Changing Political Awareness: Enterprises, Agrarian Producers, and Peasant Communities, 1969–1994. In Maxwell, C. A. and Mauceri, P., editors, *Peruvian Labyrinth: Polity, Society, Economy*, pages 107–133. Penn State Press.

Hunefeldt, C. (2018). *Fiscal Capitalism and the Dismantling of Citizenship in Puno, Peru*. Marcial Pons, Madrid.

Hunt, S. J. (1973). *Growth and Guano in Nineteenth Century Peru*. Research Program in Economic Development, Woodrow Wilson School, Princeton University, Princeton.

Hunt, S. J. (1984). Guano y crecimiento en el Perú del siglo XIX. *Hisla: revista latinoamericana de la historia económica y social.*

Hurtado Mercado, J. (1986). *El Katarismo.* Hisbol, La Paz.

Infobae. (2011, August 8). Evo Morales tendrá que disculparse con las mujeres indígenas. *Infobae.*

Instituto Nacional de Estadística e Informática (2014). *IV Censo Nacional Agropecuario.* INEI, Peru.

Instituto Nacional de los Pueblos Indígenas (2019). Oxchuc, Chiapas, primer Municipio indígena que elegirá a sus Autoridades bajo el régimen de Sistemas Normativos Indígenas. *INPI Blog.*

International Labour Office (1929). *Forced Labor: Report and Draft Questionnaire.* ILO, Geneva.

Irurozqui, M. (2000). The Sound of the Pututos. Politicisation and Indigenous Rebellions in Bolivia, 1826–1921. *Journal of Latin American Studies*, 32(1):85–114.

Iverson, P. (1983). *The Navajo Nation.* University of New Mexico Press, Albuquerque.

Jackson, J. E. and Warren, K. B. (2005). Indigenous Movements in Latin America, 1992–2004: Controversies, Ironies, New Directions. *Annual Review of Anthropology*, 34(1): 549–573.

Jackson, R. H. (1989). The Decline of the Hacienda in Cochabamba, Bolivia: The Case of the Sacaba Valley, 1870–1929. *The Hispanic American Historical Review*, 69(2):259–281.

Jackson, R. H. (1994). *Regional Markets and Agrarian Transformation in Bolivia: Cochabamba, 1539–1960.* University of New Mexico Press, Albuquerque.

Jacobsen, N. (1993). *Mirages of Transition: The Peruvian Altiplano, 1780–1930.* University of California Press, Berkeley.

Jacobsen, N. (1997). Liberalism and Indian Communities. In Jackson, R. H., editor, *Liberals, the Church, and Indian Peasants: Corporate Lands and the Challenge of Reform in Nineteenth-Century Spanish America.* University of New Mexico Press, Albuquerque.

Jaskoski, M. (2022). *The Politics of Extraction: Territorial Rights, Participatory Institutions, and Conflict in Latin America.* Oxford University Press, Oxford, England.

Kammann, P. (1982). *Movimientos Campesinos En El Perú, 1900–1968: Análisis Cuantitativo y Cualitativo (Preliminar).* Universidad Mayor de San Marcos, Seminario de Historia Rural Andina, Lima.

Kapsoli, W. (1982). *Los movimientos campesinos en el Perú: 1879–1965.* Ediciones Atusparia, Lima.

Kapsoli, W. (1984). *Ayllus del sol: Anarquismo y utopía andina.* Tarea, Lima.

Kapsoli, W. and Reátegui, W. (1987). *El campesinado peruano: 1919–1930.* Universidad Nacional Mayor de San Marcos, Lima.

Kelly, L. C. (1975). The Indian Reorganization Act: The Dream and the Reality. *Pacific Historical Review*, 44(3):291–312.

Kenner, D. and Paz, S. (2012). Interview: Sarela Paz Discusses the Indigenous Organisation CONISUR. *Bolivia Diary*, January 18.

Klein, H. S. (1992). *Bolivia: The Evolution of a Multi-ethnic Society.* Oxford University Press, Oxford, England.

Klein, H. S. (1993). *Haciendas and Ayllus: Rural Society in the Bolivian Andes in the Eighteenth and Nineteenth Centuries.* Stanford University Press, Stanford, CA.

Knight, A. (1986). Mexican Peonage: What Was It and Why Was It? *Journal of Latin American Studies*, 18(1):41–74.

Kohl, J. (2020). *Indigenous Struggle and the Bolivian National Revolution: Land and Liberty!* Routledge, New York.

Kubler, G. (1952). *The Indian Caste of Peru, 1795–1940; a Population Study Based upon Tax Records and Census Reports*. U.S. Govt. Print. Off, Washington, D.C.

Lagos, M. L. (1991). The Politics of Representation: Class and Ethnic Identities in Cochabamba, Bolivia. *Boletín de Antropología Americana*, (24):143–150.

Laing, A. F. (2018). Subaltern Geographies in the Plurinational State of Bolivia: The TIPNIS Conflict. In Jazeel, T. and Legg, S., editors, *Subaltern Geographies*. University of Georgia Press, Athens, GA.

Landa Vásquez, L. (2006). Los espejos opacos del movimiento indígena peruano. In Alayza, A. and Toche, E., editors, *Nuevos rostros en la escena nacional, Perú hoy*, pages 117–140. Desco, Centro de Estudios y Promoción del Desarrollo, Lima, 1. ed. edition.

Langer, E. D. (1989). *Economic Change and Rural Resistance in Southern Bolivia, 1880–1930*. Stanford University Press, Stanford, CA.

Langer, E. D. (2018). From Prosperity to Poverty: Andeans in the Nineteenth Century. In Santoro, M. and Langer, E. D., editors, *Hemispheric Indigeneities: Native Identity and Agency in Mesoamerica, the Andes, and Canada*, pages 151–182. University of Nebraska Press, Lincoln.

Larson, B. (1996). Andean Highland Peasants & Nation Making (1800s). In Trigger, B. G., Washburn, W. E., Salomon, F., and Adams, R. E. W., editors, *The Cambridge History of the Native Peoples of the Americas*. Cambridge University Press, Cambridge, UK.

Larson, B. (1998). *Cochabamba, 1550–1900: Colonialism and Agrarian Transformation in Bolivia*. Duke University Press, Durham, NC.

Larson, B. (2004). *Trials of Nation Making: Liberalism, Race, and Ethnicity in the Andes, 1810–1910*. Cambridge University Press, Cambridge, UK.

Lawrence, A. (2013). *Imperial Rule and the Politics of Nationalism: Anti-colonial Protest in the French Empire*. Cambridge University Press, Cambridge, UK.

Lee, A. and Schultz, K. A. (2012). Comparing British and French Colonial Legacies: A Discontinuity Analysis of Cameroon. *Quarterly Journal of Political Science*, 7(4):365–410.

Leibner, G. (2003). Radicalism and integration: The Tahuantinsuyo Committee Experience and the Indigenismo of Leguía Reconsidered, 1919–1924. *Journal of Iberian and Latin American Research*, 9(2):1–24.

Lienhard, M. (1992). *Testimonios, cartas y manifiestos indígenas: desde la conquista hasta comienzos del siglo XX*. Fundacion Biblioteca Ayacuch, Caracas.

Llamojha Mitma, M. and Heilman, J. P. (2016). *Now Peru Is Mine: The Life and Times of a Campesino Activist*. Duke University Press, Durham, NC.

Long, N. and Roberts, B. (1984). *Miners, Peasants and Entrepreneurs: Regional Development in the Central Highlands of Peru*. Cambridge University Press, Cambridge, UK.

Lord, P. P. (1965). *The Peasantry as an Emerging Political Factor in Mexico, Bolivia, and Venezuela*. Land Tenure Center, University of Wisconsin, Madison, WI.

Lowenthal, A. F. (2015). *The Peruvian Experiment: Continuity and Change Under Military Rule*. Princeton University Press, Princeton.

Lucero, J. A. (2008). *Struggles of Voice: The Politics of Indigenous Representation in the Andes.* University of Pittsburgh Press, Pittsburgh, PA.

Macera, P. (1976). *Población rural en haciendas, 1876.* Universidad Nacional Mayor de San Marcos, Dirección Universitaria de Proyección Social, Seminario de Historia Rural Andina, Lima.

Madrid, R. L. (2008). The Rise of Ethnopopulism in Latin America. *World Politics,* 60(3):475–508.

Magaloni, B., Díaz-Cayeros, A., and Ruiz Euler, A. (2019). Public Good Provision and Traditional Governance in Indigenous Communities in Oaxaca, Mexico. *Comparative Political Studies.*

Mahoney, J. (2010). *Colonialism and Postcolonial Development: Spanish America in Comparative Perspective.* Cambridge University Press, Cambridge, UK.

Mainwaring, S. (2006). *The Crisis of Democratic Representation in the Andes.* Stanford University Press, Stanford, CA.

Mallon, F. E. (1992). Indian Communities, Political Cultures, and the State in Latin America, 1780–1990. *Journal of Latin American Studies,* 24:35–53.

Mallon, F. E. (1995). *Peasant and Nation: The Making of Postcolonial Mexico and Peru.* University of California Press, Berkeley.

Mallon, F. E. (2014). *The Defense of Community in Peru's Central Highlands: Peasant Struggle and Capitalist Transition, 1860–1940.* Princeton University Press, Princeton.

Mamani Condori, C. B. (1991). *Taraqu, 1866–1935: masacre, guerra y "renovación" en la biografía de Eduardo L. Nina Qhispi.* Ediciones Aruwiyiri, La Paz.

Manrique, N. (1988). *Yawar Mayu: sociedades terratenientes serranas, 1879–1910.* Instituto Francés de Estudios Andinos, Lima.

Mariátegui, J. C. (1988). *Seven Interpretive Essays on Peruvian Reality.* University of Texas Press, Austin.

Marín, J. A. F. and Castilla, R. P. (1973). *Luchas campesinas en el Perú, 1900–1920.* Seminario de Historia Rural Andina, Lima.

Marsh, M. A. (1928). *The Bankers in Bolivia; a Study in American Foreign Investment.* AMS Press, New York.

Martínez Arellano, H. (1960). Las migraciones altiplánicas y la colonización del Tambopata. *Repositorio de Tesis - UNMSM.*

Matos Mar, J. (1964). Las Haciendas del Valle de Chancay. In Favre, H., Delavaud, C. C., and Matos Mar, J., editors, *La Hacienda en el Perú,* pages 283–394. Instituto de Estudios Peruanos, Lima.

Matos Mar, J. (1976). *Yanaconaje y reforma agraria en el Perú: el caso del Valle de Chancay.* Instituto de Estudios Peruanos, Lima.

Mattiace, S. L. (2003). *To See with Two Eyes: Peasant Activism & Indian Autonomy in Chiapas, Mexico.* University of New Mexico Press, Albuquerque.

Mattiace, S. L. (2009). Ethnic Mobilization among the Maya of Yucatán. *Latin American and Caribbean Ethnic Studies,* 4(2):137–169.

Mayer, E. (1995). *State Policy and Community Conflict in Bolivia and Peru, 1900–1980.* PhD thesis, University of California, San Diego.

Mayer, E. (2009). *Ugly Stories of the Peruvian Agrarian Reform.* Duke University Press, Durham.

Mazzuca, S. (2021). *Latecomer State Formation: Political Geography and Capacity Failure in Latin America.* Yale University Press, New Haven.

McBride, G. M. (1921). *The Agrarian Indian Communities of Highland Bolivia.* Oxford University Press, Oxford, England.

McClintock, C. (1981). *Peasant Cooperatives and Political Change in Peru.* Princeton University Press, Princeton.

McCreery, D. (1994). *Rural Guatemala, 1760–1940.* Stanford University Press, Stanford, CA.

McMurry, N. (2022). From Recognition to Integration: Indigenous Autonomy, State Authority, and National Identity in the Philippines. *American Political Science Review*, 116(2): 547–563.

McPherson, R. S. (1998). Navajo Livestock Reduction in Southeastern Utah, 1933–46: History Repeats Itself. *American Indian Quarterly*, 22(1/2):1–18.

Medrano, E. R. (2011). *Mexico's Indigenous Communities: Their Lands and Histories, 1500–2010.* University Press of Colorado, Boulder.

Meixueiro, G., Maldonado Hernández, G., and Baca Nakakawa, A. (2020). *Asambleas y Urnas, Resultados de Una Encuesta Comparativa Entre Municipios de Sistemas Normativos Indígenas y Partidos Políticos En Oaxaca.* Instituto Estatal Electoral y de Participación Ciudadana de Oaxaca (IEEPCO), Oaxaca, Mexico.

Mekeel, S. (1944). An Appraisal of the Indian Reorganization Act. *American Anthropologist*, 46(2):209–217.

Melgar Bao, R. (1988). *Sindicalismo y milenarismo en la región andina del Perú (1920–1931).* Ediciones Cuicuilco, Mexico.

Meza Bazán, M. M. (1999). *Caminos al progreso. Mano de obra y política de vialidad en el Perú: la ley de conscripción vial. 1920–1930.* PhD thesis, Universidad Nacional Mayor de San Marcos, Lima.

Ministerio de Fomento (1930). *La Labor Constructiva Del Peru En El Gobierno Del Presidente Don Augusto B. Leguía.* T. Aguirre, Lima, Peru.

Ministerio de Gobierno y Fomento (1908). *Anexos a La Memoria de La Seccion de Fomento.* Imprenta y Litografia Boliviana–Hugo Heitmann, La Paz.

Ministerio de Vivienda, Construccion, y Saneamiento (2009). Directorio de Comunidades Campesinas del Peru 2009.

Ministro del Ramo (1908). *Anexos a La Memoria de La Seccion de Fomento.* Bolivia, La Paz.

Montoya, R. (2006). ¿Por qué no hay en Perú un movimiento político indígena como en Ecuador y Bolivia? In Aguilar, R. G. and Escárzaga, F., editors, *Movimiento indígena en América Latina: resistencia y proyecto alternativo*, pages 237–241. Universidad Autónoma Metropolitana, Mexico.

Morales, W. Q. (2013). The TIPNIS Crisis and the Meaning of Bolivian Democracy Under Evo Morales. *The Latin Americanist*, 57(1):79–90.

Mörner, M. (1975). Some Characteristics of Agrarian Structure in the Cuzco Region towards the End of the Colonial Period. *Boletín de Estudios Latinoamericanos y del Caribe*, (18):15–29.

Mundim, K. (2022). Legacies of Resistance: A Long-Range Approach to Indigenous Movement Convergence in the Andes. Paper presented at the 2022 APSA Annual Meeting.

Murtazashvili, J. B. (2016). *Informal Order and the State in Afghanistan.* Cambridge University Press, Cambridge, UK.

Nathan, N. L. (2019). *Electoral Politics and Africa's Urban Transition: Class and Ethnicity in Ghana*. Cambridge Studies in Comparative Politics. Cambridge University Press, Cambridge, UK.

Ndahinda, F. M. (2011). *Indigenousness in Africa: A Contested Legal Framework for Empowerment of 'Marginalized' Communities*. Springer Science & Business Media, The Hague.

Niebuhr, R. (2021). *¡Vamos a Avanzar!: The Chaco War and Bolivia's Political Transformation, 1899–1952*. University of Nebraska Press, Lincoln.

Nugent, D. and Fallaw, B. (2020). Preface. In Nugent, D. and Fallaw, B., editors, *State Formation in the Liberal Era: Capitalisms and Claims of Citizenship in Mexico and Peru*, pages ix–xxiii. University of Arizona Press, Tucson.

O'Connor, E. (2007). *Gender, Indian, Nation: The Contradictions of Making Ecuador, 1830–1925*. University of Arizona Press, Tucson.

O'Donnell, G. (1993). On the State, Democratization and Some Conceptual Problems: A Latin American View with Glances at Some Postcommunist Countries. *World Development*, 21(8):1355–1369.

O'Donnell, G. A. (1996). Illusions about Consolidation. *Journal of Democracy*, 7(2):34–51.

Oficina Nacional de Inmigración, Estadistica y Progpaganda Geográfica (1904). *Censo General de La Poblacion de La República de Bolivia*. José M. Gamarra, La Paz.

Olson, M. (1971). *The Logic of Collective Action*. Harvard University Press, Cambridge, Mass.

Orellana Candia, A. M. (2011). Construcción discursiva de la identidad e imagen del MAS en torno al conflicto por el TIPNIS. *Punto Cero*, 16(23):36–40.

Orlove, B. S. (2014). *Alpacas, Sheep, and Men: The Wool Export Economy and Regional Society in Southern Peru*. Academic Press, London.

Paige, J. M. (1978). *Agrarian Revolution*. Free Press, New York.

Pan American Union (1918). *Bulletin of the Pan-American Union*, volume XLVII. Union of American Republics, Washington, D. C.

Patch, R. W. (1960). Bolivia: U.S. Assistance in a Revolutionary Setting. In Adams, R. N., Gillin, J., and Lewis, O., editors, *Social Change in Latin America Today: Its Implications for United States Policy*, pages 108–176. Council on Foreign Relations, Washington, D.C.

Patch, R. W. (1961). Bolivia: The Restrained Revolution. *The ANNALS of the American Academy of Political and Social Science*, 334(1):123–132.

Paye, L., Arteaga, W., and Ramírez, N. (2011). *Compendio de Espaciomapas de TCO En Tierras Bajas: Tenencia y Aprovechamiento de Recursos Naturales En Territorios Indígenas*. CEDLA, La Paz.

Paye, L., Arteaga, W., and Ramírez, N. (2013). *Compendio de espaciomapas de TCO y TIOC en tierras altas: Tenencia de la tierra de recursos naturales en territorios originarios*. CEDLA, La Paz.

de la Peña, G. (1998). Rural mobilizations in Latin America since c. 1920. In Bethell, L., editor, *Latin America: Politics and Society Since 1930*, pages 291–394. Cambridge University Press, Cambridge, UK.

Pereyra, O. (2016). Asamblea indígena aprueba inicio del proceso autonómico. Eju. September 11.

Perez, D. M. (1972). *Población rural en haciendas del Peru 1940*. Universidad Nacional Mayor de San Marcos, Seminario de Historia Rural Andino, Lima.

Peru (1929). Red general de carreteras y ferrocarriles, Peru.

Peru Dirección Nacional de Estadistica y Censos (1944). *Censo nacional de población y ocupación 1940*. Ministerio de Hacienda y Comercio, Dirección Nacional de Estadística, República del Perú, Lima.

Place, F. and Hazell, P. (1993). Productivity Effects of Indigenous Land Tenure Systems in Sub-Saharan Africa. *American Journal of Agricultural Economics*, 75(1):10–19.

Platt, T. (1982). *Estado boliviano y ayllu andino: tierra y tributo en el norte de Potosí*. Instituto de Estudios Peruanos, Lima.

Platt, T. (1987). The Andean Experience of Bolivian Liberalism, 1825–1900: Roots of Rebellion in 19th Century Chayanta (Potosí). In Stern, S., editor, *Resistance, Rebellion, and Consciousness in the Andean Peasant World, 18th to 20th Centuries*, pages 280–326. University of Wisconsin Press, Madison.

Polanyi, K. (1944). *The Great Transformation: The Political and Economic Origins of Our Time*. Beacon Press, Boston.

Ponce Vargas, M. I. (2016). *Nos Resistimos a Dejar Nuestro Territorio: Los Yurakarés Entre El Presente y Los Desafíos Del Futuro*. FUNPROEIB Andes, Cochabamba, Bolivia.

Poole, D. (1997). *Vision, Race, and Modernity: A Visual Economy of the Andean Image World*. Princeton University Press, Princeton.

Popkin, S. L. (1979). *The Rational Peasant: The Political Economy of Rural Society in Vietnam*. University of California Press, Berkeley, CA.

Portaro, E. (1930). *Estado acutal de la construcción de carreteras en el Perú*. Imp. Torres Aguirre, Lima.

Posner, D. N. (2005). *Institutions and Ethnic Politics in Africa*. Cambridge University Press, Cambridge, UK.

Postero, N. (2017). *The Indigenous State: Race, Politics, and Performance in Plurinational Bolivia*. University of California Press, Berkeley, CA.

Postero, N. G. (2007). *Now We Are Citizens: Indigenous Politics in Postmulticultural Bolivia*. Stanford University Press, Stanford, CA.

Powell, J. D. (1971). *Political Mobilization of the Venezuelan Peasant*. Harvard University Press, Cambridge, Mass.

Prefecto de Cochabamba (1915). *Informe Del Prefecto y Comandante General Del Departamento*. La Prefectura, Cochabamba.

Prefecto de Oruro (1911). *Informe Presentado Ante El Supremo Gobierno*. La Prefectura, Oruro.

Prefecto de Potosí (1916). *Informe Del Prefecto, Comandante General, y Superintendente de Hacienda y Minas Del Departamento*. La Prefectura, Potosí.

Prefectura y Comandancia General (1909). *Informe presentado ante el supremo gobierno por el ... Prefecto y Comandante General del Departamento de Oruro*. La Prefectura, Oruro, Bolivia.

Preston, D. A. (1978). *Farmers and Towns: Rural-Urban Relations in Highland Bolivia*. Geo Abstracts, Limited, Norwich.

de Quesada, A. (2011). *The Chaco War 1932–35: South America's Greatest Modern Conflict*. Osprey, Oxford, England.

Rabushka, A. and Shepsle, K. A. (1972). *Politics in Plural Societies: A Theory of Democratic Instability*. Merrill, Columbus, Ohio.

Ramos Flores, M. (2016). Santos Marka Túla y las demandas de los Caciques apoderados en la primera parte del siglo XX. *Fuentes, Revista de la Biblioteca y Archivo Histórico de la Asamblea Legislativa Plurinacional*, 10(47):24.

Rappaport, J. (1990). *The Politics of Memory: Native Historical Interpretation in the Colombian Andes*. Cambridge University Press, Cambridge, UK.

Recondo, D. (2007). *La política del gatopardo: Multiculturalismo y democracia en Oaxaca*. CIESAS, Mexico.

Regal, A. (1936). *Los Caminos Del Inca En El Antiguo Perú*. Sanmartí y cía., s. a, Lima.

Reyeros, R. A. (1949). *El pongueaje: la servidumbre personal de los indios bolivianos*. ed. Universo, La Paz.

Rice, R. (2012). *The New Politics of Protest: Indigenous Mobilization in Latin America's Neoliberal Era*. University of Arizona Press, Tucson.

Rivera Cusicanqui, S. (1978). La Expansión del Latifundio en el Altiplano Boliviano: Elementos para la Caracterización de una Oligarquía Regional. *Avances*, 2:95–118.

Rivera Cusicanqui, S. (1986). *Oprimidos Pero No Vencidos: Luchas Del Campesinado Aymara y Qhechwa de Bolivia, 1900–1980*. Instituto de Investigaciones de las Naciones Unidas para el Desarrollo Social, Geneva.

Rivera Cusicanqui, S. (1987). *Oppressed but Not Defeated: Peasant Struggles among the Aymara and Qhechwa in Bolivia, 1900–1980*. United Nations Research Inst. for Social Development, Geneva.

Rivera Cusicanqui, S. (1991). "Pedimos la revisión de límites": Un episodio de incomunicación de castas en el movimiento de caciques-apoderados de los Andes bolivianos 1919–1921. In *Reproducción y Transformación de Las Sociedades Andinas Siglos XVI-XX*, volume 2, pages 603–652. Abya-Yala, Quito.

Rodríguez Ostria, G. (1980). Original Accumulation, Capitalism, and Precapitalistic Agriculture in Bolivia (1870–1885. *Latin American Perspectives*, 7(4):50–66.

Rodríguez Ostria, G. (2014). *Capitalismo, modernización y resistencia popular 1825–1952*. Vicepresidencia del Estado de Bolivia-Centro de Investigaciones Sociales, La Paz, Bolivia.

Roessel, R. and Johnson, B. H. (1974). *Navajo Livestock Reduction: A National Disgrace*. Navajo Community College Press, Chinle, Arizona.

Rothschild, J. (1981). *Ethnopolitics: A Conceptual Framework*. Columbia University Press, New York.

Salcedo, T. (1921). *Las Comunidades Indígenas y La Industria Agrícola En El Departamento de Ayacucho*. PhD thesis, Universidad Nacional de San Agustín, Arequipa.

Sambanis, N. and Milanovic, B. (2014). Explaining Regional Autonomy Differences in Decentralized Countries. *Comparative Political Studies*, 47(13):1830–1855.

Sapienza, A. L., Fracchia, A. L. S., and Peláez, J. L. M. (2020). *The Chaco War, 1932–1935: Fighting in Green Hell*. Helion Limited, Warwick.

Schurz, W. (1921). *Bolivia: A Commercial and Industrial Handbook*. Special Agents Series 208. U.S. Government Printing Office, Washington, DC.

Scott, J. C. (1977). *The Moral Economy of the Peasant: Rebellion and Subsistence in Southeast Asia*. Yale University Press, New Haven.

Seligmann, L. J. (1993). The Burden of Visions amidst Reform: Peasant Relations to Law in the Peruvian Andes. *American Ethnologist*, 20(1):25–51.

Seligmann, L. J. (1995). *Between Reform & Revolution: Political Struggles in the Peruvian Andes, 1969–1991*. Stanford University Press, Stanford, CA.

Sheridan, T. E. (2012). *Arizona: A History, Revised Edition*. University of Arizona Press, Tucson.

Shesko, E. (2020). *Conscript Nation: Coercion and Citizenship in the Bolivian Barracks*. University of Pittsburgh Press, Pittsburgh, PA.

Sistema Integral de Modernización Catastral y Registral (2016). Ejidos Certificados, Parcelas Certificadas, y Parcelas con Dominio Pleno.

Sjaastad, E. and Bromley, D. W. (1997). Indigenous Land Rights in Sub-Saharan Africa: Appropriation, Security and Investment Demand. *World Development*, 25(4):549–562.

Smith, B. C. (1985). *Decentralization: The Territorial Dimension of the State*. G. Allen & Unwin, London.

Smith, B. T. (2020). Communal Work, Forced Labor, and Road Building in Mexico, 1920–1958. In Nugent, D. and Fallaw, B., editors, *State Formation in the Liberal Era: Capitalisms and Claims of Citizenship in Mexico and Peru*, pages 273–298. University of Arizona Press, Tucson.

Smith, D. A., Herlihy, P. H., Kelly, J. H., and Viera, A. R. (2009). The Certification and Privatization of Indigenous Lands in Mexico. *Journal of Latin American Geography*, 8(2):175–207.

Smith, G. (1991). *Livelihood and Resistance: Peasants and the Politics of Land in Peru*. University of California Press, Berkeley, CA.

Smith, S. M. (1977). Labor Exploitation on Pre-1952 Haciendas in the Lower Valley of Cochabamba, Bolivia. *The Journal of Developing Areas*, 11(2):227–244.

Soifer, H. D. (2015). *State Building in Latin America*. Cambridge University Press, Cambridge, UK.

Soliz, C. (2021). *Fields of Revolution: Agrarian Reform and Rural State Formation in Bolivia, 1935–1964*. University of Pittsburgh Press, Pittsburgh, PA.

Soliz, M. C. (2014). *Fields of Revolution: The Politics of Agrarian Reform in Bolivia, 1935–1971*. PhD thesis, New York University, New York.

Sorens, J. (2012). *Secessionism: Identity, Interest, and Strategy*. McGill-Queen's University Press, Montreal.

Starn, O. (1999). *Nightwatch: The Politics of Protest in the Andes*. Duke University Press, Durham, NC.

Stauffer, C. (2018). Native Peoples Sour on Morales, Bolivia's First Indigenous President. *Reuters*.

Stein, S. (1980). *Populism in Peru: The Emergence of the Masses and the Politics of Social Control*. University of Wisconsin Press, Madison, WI.

Stern, S. J. (1993). *Peru's Indian Peoples and the Challenge of Spanish Conquest: Huamanga to 1640*. University of Wisconsin Press, Madison, WI.

Streeck, W. and Thelen, K. A. (2005). Introduction: Institutional Change in Advanced Political Economies. In Streeck, W. and Thelen, K. A., editors, *Beyond Continuity: Institutional Change in Advanced Political Economies*, pages 1–39. Oxford University Press, Oxford, UK.

Sub Central de Pueblos Indígenas: Mojeños-Yurace-Chimane del TIPNIS (2012). Resolución No. 1: Rechazo a que la Carretera Villa Tunari-San Ignacio de Mojos Pase por el TIPNIS y Resistencia a la Aplicación de la Ley no. 222 en Nuestro Territorio.

Summerhill, W. R. (2006). The Development of Infrastructure. In Bulmer-Thomas, V., Coatsworth, J., and Cortes-Conde, R., editors, *The Cambridge Economic History of Latin America: The Long Twentieth Century*, volume 2, pages 293–326. Cambridge University Press, Cambridge, UK.

Superintendencia Nacional de los Registros Públicos (SUNARP). (2016). Guía general para comunidades campesinas. Servicios Graficos, Lima.

Tarrow, S. G. (2011). *Power in Movement: Social Movements and Contentious Politics*. Cambridge University Press, Cambridge, UK.

Taylor, G. D. (1980). *The New Deal and American Indian Tribalism: The Administration of the Indian Reorganization Act, 1934–45*. University of Nebraska Press, Lincoln.

Taylor, L. (1984). Cambios capitalistas en las haciendas cajamarquinas. *Apuntes. Revista de ciencias sociales*, pages 79–110.

Teijeiro, J. (2007). *La rebelión permanente: crisis de identidad y persistencia étnico-cultural aymara en Bolivia*. Plural editores, La Paz.

Thompson, E. P. (1971). The Moral Economy of the English Crowd in the Eighteenth Century. *Past & Present*, 50(1):76–136.

Thurner, M. (1997). *From Two Republics to One Divided: Contradictions of Postcolonial Nation-making in Andean Peru*. Duke University Press, Durham, NC.

Ticona Alejo, E. (1996). *CSUTCB, trayectoria y desafíos*. CEDOIN, La Paz, Bolivia.

Ticona Alejo, E. (2003). Pueblos indígenas y Estado boliviano. La larga historia de conflictos. *Gazeta de Antropología*, 19(10).

Ticona Alejo, E. (2010). *Saberes, conocimientos y prácticas anticoloniales del pueblo aymara-quechua en Bolivia*. Plural editores, La Paz, Bolivia.

Tilly, C. (1978). *From Mobilization to Revolution*. Addison-Wesley, Reading, MA.

Tockman, J. and Cameron, J. (2014). Indigenous Autonomy and the Contradictions of Plurina-tionalism in Bolivia. *Latin American Politics and Society*, 56(3):46–69.

Tockman, J., Cameron, J., and Plata, W. (2015). New Institutions of Indigenous Self-Governance in Bolivia: Between Autonomy and Self-Discipline. *Latin American and Caribbean Ethnic Studies*, 10(1): 37–59.

Treisman, D. S. (1997). Russia's "Ethnic Revival": The Separatist Activism of Regional Leaders in a Postcommunist Order. *World Politics*, 49(2):212–249.

Trejo, G. (2012). *Popular Movements in Autocracies: Religion, Repression, and Indigenous Collective Action in Mexico*. Cambridge University Press, Cambridge, UK.

United Nations (2008). UN Declaration on the Rights of Indigenous Peoples. Technical report.

Urgente (2019). Los indígenas fueron tratados peor en la República que en la época Virreinal. https://urgente.bo/.

Van Aken, M. (1981). The Lingering Death of Indian Tribute in Ecuador. *The Hispanic American Historical Review*, 61(3):429–459.

Van Cott, D. L. (2001). Explaining Ethnic Autonomy Regimes in Latin America. *Studies in Comparative International Development*, 35(4):30–58.

Van Cott, D. L. (2005). Building Inclusive Democracies: Indigenous Peoples and Ethnic Minorities in Latin America. *Democratization*, 12(5):820–837.

Van der Windt, P., Humphreys, M., Medina, L., Timmons, J. F., and Voors, M. (2018). Citizen Attitudes Toward Traditional and State Authorities: Substitutes or Complements? *Comparative Political Studies*.

Vaughan, M. K. and Lewis, S. (2006). *The Eagle and the Virgin: Nation and Cultural Revolution in Mexico, 1920–1940*. Duke University Press, Durham, NC.

Walle, P. (1914). *Bolivia: Its People and Its Resources, Its Railways, Mines, and Rubber-forests*. T. F. Unwin, London.

Wallerstein, I. M. (2005). *Africa: The Politics of Independence and Unity*. University of Nebraska Press, Lincoln.

Ward, A. R. (2011). An Interview with Hugo Blanco Galdos. *Interventions*, 13(4):651–663.

Washbrook, S. (2012). *Producing Modernity in Mexico: Labour, Race, and the State in Chiapas, 1876–1914*. OUP/British Academy.

Washburn, W. E. (1984). A Fifty-Year Perspective on the Indian Reorganization Act. *American Anthropologist*, 86(2):279–289.

Watters, R. F. (1994). *Poverty and Peasantry in Peru's Southern Andes, 1963–90*. Springer, London.

Weisiger, M. (2007). Gendered Injustice: Navajo Livestock Reduction in the New Deal Era. *Western Historical Quarterly*, 38(4):437–455.

Weisiger, M. (2011). *Dreaming of Sheep in Navajo Country*. University of Washington Press, Seattle.

Wilkins, D. E. (2007). *American Indian Politics and the American Political System*. Rowman & Littlefield, Lanham, Maryland.

Wilkins, D. E. (2013). *The Navajo Political Experience*. Rowman & Littlefield, Lanham, Maryland.

Williams, D. (2007). Administering the Otavalan Indian and Centralizing Governance in Ecuador, 1851–1875. In Becker, M. and A. Kim Clark, editors, *Highland Indians and the State in Modern Ecuador*, pages 22–36. University of Pittsburgh Press, Pittsburgh, PA.

Wilson, F. (2018). Leguía y la política indigenista. In Drinot, P., editor, *La Patria Nueva: Economía, Sociedad y Cultura En El Perú, 1919–1930*, pages 139–168. UNC Press, Chapel Hill.

Winder, D. (2014). The Impact of the Comunidad on Local Development in the Mantaro Valley. In Long, N. and Roberts, B. R., editors, *Peasant Cooperation and Capitalist Expansion in Central Peru*, pages 209–240. University of Texas Press, Austin.

Wolf, E. R. (1957). Closed Corporate Peasant Communities in Mesoamerica and Central Java. *Southwestern Journal of Anthropology*, 13(1):1–18.

Wood, E. J. (2003). *Insurgent Collective Action and Civil War in El Salvador*. Cambridge University Press, Cambridge, UK.

World Bank (2002). *Chile's High Growth Economy: Poverty and Income Distribution, 1987–1998*. World Bank Publications, Washington, DC.

Wright, T. C. (2001). *Latin America in the Era of the Cuban Revolution*. Praeger, Westport, Connecticut.

Yashar, D. J. (1998). Contesting Citizenship: Indigenous Movements and Democracy in Latin America. *Comparative Politics*, 31(1):23–42.

Yashar, D. J. (2005). *Contesting Citizenship in Latin America: The Rise of Indigenous Movements and the Postliberal Challenge*. Cambridge University Press, Cambridge, UK.

Zimmerer, K. S. (1997). *Changing Fortunes: Biodiversity and Peasant Livelihood in the Peruvian Andes*. University of California Press, Berkeley.

Zubrzycki, G. and Woźny, A. (2020). The Comparative Politics of Collective Memory. *Annual Review of Sociology*, 46(1):175–194.

Zuñiga Navarro, G. (1998). Los procesos de constitución de territorios indígenas en América Latina. *Nueva sociedad*, (153):141–155.

# INDEX

Page numbers in italics indicate figures and tables.

GPSR Authorized Representative: Easy Access System Europe - Mustamäe tee
50, 10621 Tallinn, Estonia, gpsr.requests@easproject.com

www.ingramcontent.com/pod-product-compliance
Lightning Source LLC
Chambersburg PA
CBHW020843270326
41928CB00006B/522